We Need A Movement:
Four problems to solve
to restore rational government

Dedication

To caring people everywhere who sustain those around them.

WE NEED A MOVEMENT:
Four problems to solve to restore rational government
John Jensen
CreateSpace Publishing
  ISBN-13: 978-1977510105
  ISBN-10: 1977510108

Table of Contents

Preface, vi.

PART ONE. THE PROBLEM OF MEANING, 1

1. The power of a *mythus*, 1 – 2. Goodness as our ground, 3 – 3. Good of the whole, 7 – 4. Right and wrong matter, 11 – 5. Need for unconditional love, 13 – 6. Mobilizing yourself, 16 – 7. Consider dedication, 19 – 8. The role of a movement, 25 – 9. Limitations of the innate valuing process, 30.

PART TWO. THE PROBLEM OF SELFISH POWER, 32

1. The core problem, 32 – 2. Selecting a lens for change, 33 – 3. How civilizations are overturned, 36 – 4. The creative minority turns dominant, 38 – 5. Full employment, 41 – 6. How we went wrong, 43 – 7. The attack on truth, 46 – 8. Impact of racism, 48 – 9. Participating in oppression, 53 – 10. Who is society for?, 55 – 11. People lose faith in the system, 59 – 12. Meritocracy and advantage discriminate, 62 – 13. Market forces can unbalance the system, 64.

PART THREE. THE PROBLEM OF MEDIOCRE THINKING, 66

1. Don't do stupid stuff, 66 – 2. How mediocre thinking is a problem, 69 – 3. Sources of mediocre thinking, 72 – 4. Correct thinking, 90 – 5. Acting on ideas, 92 – 6. A change narrative, 93 – 7. Align with evidence, 96 – 8. The appeal to churches, 99 – 9. Religion without control, 105 – 10. Use resources wisely, 108 – 11. Convey a group perspective, 109 – 12. Change negative attitudes, 112 – 13. The necessity of limitation, 114 – 14. Use power carefully, 118 – 15. Learn from emotions, 120.

PART FOUR. THE PROBLEM OF ORGANIZATION, 126

1. Movement inward and outward, 126 – 2. Four ways to start, 127 – 3. Orient newcomers, 130 – 4. Ask for a response, 136 – 5. Choose planners, 138 – 6. Functions of the planning team, 141 – 7. Communications for planning, 145 – 8. The key role of supervision, 148 – 9. Start rapidly, 154 – 10. Increase numbers quickly, 158 – 11. Lead, 160 – 12. Conduct campaigns, 162 – 13. Canvassing, 167 – 14. Act on ideas learned, 173 – 15. Become fluent with ideas, 175 – 16. Allay fear, 184 – 17. Study and share, 185 – 18. Questions for discussion, 186 – 19. The issue of fairness, 194 – 20. Mass action and personal contact, 199 – 21. Face to face needs, 202– 22. Connect through evidence, 207 – 23. Ordinary communication, 211 – 24. Healing by respect, 213 – 25. Resolve conflict, 217 – 26. Learn deeply, 222 – 27. Turning points for action, 227– 28. A spectrum of goals, 234 – 29. Agreements, principles, and processes, 238 – 30. Key electoral changes, 240 — 31. Communicate with opponents, 244– 32. Arguing with extremists, 254– 33. Obtain the skills you need, 264 – 34. A continuum of change, 268 — References, 280– Recommended Reading, 297 – Appendix I. Promotional flier, 299 – Appendix II. Ideas to master, 299.

Preface

In her book *Hope in the Dark: Untold Histories, Wild Possibilities,* Rebecca Solnit recounts inspiring examples of activists working together to achieve social change. Yet near the end she notes, "You are part of the system, and you need, we all need, to change that system. Nothing less than systemic change will save us…How will we get to where we need to be? No one knows…" (1). She expresses the widespread discouragement about how our system is running, and that the means of change are not in common view.

But imagine for a moment that person to person contact is the strongest underutilized force for change.

Assume also that a large number of people learn how to help others adopt constructive ideas. Imagine then that this large number blankets every corner of the country, communicating good ideas face to face, *and assume that we can carry out what we imagine.* That is the means we explain here.

Cesar Chavez, a bold, relentless, fearless person whose efforts for farm workers changed labor conditions in the U.S., expressed it most simply. "Organizing is easy," he said once, "just paint a picture and color it in." We explain the needs, their urgency, and what to do about them. We compose a narrative and get it to society; create a picture that makes sense to the public, and deliver it. To frame the issue in reverse, we ask, "What factors have injured our system the most, which if corrected would help it work better?"

The answer lies in three problems we examine in detail. The nation needs to:

1. Change its governing belief from self-interest to the good of the whole.
2. Counteract the selfishness of the ruling elite.
3. Correct pervasive mediocre thinking.

An accurate picture of these three problems needs to be spread throughout the nation to engage mainstream understanding, and influence the selection of representatives and the framing of laws and policies.

How do we do this?

The boldness we noted in the efforts of Cesar Chavez is likely to have further play. The 2016 presidential election challenged common wisdom as Donald Trump won despite an unfavorable rating eight points higher than his favorable rating and other features normally deal-breakers. Browsing through a thesaurus later, I ran across the word "dangerous." Thinking about its synonyms, "I'm probably going to need these," I continued on to "dare" and at once the picture came clear: **boldness, primary process**.

That was what he did. Though many other influences were at work, a particular quality had an impact. He dared to tell off everyone about whom others said, "You mustn't alienate them." He dared people to attack him, because "I go after those who attack me." He dared people to stop supporting him even based on his actions. "I could shoot someone" asserted a new moral norm: "Even my misdeeds won't hurt me."

Rather than his stands on issues, his point was his own will. He would not placate and win by saying what people wanted to hear. He projected his power rather than ideas; strength, confidence, and treating critics like a boxer saying "My opponent won't lay a glove on me" ("They're weak"). Even his occasional foul language probably helped him, because while offending some, it increases a speaker's perceived authenticity: "He wouldn't say that unless he meant it" (2).

But the winning element was not negativity. Boldness serves even better from admirable people like Washington, Lincoln, and Roosevelt. The point instead is that *strengths are so determinative they can override a host of negatives*. Trump won because his boldness encouraged people to hope that he would drive the change they wanted. *Had he not been bold, they could not have believed he would bring change.* They expected he would eventually get the details right and forgave him for pronouncements left like wandering comets.

A better message could have obscured this lesson. People might say,

"Well, the negatives worked against him, but his stands on the issues won it," but issues were not his ground. As an appeal to the working class, Hillary Clinton had a plan for putting America back to work while Trump dared even more—dare China, auto companies, Mexico, NATO countries, and the Washington establishment. The dares said he would push others to the limit.

And why do that? In contrast to Clinton asking voters to "sing in gentle harmony," Trump emphasized, *"There are bad people out there,"* bad enough that a powerful person must seize the situation ("I'm the only one who can do it"). His boldness matched the scope of the problem he promised to solve.

The lesson for activists is that people wait for determination comparable to the problem they face. We do not offer chewing gum when someone loses their leg. Our response must match the need. Confronting a mountain of problems, we need a mountain of boldness and will, not just good ideas.

With it, people open the doors of their lives to everything else. Ideas become credible, actions doable, and mutual support has meaning. A good message alone does not move people to follow us, nor inspire them to draw deeply on themselves. They look for energy they can personally attach to.

Below we invite you to find your own indomitable core. If you are fearless, frank, relentless, and impervious to attack, you will attract people. They will listen to your ideas and may follow your lead. To change society, you will need to learn how your personal power can have an effect, following Siddhartha's model: "I go to my goal like a stone goes through water."

While a single candle can light the world and individuals have their effect, the scope of needs today is different. We might imagine the energy in a population of 300 million-plus as a lake, pooled in one place yet representing potential force. In circulating, it presses against boundaries all around it, yet goes nowhere, only returning constantly to itself.

But imagine that a bank breaks, turning the lake into a river. Energy goes somewhere, doing work, surmounting obstacles, enlivening life along its banks. In that picture, we unite with others to affect big problems. We go somewhere.

Maybe you work in political campaigns and they succeed just enough to keep you engaged. Or you are in a community organization or association that contributes. But despite a million and a half of them in the U.S., big problems still loom like economic inequality, racism, classism, climate change, education, health care, financial security, criminal justice, and world conditions—all begging for effective intervention.

A clear focus is indispensable. When I was young, my father taught me how to use tools. Facing a nail with a hammer in my hand, I would swing at it, bend it, my father would shake his head and say, "Give it another," and I would bend it more. Eventually I learned that I had to aim exactly, and if I did the nail would seat perfectly. We accomplish what we want by focusing our effort.

One writer suggested that all accomplishment depends on "strenuous limitation" illustrated by a mill race. Water gathers power only when channeled. Random protests, expensive lobbyists, creative media, and clever campaigns may not achieve their purposes because continually addressing one piece at a time. Our need instead is to assemble elements that solve many pieces together, and unite dispersed energy into a coherent stream. This depends not merely on numbers holding general agreement. To make a difference, each must know and do their part gladly because they value what they accomplish. Everything hinges on becoming a collective but thoughtful force.

The Preamble to the Constitution describes a channel for it. Patriots actually believe in and live by the founding principles of their nation:

> We the people of the United States, in order to form a more perfect union, ensure domestic tranquility, provide for the common defense, and insure the blessings of liberty for ourselves and our posterity, do hereby establish the Constitution of the United States.

"We the people" seek outcomes like "perfect union," "domestic tranquility," "defense," and "blessings of liberty" for "ourselves and our posterity." Our country instead has veered of late toward interest groups instead of a *we*, polarization instead of perfect union, inter-group hostility instead of domestic tranquility, and worse prospects for our posterity than we received.

Two massive forces drive this misdirection: the self-interest of leaders who misuse power granted them, and mediocre thinking tolerated throughout society. With these reined in, a host of specific problems could yield quickly. A movement seeks unselfish leaders for society who have good thinking. To find them, large numbers need to agree on a direction and develop the skills in communication, leadership, and service to pursue it.

Given recent politics, the United States may wish to consider such a shift. An approach in psychology called the Theory of Positive Disintegration says that when people encounter difficulties, aspects of their thinking loosen up. The depth of their coming apart is the depth of change possible, so that for a minor distress, a minor change suffices. But the deeper the disintegration, the more profound the change can be. People lose their job, marriage, friends, and money, and when their children no longer speak to them, they "hit bottom" and decide to rethink their life. Their need then is for guidance and support that help them find a healing pathway.

The same experience can strike a society, and it needs a similar response—to recognize what is broken, decide to change it, and get help to plot a way back. Problems can present opportunities. "Never let a good crisis go to waste," advised Rahm Emanuel.

This book began in 1966 when as a Catholic priest I came upon organizing methods that had a startling impact, but over time many other influences contributed: being raised in a politically active family, learning Russian language and history in the Army Counter-Intelligence Corps, a study of mass movements and social change, attempts at community organizing, holding elected municipal office, developing and consulting on classroom methods, working as a clinical psychologist, and learning valuable lessons from insightful people (3).

While others may analyze social change through politics, economics, media, demographics, or culture, we propose here using a force 100 percent available in its smallest and largest dimensions, *connecting with others*. When we rely instead on impersonal technology or mass appeals, we are helpless when they fail us. Developments drift off because others do what they please, but when we manage our field of activity directly, only our willingness to expend the effort limits us.

The ideas below are largely known already as information, but our culture has separated them from how to apply them. Significant facts are ignored. Mainstream thinking may know a critical truth and wave it goodbye as it dissolves in our collective sinkhole of forgetfulness. The broad need is to focus the nation on grasping and acting on what is obvious and urgent.

We need the lessons of ancient and recent history, but also to understand people's tendencies, feelings, limitations, and reasoning in order to appeal to them. Simple activities can have an impact. The fields of psychology, public speaking, politics, education, and sales taken together tell us *how to convey an idea to nearly anyone under any conditions*. If we are frustrated at someone's resistance to our golden idea, we should look first to our own skills rather than to their apparent obstinacy. We need to knock on the right door.

Here we return often to communicating in different ways for varied purposes but the breadth of relevant concerns has led to structuring the book around individual sections, each a brief essay about one issue under the four major topics. The book overall, however, is meant as an integrated framework, not just a compendium of techniques to pick from. Learning it should help activists spot quickly why their effort may bog down and how to turn it around, though the book is only a starting point. Many brief sections already have volumes of their own written by other authors. Our aim here has been to assemble overlooked factors that together can aid broad-based public action.

The challenge of changing society parallels my difficulty writing this book. Through decades of effort, I could not push beyond my understanding but only recognize that it was insufficient. My problem was in thinking, and we could say the same about society. Everyone is entrained in a personal understanding that sets the boundaries of their actions. In proceeding along a familiar channel, they may not turn when a turn is indicated.

A state teacher of the year explained the problem in reference to educators. You could divide them, he told me, into speedboats, reefs, and barges. The speedboats dash about, pursuing innovations enthusiastically. Though small in number, they propel change. The reefs are those who resist change on principle and will sink any new thing given a chance, while the bulk of the staff are barges. They have little flexibility to change course, but carry the load forward once pointed in the right direction.

So also with the public in general. Most move forward on the track they understand, some give fresh energy to a new one, and others sabotage it if they can. In seeking change ourselves, we accept that we push past an edge into an unknown.

One day walking up a quiet residential sidewalk, I passed the home of a family of large ants scurrying back and forth within a few feet of their hole. A hundred feet further on, I caught up with an ant of the same kind striding confidently up the center of the sidewalk.

"Hey buddy, you're a long way from home!" I said to him.

"Just checking out the neighborhood," I'm sure I heard him answer. "Somebody's gotta do it."

If you are like the exploring ant, my heart goes with you. Some explorers don't return, but like the ant declared, "Somebody's gotta do it."

For you personally the effort may be more challenging than you expect, and take more out of you for a longer time than you imagine, but you start with enough concern to get you moving. You will need a plan you can do a step at a time. The one explained below contains a direction for action, pitfalls that can obstruct it, and ideas that help it along.

Successful activity involves personal change, perhaps even substantial. The reason is that ultimately we cannot act differently from who we are. We cannot *drive* ourselves to act for long in ways that do not fit us. This means that social change depends on people changing, beginning with ourselves. Our determination to remain as we are is an ongoing stumbling block to movement participation, but since all our actions arise from our feelings and thoughts, to improve our actions *we have no choice but to master feelings and thoughts*. To put it another way, you will not act differently from how you think. If you now are passive, waiting for someone else to do something, that is how you are thinking, and that is what must change.

As a practical beginning, readers might set out to assimilate and be able to explain each section of this book. Explaining is important because it helps our mind divide a big idea into units of the size it can think about. The book has four parts. The first concerns the difficulty of defining meaning. People unite around an idea that matters to them. The second and third parts address the two main causes of society's woes—the selfish power of the dominant minority, and the widespread indifference to mediocre thinking. The fourth part describes the internal workings of an effective movement. Each part invites a type of response:

The first, about finding meaning, asks for a change of heart and invites you to sort out your lifetime values. It readies you to apply the practical steps that follow, and grounds you in a viewpoint that will help you and society solve problems far into the future.

The second concerning selfish power explains the central argument for what needs to change. System-wide problems call for system-wide solutions that help society endure beyond the current presidential cycle. The content of these two parts needs to be spread broadly.

The third part concerns mediocre thinking, the departure from rationality that encourages emotion-driven, ideological, ineffective policies. It comprises a lens through which to assess the ideas of leaders and the public, recognize poor quality thinking, and understand how to respond. Running law-making through the gauntlet of a structure prone to gridlock and misdirection has let us down.

The fourth part describes the inner life of the movement—the activities that motivate people to cooperate, become fluent with ideas, and act on them. Explanations on group design, resolving problems, and setting direction help organizers avoid pitfalls that can sabotage progress.

The references note sources for many ideas, and some expand on points in the text. Often I have relied on my memory of details, so if others' research can correct them, I welcome the correction. Evidence is our common ground. And while America, Alaska, family, and my Catholic upbringing formed my own early frame of reference, the principles below apply across the world to people of all nations and beliefs. They concern how people treat each other so everyone prospers.

John Jensen

December 2017

I

PART ONE. THE PROBLEM OF MEANING

1. The power of a *mythus*

Despite their individual qualities, people in any large group tend to possess a common picture of who they are, values they share, and activities that matter to them. The word applied to this belief is a *mythus*, described also as the dominant narrative or mainstream thinking. A slogan may capture it, like "Remember Pearl Harbor," "United We Stand," or "Preserve the Union." Regions may have their own *mythus*, such as how slavery and its aftermath defined attitudes differently in the American south and north. George Washington pleaded to the Constitutional Convention to create a constructive *mythus* for the new nation in words carved into the stone arch at Washington Square Park in New York City so later generations would not forget them: "Let us raise a standard to which the wise and honest may repair. The event is in the hand of God."

The *mythus* of the time guided my town and my own early life. Growing up in Alaska in the 1940s, even young I heard the words, "the war effort." Our town did what was expected. I got no cap pistols one year, and could not swallow the butter substitute that arrived by boat. In an air raid drill, we kindergartners, somewhat puzzled at adults' seriousness, trooped uphill from our small school to hide under alder trees in case our school were bombed. Men still in town joined the National Guard and practiced their marksmanship, and my mother, remembering those years, commented later, "Gosh, we worked *so* hard."

A shared commitment to the war effort generated spontaneous cooperation. Roosevelt asked an auto manufacturer, "Could you build tanks?" and the man replied instantly, "Sure, where can I see one?"

Pearl Harbor hurled us into the war in the Pacific, but we hesitated for months about Europe. Drawing us toward war were the plight of our British allies and newsreels of events in Europe–Hitler screaming at crowds, soldiers goose-stepping, and bombs exploding. People's own eyes told them, "This is your enemy." The *mythus* was the logical conclusion of vivid evidence.

A belief developed this way, however, *can be fatal* by waiting till near-breakdown before responding. Many problems do not burst into our awareness but are systemic—important but not acute. People may quietly accept being oppressed and ill-served for generations. Declining fresh water, melting polar ice, rising sea level, a heating planet, tides of refugees, and economic inequality do not present a specific enemy, a watershed event, nor a simple channel of effort, yet all can devastate us. Thoughtful plans are needed long before disaster strikes.

Leaders influence the picture we act on and the emotions enlisted. Anger at the establishment helped elect Donald Trump, but negative emotions readily unbalance collective judgment. A public in the grip of anger or fear is easily manipulated, and an enemy explained how this is done. Gustave Gilbert, an intelligence officer, interviewed Herman Goering facing trial as a war criminal after World War II:

"We got around to the subject of war again and I said that, contrary to his attitude, I did not think that the common people are very thankful for leaders who bring them war and destruction."

"Why, of course, the people don't want war," Goering shrugged. "Why would some poor slob on a farm want to risk his life in a war when the best that he can get out of it is to come back to his farm in one piece. Naturally, the common people don't want war; neither in Russia nor in England nor in America, nor for that matter in Germany. That is understood. But, after all, it is the leaders of the country who determine the policy and it is always a simple matter to drag the people along, whether it is a democracy or a fascist dictatorship or a Parliament or a Communist dictatorship."

"There is one difference," I pointed out. "In a democracy the people have some say in the matter through their elected representatives, and in the United States only Congress can declare wars."

"Oh, that is all well and good," said Goering, "but, voice or no voice, the people can always be brought to the bidding of the leaders. That is easy. All you have to do is tell them they are being attacked and denounce the pacifists for lack of patriotism and exposing the country to danger. It works the same way in any country" (4).

Goering's point, tragically, applies to us. That very sequence of events led the U.S. into the second Iraq War. Leaders who wanted war promoted weak evidence to create fear, telling the nation it could face nuclear attack if it did not act at once, and an anxious, ill-informed Congress went along. Leaders knowingly exaggerated data to scare the nation into a war meant to secure Iraq's oil, a deed many regard now as the worst foreign policy blunder in our nation's history (5). The action taken, despite a flood of international protest, illustrates also how leaders captured in a bubble of their own thinking can damage their people.

We need a *mythus* that expresses a constructive goal and means. The Civil Rights Movement recognized that only positive principles could bring about the changes needed. Martin Luther King, Jr. pointed out that "love is the only force that can convert an enemy into a friend." We need to understand how to apply that timeless truth.

2. Goodness as our ground

Focus on what you want rather than on what you don't want. The road to love passes through goodness, and we can describe basic good as meeting human needs. Abraham Maslow suggested that we address a spectrum of them somewhat sequentially beginning with survival—food, water, and shelter. Having them for today, we save them up for tomorrow and plan for safety and security. Our physical needs met, we turn attention to connect with others, form into groups, and figure out how to understand our world. Social relations and learning loom larger, and further fulfillment comes in care for others and creating what our culture values (6).

Development along this continuum proceeds from the personal to the social and public, from the concrete to the intangible, and from necessities to options. Basic needs come first because of our limited energy. We must survive and cannot do everything at once. A social system helps people cope with necessities so they can move themselves toward higher values, but the conditions we put up with define how far we allow our values to define our lives. We do not want starving children begging in the streets, for example. If they are going to starve, we would rather have them out of sight because it bothers us, but that it bothers us may signal civilization taking hold. It is a bad sign if hungry children do not bother us.

While active people think first about action, their values eventually determine their results. The fact behind history's axiom, "Character is destiny," is that the qualities of our identity are the capabilities we use in what we do. Our good values generate good efforts that construct civilization. To grasp this simple idea, however, we must weigh realities lacking concrete form, engaging with intangibles like loyalty, love, and justice that make solutions work. Neighbors may connect through mutual harmony, or take up a common task through responsibility.

Values can jump continents, their non-materiality allowing them to span distance. Religions generate common effort as they picture God's plan similarly worldwide, the plan's etheriality allowing it to be universal as are values behind democracy, freedom, and equality before the law. We encounter such principles in the Gettysburg Address and our nation's founding documents. President Roosevelt declared an intangible to be key in overcoming the Great Depression: "The only thing we have to fear is, fear itself!"

When we fail to address intangibles, our practical actions misfire. Encountering blatant racism, for instance, we usually leave it alone. We might believe we cannot change such an attitude, but even checking its expression may be a low priority, so that we teach each other to be indifferent to important principles violated. Public figures may lie, and associates who could correct them but gain from their favor keep quiet so that a lesser gain displaces a value, and people begin to assume that that is how things work. Warping an intangible, we inevitably warp its application.

Every public issue involves goodness. Many believe we can do without it, that refuting lies and correcting racism do not matter, but society slowly comes apart as we let destructive values govern. When a previous effort did not solve a problem, conditions evolve, new players enter, and again we consider, "What good can we obtain here?" beginning back in simple things. Leaders should not lie, cheat, steal, and manipulate others for their own ends. Citizens should be fair and just, keep their agreements, restrain wrong-doers, and remove oppressive force and toxic influences. A disintegrating society ceases to be vigilant about conditions basic to its survival.

A movement particularly needs grounding in moral excellence, a resistance to evil, and the exercise of virtue typically shown in responsibility and kindness toward others. Such qualities separate those we jail from those with cities named after them. Putting the good to work engages the great creative motor of human activity, and in the end can overwhelm arms. Greeks enslaved by the Romans became their teachers and spread science, learning, and culture throughout the known world. For centuries missionaries have devoted their lives to delivering virtues of human decency and service everywhere, and outstanding teachers present a vision of goodness to guide students' lives.

Goodness is so fundamental that we refer to it even when we are selfish, seeking good *for us*. Even a potential suicide thinks, "I'll be better off." The main task of life is to remain in goodness, and the second, to manifest it. Be good and do good. We show we love others by the good we offer them, but also may notice that leaving them alone will do better than our help.

Face the reality of U.S. mistakes. A window into the goodness needed in social policy is how its opposite worked when leaders co-opted us for unworthy motives. Three big mistakes in U.S. history have been slavery, conquest, and colonialism—all errors against goodness. We shield from children that people like themselves did these things, that their playground aggression echoes the injury their ancestors caused and may foreshadow damage they will inflict as adults.

Beyond its toll in individual suffering, slavery nearly fractured the nation and has had painful effects to the present (cf. Part Two, 8. *Impact of racism*). That so many accepted it as right for centuries prompts concern. Was the governing minority insane from an inheritable gene it passed on to us? Ask an open-minded person, "Tell me, was slavery a good idea or did people suffer brutal injustice?" For the few who actually defend it, find a detailed description of it and go over how they would feel living it themselves. Ask gently, "So you're okay with lynching?" or "So if you lived there, you would bring your children to a picnic where the entertainment was lynching a black slave?"

Similarly with our near genocide of ten million or more American Indians while taking their land and livelihood. Americans told themselves not only that they could do it but that because it was inevitable, it had to be correct: *Manifest Destiny.* Does our frozen conscience even shudder when we kill people to take their land? How should an enlightened conscience regard that period?

The war in Vietnam began from our support for French colonialism. But why should Americans die supporting wealthy people exploiting the poor? It was justified by ideology, Communism versus Freedom, thinking so patterned we could not separate valid from spurious. International terrorism has metasticized from our invasion of Iraq. We have done poorly distinguishing good from bad.

We may discover later that good arises after destruction, and rationalize our deeds—former President Bush predicts eventual good from the Iraq war. Let's hope. And after Roman armies killed hundreds of thousands in France, civilization took hold in western Europe. We respond to the conditions left to us, but face a different question up front deciding to do good or evil. We are morally bidden not to use the worse means as we understand them. While we may argue complex situations, a telling clue is *Cui bono?* (Who benefits?) If our action benefits ourselves, then self-interest is our motive, and the loss others suffer for our gain measures the evil in our deed.

People may perform the good instrumentally, being good because they benefit from it, but as a value we rank it more significant than life itself. Better a short one doing good than a long one doing evil. We remain moral by holding to the good even when it stretches us, by not taking personal offense at others' evil deeds even as we work to counteract them, and by not descending to the unworthy actions of our opponents. We are compassionate toward others and rely on truth to advance the good.

To develop our ability at this, we need only attend steadily to a single question: *What is the good here and now?* Just recognizing it where we are trains our mind to grasp the conditions that obtain it. Cause and effect become plain to an awareness wired to appreciate them. If we want our actions to result in good, we need only foresee how they will cause it. Imagine on the other hand a resentful man who thinks, "I feel like punching someone." He goes out for an evening, and later punches someone even though blaming the other for the incident. His deeper current of thought set him up. For us, attending to the good sets us up to make it happen.

3. Good of the whole

Apply the good of the whole to society. Society's entire activity is meant to meet the needs Maslow identified, but it can assign more of its resources to one need over another, inviting clarity over a basis for doing so. The issue is ancient. Over two millennia ago, in a Greek culture that believed ideas should guide behavior, Socrates explained the purpose of governance:

> (I)t's not the concern of law that any one class in the city fare exceptionally well, but it contrives to bring this about in the city as a whole, harmonizing the citizens by persuasion and compulsion, making them share with one another the benefit that each is able to bring to the commonwealth. And it produces such men in the city not in order to let them turn whichever way

each wants, but in order that it may use them in binding the city together (7).

The issue for Socrates was whether the interest of governance was for a class or the whole city. When the arguments were done and benefits allocated, would the few or the many prosper, and would the many experience a sense of unity around this purpose? He believed the city should enhance the lives of all, each person rather than a few lucky citizens. For us, good of the whole should include individuals, all demographic categories, the natural environment, and the social world, and weigh preferred outcomes against all other impacts.

On the personal level, the choice is usually between selfish and unselfish, benefiting ourselves or what lies beyond us. At the limited end are our family and group while we dismiss everything else, but how far does the whole extend in the other direction? On the basis that "You break it, you own it," are families fleeing danger in Central America in our whole? We sold them weapons, and our drug trade supplied them money and inflicted violence, so are we responsible for their fugitives?

Those claiming class privilege might answer, "Do people today whose ancestors were slaves in our cotton fields finally qualify to be in our whole?" If not, on what basis? And about millions fleeing destruction in the Middle East, other countries ask, "What can we do?" and "Are we willing to do it?" If we can do nothing, okay, we can't. But if we can, that human disaster enters our whole to be weighed along with everything else.

Politics today argues the issue Socrates explained. A fact of history is that power has been unequally distributed, which has made freedom from oppression a daily concern for entire populations. Theories of democracy gradually incorporated freedom as a value important for all, yet the ruling classes historically developed the theories because they wanted freedom for themselves. It was not power that rankled, but power over them, so that in proposing freedom as a social standard, they did not think to include others. *Our founders left out slaves, foreigners, Native Americans, females, young, and poor.* In sum, anyone lacking social influence was excluded from the freedom white property owners enjoyed. As George Orwell put it, "Everyone is equal, but some are more equal than others." Over the years, freedom as actually applied has often meant a ruling elite freed from social restrictions and able to exert financial and economic power over the lower classes.

Today the optics of freedom from government interference play well before independent-minded citizens of all economic strata who are certain that less government is always better, and do not want to pay taxes, obey laws, or take care of others. But the downside of this attitude is granting the elite more power over those without it. People unaccustomed to weighing values may not even notice a problem: *how to balance freedom for the individual with responsibility for the whole.* Both ideas are abstractions not easily assimilated by minds riveted to the concrete and self-interested, and hence require constant, patient explanation and application.

The difficulty is even more acute now as civilization has evolved. Though we all value freedom-as-choice ("Should we go to Yosemite or the Everglades for vacation?"), factors beyond our control define our actual options. With no resources, we cannot go to either one though we may still feel free to choose. We are each vulnerable now to more deeds from more people that affect our personal resources; to changes in climate, economic patterns, depletion of resources, and dysfunction in society's agencies. All of us depend on society's overall operation.

Our military deployed across the world acknowledges a whole in terms of quelling violence—a fundamental need—while helping to sustain a very American attitude: For us to prosper, others must prosper too. The world ultimately will sink or swim together. For the last seventy years, the U.S. has been the world's principal influence for maintaining peace, but the limitation of our model is that it may rely too much on force that can only establish a temporary umbrella of safety.

An element of proportion matters. Imagine, for example, that we set up a billion dollar American School-Hospital Complex in a welcoming foreign country, so generations there could grow up grateful that the Americans changed their lives. Despite its practical challenges, this is not unthinkable. If a billion-dollar cost seems high (especially if built for others and not ourselves), for the four trillion dollar round number price tag on the war in Iraq, *we could have constructed four thousand such billion-dollar American Complexes.* Savor that for a moment. For what we have already spent and will spend just for the second Iraq war, we could have built 4,000 billion-dollar education-and-health facilities–and have built none. Were we perhaps a little lean on health and learning, and a little heavy on force?

What do we stand for? Those promoting "America first" might notice that we already point war machines at others in the Middle East at the cost of trillions. The question is not whether we spend money for others. An Amazon of our resources flows to them. Our question is the shape of the society we leave behind when we are done fighting. An entire class of leaders has acted foolishly. They missed a lesson and ignored values, sought change through coercive power that can only occur through cooperation.

Behavior teaches principles. Force is but one among many influences and used alone has unpredictable outcomes. We ourselves armed Bin Laden because we thought it wise to supply weapons to our enemy's enemy, and sold them to Iran which for decades now has been an antagonist. During the Black Power Movement in the 60s, many of its supporters carried weapons, yet Stokely Carmichael accurately cautioned that if you give people a gun without educating them, *they might point it at you.* Constructive change means we change how people think, how they discriminate one good from another.

To draw on constructive principles, we need to think better (cf. Part Three), and understand the implications of the factors before us. Where cause and effect are unclear, we should always choose the highest value available because vast changes can begin from seemingly minor events. The butterfly effect altering a massive weather front applies to social trends. Middle East tensions have been dramatically exacerbated now for a decade and a half by an American president's determination to remove an Iraqi president, and we are just past a century of "one thing leads to another."

A wrong turn by his limousine driver brought Archduke Ferdinand before his assassin, igniting the First World War, which generated the forces erupting in the Second World War, which led to the Iron Curtain, the Cold War, and present tensions with Russia. Four generations of suffering followed an obscure beginning, and millions eventually died because of one person's character. As a young man Joseph Stalin figured out how to gain political influence by killing people, suggesting that we examine the qualities of people we decide to trust, that we watch how their actions reveal their values and judgment.

An essential discipline is to cease thinking first of advantage and turn instead to a balance of values: How is everything affected by what I am about to do? In campaign advertisements, a Congressman facing re-election repeated that he had "always put his state first." His state would come before good of the whole, equity with another state, benefit to the nation, spending federal money fairly, and world needs. These would always be second. In every situation, he would seek advantage for his state, a sentiment many of our nation's Congressmen seem driven to re-emphasize to their constituents.

Perhaps that Congressman exaggerated to be elected, but may have assessed his people accurately: "In any contest of values, forget parity, fairness, and justice and just get as much as you can for us. We like federal spending here more than we dislike inequity or an inflated Federal budget." Yet on the other hand, people increasingly recognize how they are affected by the condition of the world itself–its violence, its climate, its resources, its politics–and may be able to think bigger.

Leaders need the courage to explain what enables society to work, that Federal money is available only because the group succeeds apart from any individual's success, and that mature people pay for what they want. The nation's productivity deserves care instead of waste. When lesser desires receive a lopsided boon, urgent needs go begging. The good of the whole is a touchstone for weighing among priorities.

4. Right and wrong matter

Reflect on moral intangibles. Committing to goodness helps us recognize right and wrong, and the positive outcomes of doing right. Waste and inefficiency are wrong because they undermine constructive achievement, but we recognize child hunger and prisoner torture as wrong because violating human dignity. Many people's model of the world, however, has a blank where valuing human beings should be. This "failure to grasp" matters because we treat differently those we value. Society prospers when it responds at least to obvious right and wrong. Compare your own answers to those of political opponents:

Is it right for the U.S. to dismiss global warming when melting polar ice already on track will submerge world coasts where nearly half the world's population lives (8)?

Is it right that we have the highest rates of teen death and child poverty among developed nations?

Is it right that 16 million children nationally and almost a third of those living among lawmakers in the nation's capital do not get the food they need?

Is it right to roll back decades of environmental protection and make practically every kind of pollution easier in order to increase profits?

Is it right that the U.S. is the only industrialized country without a nationwide system of child care for working parents?

Is it right to subject poor children to inadequate diet, medical care, housing, and education, and expose them to toxic chemicals?

Is it right that we have the world's highest rate of incarceration–two million people, a quarter of the entire world's prisoners–yet the highest homicide rate among rich countries? Spend billions on new prisons and short change crime prevention and rehabilitation? Continue to lock up people who can't pay fines, a practice outlawed two centuries ago as inhumane?

Is it right that in our justice system an accused "is better off being rich and guilty than poor and innocent"?

Is it right that roughly two-thirds of juveniles in detention centers may have one or more diagnosable psychiatric disorders?

Is it right that we are the last western nation to treat health care as a human right?

Is it right that only half of minority children earn a high school diploma?

Is it right that some schools have everything they want and others struggle?

Is it right that the bottom forty percent own about a fifth of one percent of the nation's wealth and the top ten percent own eighty-five percent of it?

Is it right that we spend hundreds of billions annually on the military while schools, health clinics, courts, mass transit, bridges, and water works decay?

We do not ask such questions just for people to agree, "No, it's not right!" The questions instead teach them to think in terms of right and wrong. Asking "Is it right?" a dozen times logs in that issue as perhaps worth their attention.

5. Need for unconditional love

Individuals make up the whole, so the good of the whole implies care for them. Rowers in a lifeboat would care for each other because needing their help, but would do the same for family not rowing. Being "in the same boat" implies care for all, love toward everyone, enhancing others' well-being, expressing goodness toward them.

Love as a social standard can be confusing, however. People can *want* another and mistake it for love. They really wish to obtain the other, like saying, "I really love chocolate," and may not understand that love calls them to contribute unselfishly to another's well-being.

We become loving people through a general will to enhance others. As we are curious how to do that, the intent strengthens us and can persist across all cultures and relationships. Thinking steadily about others' well-being, we sometimes set aside our preferences or give up our comfort for their sake. In countless situations love elevates the human condition, and the single most important fact an individual might know is that they are loved. Receiving it even once can leave a lasting effect (9).

Notice how you practice conditional and unconditional love. We understand love better by separating these two forms. Placing a condition on our love, we set a value above love itself. We say it is okay if it meets the other standard like, "I'll love you if you love me," equal return for equal investment, limiting our love by what we gain from it. Or we may love people if they are good to us and withdraw it from those who do not provide us what we want. And discovering we do not respect someone, we lose interest in their well-being so that their condition pre-empts our condition. We allow a negative in them to overcome the positive in us, and to simplify our lives may love only those of our status or family.

Exchanging comparable gains may still manifest love through a society's collective will to enhance citizens' well-being. Often society must limit its use of resources—"We will help you under these conditions," and sometimes say, "Go off with your own people and love them." If everyone agrees on following rules, raising boundaries, and reducing others' burden on themselves, a society may remain strong. Partial good through constructive agreements freely made is better than none.

Optimal society has a different premise: "Whoever you are, we are rooting for you. We are glad for your life and progress, and will help you as we can." Unconditional love expects all to benefit regardless how culturally or racially different or socially acceptable they may be.

"Love even me?" they ask.

"Yes," we answer.

Love "regardless" says we love others because of who we choose to be, a steady beacon of outgoing love. Only so can we express the highest quality of love, not by its benefit to us or by how others meet our criteria. We put out the best we have, and the good (and occasionally even the others) draw from it.

Kindness is unconditional love. Mother Teresa's shelter for the homeless in Calcutta was reported to have supplied food and shelter, the most basic deeds of love, to 36,000 people without charge. After only a stay at the shelter, 18,000 regained their health and resumed a normal life. Unconditional love gives people confidence to join society. They begin to believe they can count on those they do not know to look out for them, to treat them and their needs with respect. With a cushion of safety, they more easily find their own footing. We make life better, easier, and happier for them gratuitously rather than for payback.

Unconditional love shows also in kindness of thought. When others matter to us, small gestures reveal how we think of them—a tone of voice, an idea noted, or another left unsaid. Kind thought looks for a positive intent in their actions, withholds premature judgment about puzzling circumstances, checks gossip before it starts, and has rapid organizational impact. People may disagree but difference does not require conflict. We each have an individual view of what is correct and to be done. And when others diverge from our expectations, with no negative intent we easily judge how we think they should have done it. This can happen between teammates, in relationships, in families, or in any organization, but we can resolve such issues kindly.

People recognize quickly when unconditional love and kindness are missing. They sense it when they are judged, even if it is not expressed aloud. They pull back, are more careful, less outgoing, more isolated, and may often adapt. Instead of doing what they think best, they protect themselves from criticism by choosing from fewer options drawn from mediocre thinking. We can elicit others' poor thinking just by having a negative attitude toward them.

Instead we wish to view them kindly. We assume till demonstrated otherwise that they do the best they can with what they know, that all of us are flawed and limited and need each other's help. While in another organization criticism might arouse defensiveness, in ours it should be seen as a "heads up" we appreciate because it helps us avoid mistakes. We count on the group's loyalty to our well-being to point us correctly.

Expressing love has no end-point. We love as far and as fully as we can, and accept difficulties and obstacles as conditions of reality and not as mistakes. We make ourselves present to problems, adopting an attitude in a sense like the military. A pilot later may be shot down or troops blown up, but a military life implies accepting the possibility of loss before it occurs. Soldiers put themselves "in harm's way" because they value their mission. The parallel for us is accepting sacrifices for a value beyond today's advantage—perhaps protecting our nation, securing a future for our family, or advancing toward an enduring society.

Three clues hint at the condition of our love:

1. Do we want to be loving, to be alert to the well-being of others? If we do not even want it, we are unlikely to do it. And if we do want it, how long does the intent persist?

2. How much time do we spend in negative emotions? We can deduct nearly all that time from our loving state. Negative emotions that saturate our inner world make it harder for us to be loving toward others, though we can still do the right thing despite them.

3. If we were to ask people who know us, "Am I a loving person?", on what basis would they say yes? What do they see in us?

6. Mobilize yourself

The activity of mobilizing. Mobilizing means assembling scattered resources into a single strategy or plan. Each of us has different skill and knowledge, but the gathering process is the same for all: *we organize around what we want.*

If I determine that gratitude is an important resource for me and want to feel it, for instance, I turn my mind to an aspect of my life that gladdens me. As I put my attention on it, my internal energy shifts. Lightness and positiveness infuse the picture emerging in my mind, and my fresh focus on it binds with the energy of the picture to spread gradually through my feeling sensation, and I begin to feel grateful "all over."

Our images of people we love affect us that way when we think about them. In a sense we draw ourselves into a corner of our mind where love is present, and that corner becomes the self we act from just then. As we let it occupy the field of our attention, our loving state makes it easier for us to be loving toward anyone then. Upon deciding that is what we want, focusing on love expands it in our mind's eye and connects our internal energy to the entire spectrum of our past experiences of love.

We get better at doing this as we notice how even subtle choices can alter our internal experience. If you would like a more vivid sense of this process, after calming yourself (such as with even breaths for a couple minutes), try to place your attention steadily just on the word "joy" and watch what happens inside. Perhaps a part of you wants to argue with it, while another part accepts and moves toward it. Different memories associated with the word flash before your awareness, and it becomes plain to you that you have the power to select which association to follow. An active feeling of joy may edge into your awareness as you welcome it. To appreciate the impact of this inner process, watch it happen in reverse when you concentrate just on the word "sad" or the word "anger."

By the changes occurring inside you as you attend to even one word, you recreate yourself. We each gradually generate a different inner being by our steady direction of attention, and the self we assemble determines what we can do. The ideas below can contribute to your choices.

Act on your deepest motives. Upon declaring the good of the whole as our national *mythus,* we need to understand how it translates into personal actions and then do the actions. Initially we watch how we affect others, and choose to benefit instead of harm them. In a complex society, however, even this simple guideline can be confusing. Motives do not spring spontaneously from nowhere, but rather depend on a field of understanding. Information comes together that first makes sense, and then appears desirable and urgent. Chavez suggests that to deliver it to society, *we paint a picture and color it in.*

A car salesman illustrated the effort. One morning he saw a man on his lot examining a vehicle. He went out, began talking, and spoke for eight hours straight until the man bought the car. He answered all the questions the customer could ask but had to master them beforehand; learn every point about the car, the financing, and the purchase process; integrate them into a narrative, connect with the customer, and deliver the details. He presented a coherent picture conveying assurance.

Think about your wish to remedy world needs. You have perhaps pondered this for years, practiced skills, engaged in many actions, learned much, and now face your graduation question. To a sincere person headed for another continent who could be a leader in helping change the world, do you know what to tell them? Is the subject at least as demanding as buying a car, and could it take you eight hours to explain?

This is not about other people yet, but about you, like going to a potluck and deciding what to bring. What skill, dedication, and readiness to learn do you place on the table for the world to use? It is at least arguable that the first rule of success is showing up. You begin by bringing your talent, but by itself its effect will be limited. Urgent outcomes depend on large numbers, so your own path must reach others. The critical point is not individual activity—you and I doing what we can. Only large numbers can affect the scope of present problems. We depend now on cause and effect working with entire systems, and to understand this must think differently.

Visiting a friend many years ago, I met his grandfather who had been a labor organizer in the 1930s. When I described my interest in social change, he smiled sympathetically and said, "Nothing happens without first being made necessary."

If I wanted change, the price was causing it. Every facet of our goal must be made to happen. Conscious effort must alter conditions. Nothing can be presumed to occur by luck, magical thinking, or random good will. In the Great Depression, industry was arrayed against working people. Only the sustained effort of the labor movement, often entailing great individual sacrifice, was able to turn a corner and even then only because helped along by the demands of the Second World War. In the last seventy years the need for large numbers to address the entire system has only increased.

Gathering such a force depends on committed people, so we think about what moves us personally: perhaps the trusting faces of children looking forward to the world they will enter, or dying animals helpless as their habitat disappears, or numbers of people aimless, oppressed, discounted, and discouraged. We allow a value to affect us and awaken our will to respond.

In reconstructing our values, we may find ourselves out of step with our surroundings. Others approve us for adapting to what they think; to rules, customs, and conventions. They may not sympathize with a values-driven life, nor with our fresh boldness. Power may still appear to lie with others—those in positions of influence, the chorus of our friends' voices, or the priorities of demographic groups. We cannot see up front where intentional group activity will make a difference, so we defer to others and remain passive. Author Elizabeth Janeway pictured this state of mind: "Many people who want to change the world do not know what to do with themselves on a rainy Sunday afternoon."

You are free, of course, to ignore personal discipline about all this and do as you please. You can direct your life where you want like a fish follows the shiny thing in the water. But if the shiny thing contains a hook, you cease being free. What you chose before takes you now where you do not choose to go. Choices by you and others have shaped your society, but if you are not satisfied with it, the activity that achieved it can alter it. Understand the outcome of your actions and choose the constructive. If you tolerate the other kind, your society will draw you, like a hooked fish, to an unsatisfactory place.

7. Consider dedication

Grasp your power to be an original cause. Society can go off track quietly, and a better design may not spontaneously present itself. No lucky accidents nor inspiring leaders have remedied our need so far, and we cast about for what to do.

Our best hope lies with a large number who understand how people change and exert the effort implied. To step back from our narrative for a moment, as you read this, *what is going on with you?* In following our theme to this point, you may experience the beginning of a key idea– that dedication concerns absorbing a dominant meaning, an idea significant enough to change the direction of your life.

Deciding we want that direction deeply enough to act steadily toward it, we seize upon our will as an origin, a moment of creation, a first cause prior to which there is no identifiable starting point. When a good thing before us simply waits to be done, we look to the power of our will to do it, declaring:

"It begins with me."

"I can do this."

"I am going to run with this."

"This needs my help"

"This means a lot to me."

"I will find a way."

We set forth an aim, determine to pay its price, and do not blame others for obstacles we encounter. With an internal act, we weigh our values, alight on what satisfies us most and longest, and undertake it. We may recognize this state of mind when we set out to get an education, start a business, invent a tool, or produce art or ideas. Encountering difficulties, we find the strength to move on, and weigh what we need to learn.

What are you dedicated to just now? After handling essentials of food, rest, and income, you reveal it by where you are drawn spontaneously: *Now I can get back to my video game.* Or to my family, sports, friends, or interests. The attraction you feel probably channels your dedication, but spontaneous impulses may not point you in a positive direction. Any of us can have a gut-level sense of family concerns that generate an uneasy dread, or an unsettling view of our future, or that others have treated us unfairly, or we worry about work pressures, or we resent other races or classes. A familiar unhappy feeling may propel our actions, and upon regretting words we spoke, we may wonder, "Why did I react so harshly?"

Such words issue from a deeper layer of our mind: "Out of the abundance of the heart, the mouth speaks." Our ongoing emotions color the central channel of our thoughts which then direct our actions. When resentment feels right to us, we look for ways to express it while rationalizing its destructive effects, which may help explain events in 2016 (10).

A movement aims not just at a few policy changes but at enabling them to work long-term. Our steady effort at this arises from our ongoing thoughts and feelings that overcome doubts and advance our purpose ahead of other priorities. We awaken this attitude easiest as we bond with others, adopting the viewpoint of dedicated people by sharing experiences with them (much more on this later), and also by engaging with ideas that make us better at what we do. Dedication implies disciplining ourselves, which means applying an idea. One habitually late joins a group that values arriving on time, and he disciplines himself to be punctual. Mastering the detail of the moment prepares us to address substantial concerns.

We reveal the importance of our purpose by what we relinquish for it, the sacrifice we accept. The word joins two Latin words, *sacrum* and *facere*, meaning "to make something holy" or "do a holy deed," and refers to the depth of our self-giving apart from its wisdom or outcome. The summit of sacrifice is the gift of our life, which helps to explain Jesus' mission and also battlefield courage. Many of us might give our death in a single heroic gesture and have it over with, while giving our life may be even harder, devoting ourselves to a value a day at a time for our remaining decades. The sacrifice we accept for others' well-being marks our love and dedication.

Gladness is a sign of dedication, a happy immersion in what we do. Life might leave us frustrated or disappointed because we cannot do everything we want, and we could assume that big sacrifice generates more frustration and loss. But the dedication suggested here affects us differently because it gives meaning to our actions. We are eager to sacrifice because the meaning we came to establish is before us.

General Norman Cota, the highest ranking officer to land on Omaha Beach on D-Day, demonstrated the difference. At a moment when the invasion force appeared halted at the water's edge, he came upon soldiers pinned down by heavy fire before an opening in the defenses.

"Gentlemen, we are being killed on the beaches," he shouted over the gunfire. "Let us go inland and be killed." Pistol in hand, he ran through the opening, troops following, and they took the pillbox ahead of them.

Infantry about to launch an assault may tell each other, "See you on the other side," meaning, "We may not survive, but that is not the end of it." We wish to be so eager for the purpose we love that our actions do not entail loss. We redirect our time because we want to, because our goal inspires us. We fuel ourselves with reminders of its worth, and feel grateful for the privilege of pursuing it.

Dedication transforms our attitude toward difficulties. We seize them. They are our environment. They are to changing society what physical contact is to football. A hit is just a condition of where we work and does not mean we do something wrong. We expect opposition, which in our own lives takes up any space we allow it so that we proceed to where our advance meets resistance. Unless we do so, other priorities govern and what we do not want displaces what we do want. Weeds consume our lawn, dirt fills our house, rain penetrates our roof, and manipulative people jerk us about. Presence of limitations just means that no one has managed them, so we welcome and cope with them.

But the greater the effort the task calls for, the more completely we must call on ourselves. People who master a field of skill typically spend ten years and more at it, and reveal their competence by the scope of the problems they handle routinely. Charles Kettering, an inventive genius and one of the architects of General Motors, had a motto: "Problems are the price of progress. Don't bring me anything but trouble. Good news weakens me." He refused to allow setbacks to infect his optimistic determination.

Difficulties may be so massive that for a long time we can only pick at their edges, and may be daunted at how many remain. With so far to go, we think, we might as well give up and let chaos devour society, but we can instead bring the right attitude.

We seek not just activity but excellence in it, accomplishment that exceeds expectations. The minimum is insuring nothing wrong with what we do, like, "We don't let anything leave our shop containing a factual mistake." Excellence means the confident mastery expressed by a sign on a factory wall during World War II: "Any impossible task can be divided into 39 steps each of which is possible." We push ourselves to the edge of our capability.

We can welcome difficulties also because they change us inwardly, even if we cause them by being reactive or narrow. Offered a clue to how we might do better, we deserve to be delighted, and accept other difficulties because we are there to remedy them and have them fixed in our cross hairs.

What we do today is important because we change history. Think about it: what we master today is the history of tomorrow. Such a deal! We get to change history before it ever happens! In fact, the only way we change history is before it happens. In focusing on the mastery, the perfection, of what we have under our control now, we make possible a future—which then becomes more history–that otherwise would not be. This allows us personal peace about conditions beyond our grasp. By doing our best with today's task, we know that we have contributed to the future what was in us to do.

To influence others, we go before them in self-giving. With ourselves in hand, we invite them to join us and let them lean on us until they find their own footing. Incorporated into our group, they assimilate our standards and values. We sustain their well-being out of our loyalty to them whether or not we "get along with them."

Reaching our goal usually requires more from us than we foresee. We free ourselves from the play of circumstances, move beyond small wins and losses to nourish ourselves instead with clarity about our values. If forces defeat us, we can give up or pick ourselves up and continue. We want something strongly enough that it restores our focus, and moves us to refine our thinking and actions. Our society's survival needs to matter to us as much as our paycheck affects our personal economics. We ask, "How important is this? Is it true, necessary, kind? Do I do the work needed?" A master salesman's motto was, "Achievers make a habit of doing what ordinary folks are not willing to do," suggesting that to achieve a goal, we habitually do the challenging thing until it becomes easy.

Upsetting events may generate urgency to succeed "now or never," but such thinking can lead to fitful effort that eventually fails. We run a marathon, though circumstances at times signal a dash. Qualities matter most to us that last a lifetime. In the trade journals my father received when I was young, I read about people who succeeded by doing more than they were paid to do, going the extra mile in service. At the time I thought, "That sounds easy enough." Stepping up our effort makes our work more satisfying and successful, and becomes an approach to life.

A type of attitude seems valuable. When my son was on an ice-breaker carrying tourists to the North Pole, he and other officers were assigned regularly to go up top, scan the horizon with binoculars, and pick out polar bears among the snow and ice. He found that he could do this for up to three hours at a time, often remaining beyond his assignment.

"It was a special kind of concentration," he said later. "You could not do this if you were thinking about anything else or making conversation. You had to be doing only this." Clients on the trip would occasionally join him, look through binoculars for a couple minutes, and leave. Why one person sticks to a task and not another must be their view of it. *The patient person does not ask to be relieved of the difficulty of the moment.* Regardless what it contains, they say, "What I do now is sufficient. This moment is okay, and because it is okay, I can plant myself in it for as long as it takes." And if the moment is okay, one can accept its limitations–being uncomfortable, starting a learning curve, anxious about mistakes, or uncertain of one's ground. We can forgive those conditions, dismiss our discomfort, and do our best with the action.

We want to encourage this attitude in each other, and may know people who have it already, who have persevered at care-taking for others, endured reverses, or pursued a purpose to benefit society. People can learn the activities of a movement quickly, but the character to sustain them develops from steady internal effort. Go to such people, tell them what you value about them, and explain how they might apply their ability. Suggest an issue they might like to work on, and introduce them to your group.

Your own effort is significant in whatever form you give it. For the scope of today's problems, however, it must eventually incorporate others. Movements of history prevailed as numbers insisted publicly and vocally on changes they demanded, but in today's complex world, different features will enable one to succeed.

8. The role of a movement

"Aren't things getting better all over the world? Less war, suffering, and poverty, and more education, food, and democracy?"

In many ways that is true, but people as a body have a stake in what remains. Whenever public opinion is confused, it can be manipulated. The influential can easily steer decisions their way at the expense of long-term values, so that in recent years *democracy worldwide has retreated* as autocrats have gradually become dictators. Even small successful changes can occur under an oppressive social structure that does not change.

Problems such as a warming climate do not lend themselves to piecemeal initiatives but require international cooperation. Power is a worry. Military overreach historically has often led to disaster, so we wonder how the range of American values represent us abroad. National education, health care, and justice systems labor under politicized, fragmented, ideological policies.

"Is this a political effort?"

Much of it is, but for the depth of change needed we must affect mainstream thought. What people want guides their vote, suggesting the need to educate them about threats to civilization. Conveying this larger field of understanding is critical because even big problems can seem invisible. About any random group—scores on a sidewalk downtown—ask, "How many of them work for the survival of civilization?" The answer of course is zero or perhaps one. Almost no one thinks in those terms. They take civilization for granted, are absorbed in their own experience, and at best "do their part." But anything we think about rarely we turn over to people who think about it continually. And when the few who think about the direction of civilization violate the good of the whole, conditions worsen.

Why do we need a movement when people already show their opinion with mass demonstrations, anger at their representatives, investigations, and even shootings?

If representatives took care of problems, there would be no demonstrations. But they do their job so poorly today that fed-up people challenge the system bluntly even though blunt pressure cannot manage the problems. For society to work as a system, it must correct precise functions. Imagine coming upon a neighbor whose car is out of gas and he asks for a push to a gas station. We bring our car behind his and give it a nudge but it doesn't move because he is standing on the brakes.

It is something like that in society. Representative government misleads us by urging us to trust our delegates to move the necessary levers whether they do so or not. A few hundred powerful people can ignore millions venting their ire, so we need to understand how to release the brakes. We may feel helpless, particularly when officeholders work overtime for changes in the wrong direction, but we cannot simply declare periodically how upset we are.

Many have hoped that communications technology, big data, intensive polling, tools of force, and millions working at improvements would make the difference. But even a national organization with numbers, money, and publicity may stalemate. Gains remain in a niche, progress slows, and public attention shifts, leaving us wondering what we missed. Our influence dissolved too far from the levers of change.

Familiar ideologies are not likely to remedy this—they have already been tried–and asking people to think differently may not work because old ideas suck people back into them like quicksand. And changing just people's actions by pressure or manufactured crises may not hold. If their new effort does not succeed quickly, they give it up. We need to supply the elements of sustained change.

How does a movement think differently from the mainstream?

Even offering a message of large scope, a movement adapts it to the receiver. If people are immersed in a niche we fail to address, they do not hear us. Either we enlarge their thinking or address their niche. And does our message reward a few or benefit all? And do we deliver our ideas through people's efforts or rely on expensive advertising? Depending on technology, we are stuck when it fails us. People's effort needs to persevere, suggesting ongoing training and development. And even numbers can lose their way, presuming a need for thoughtful planning.

Principally, we need to shift attention from small problems to the big one, improving the larger system so smaller efforts can succeed. We do not limit the ocean's rise only in front of our coastal town, air temperature only in our state, or income inequality only in our neighborhood. Ignoring a problem's larger dimension can leave us helpless against its local forms. Familiar hurdles recur: how to think for the whole instead of the part, have a life of ideas, work in groups, balance emotions, build dedication, and convey a viewpoint. Yet these competences need to develop along with action. Education by itself has not caused change.

A movement perfects campaigns. Political effort may have limited objectives: we can expand them. Poor public thinking may hamstring progress: we can improve thinking. People go in and out of activity: we can help them stay active. Leaders may not act in the best interests of all: we can choose better leaders. We address salient factors.

What is different about a movement's approach to problems?

It is active rather than passive. Passivity does not work. People often let troublesome issues languish till they explode, as in the American Revolution, the World Wars, or the Great Depression. Chaos does not work. Some public figures prefer it as their force for change and would sacrifice human needs to implement their ideology. Passive resistance–like non-violent protest for the independence of India or our own Civil Rights Movement—has limits. Stopping a bad thing does not start a good one. India competes for being the most unequal country in the world, and the U.S. still experiences endemic racism, injustice, and economic inequality. We particularly want systems that meet needs long-term. If these fail, individual benefits disappear quickly. The challenge is not how to solve separate problems, but rather how to develop collective will toward a more comprehensive aim.

What qualities does a movement need now?

Credible people must communicate reasonable ideas with integrity. A movement needs a broad-based ideal that attracts people's loyalty and effort, gets them into action, and initiates an internal group life that sustains them. For this, four factors work together: **engaging in learning and action toward a common vision with an internal life of mutual support.** Each factor supplies an essential quality.

Vision. People do only what they grasp. For an enduring effort they need a plan that unites varied interests. The vision generates hope and purpose, and gives due proportion to values and activities.

Learning. People need to absorb the knowledge and skills that help them change society: principles and practices that bond them as a team, the effect of their values, how to conduct movement activities, and the impact of the latter on society. Without continued learning, their effort inevitably deteriorates.

Action. The main action is communicating ideas. We affect society as we spread good ideas and help others apply them. We implement the vision.

Mutual support. Personal connections sustain people day to day. They hold their direction and become stronger operating as a team, encouraging each other, and addressing individual needs.

Unconditional love needs to infuse the four factors. Vision means loving a future we picture. We want good in what we move toward. Learning means loving ideas that help us along, not just gathering them. We value them for the good they represent. Action means loving those whose lives we hope to enhance, and mutual support means loving our allies and co-workers. The four factors combine to strengthen our commitment to our purpose.

What are the typical activities of a movement?

Sixteen describe what movement members do:

1. Change perspective. We develop a frame of reference enabling us to work together. We listen carefully to each other.

2. Invite people one at a time. Two people become four by inviting two more. If we want others to come to a party, we ask them.

3. Develop an argument. We need a common view about our purpose and the means to achieve it that we can present to the public.

4. Help people become articulate. We must be able to explain to opponents and the undecided why and how to change. We develop skill at conveying our ideas.

5. Plan for group action. We can encounter dead ends among our options for activity. We plan how to put limited numbers and resources to best use.

6. Provide group support. Action for social change can be tiring and confusing. A supportive group helps sustain people's motivation.

7. Unite around the good of the whole. We take responsibility for all needs that help humans and the biosphere prosper.

8. Dedicate to a purpose. It is not enough that we subscribe to a value. To change society, we reorganize our personal thinking and activity around that purpose.

9. Learn what is needed. To enhance the good in society and the physical world, we continue learning.

10. Question ourselves. It is nearly impossible to reach adulthood without adopting narrow assumptions. Unless we question ourselves and each other, we impose our mistakes on society.

11. Reason with evidence. Sound social policy relies on evidence available to everyone. Without commitment to it, we float among unverifiable opinions.

12. Develop a long-view narrative. Conditions affecting the most people for the longest time play out over generations. We account for time spans.

13. Multiply numbers. Super-majorities may be needed to alter critical policies, so we learn how to multiply numbers.

14. Elect creative representatives. Civilizations rise as leaders are creative for the good of the whole and fall as they are not. We help good people win elections.

15. Remedy society's problems. Activists knowledgeable, united, and numerous solve society's problems by group planning and action.

16. Avoid pitfalls. Complex systems are vulnerable to pitfalls that sabotage progress, so we identify and avoid them.

9. Limitations of the innate valuing process

Use reflection to guide instinct. Determined to advance the good in our life, our perennial problem is figuring out what it is. The answer often is unclear.

We do not change like animals, trees, and grass do. As best we can tell, the latter always try to be the best animal, tree, or grass they can be. Their instincts, their inherent programming, moves them to maximize their potential and enhance their survival. We, on the other hand, balance among conflicting purposes and must understand them in order to sort them out. We surpass the limits of our instincts by conscious reflection. Our inherited physical makeup only prepares us to have children and sustain the human race. Everything beyond a hardscrabble, hand-to-mouth existence like chimpanzees depends on ideas. The good ones enhance human existence and the bad ones do not, but we constantly misjudge which is which.

A parallel we have to animal instincts is a generalized drive for survival, the innate valuing process, built into our physical makeup that orients us toward our well-being. It operates in microseconds when we start to fall and our muscles catch us. Sometimes falling is a good idea (such as on hearing a gunshot) and we can train ourselves to do that, but the human system has evolved spontaneous responses to keep us alive. We avoid threat, spit out rancid food, and approach people who seem to welcome us. Our innate valuing process alerts us to circumstances that appear good for us.

But if we do not use reflection to temper our instincts, they can destroy us. In modern society we tend to eat more fat and sugar than we need, for instance. Since doing so is clearly against our well-being, why do we do it? As early humans, we would have consumed enough fat and sugar just by eating whatever we killed or harvested, but our instincts do not regulate our independent desire for them. Our developed cravings for fat and sugar roll on unchecked unless deliberate thinking determines otherwise. Vendors noticing we ignore that effort then sell us fat and sugar with the nutrients removed, so that government statistics indicate over two-thirds of U.S. adults overweight, and over one-third obese (11).

Relying on animal-level reactions where rational thought is required, we suffer the consequences and can grasp what they mean for our nation's most basic strength. If a foreign country that wished to weaken the U.S. had achieved these outcomes through manipulating our food supply, *would it conclude from these statistics that it was winning?*

Instincts that alert us to our own immediate wants, furthermore, do not serve us well for needs dispersed and distant. Gains today may hurt us later, so with our brain we must weigh short and long-term benefit. Some for us deprive others. An offer might attract us, but the details fall through. We may trust people whose promises fail us. Strident voices may divert us and fascinating stories mislead us. And choosing between near-good and far-good, between self-care and group-care, can confuse us because both options appear good.

We typically resolve self-care first, and then with our own position secured look to group needs. In a wagon train headed west in the 1800s, a head of household might prepare himself for the day, look after his family, and then with spare energy check on others in the wagon train. Primary loyalty goes to those closest, but with a small lapse in attention one may take the wagon train for granted and dismiss the needs of those further back. Especially when laggards appear to belong to someone else, we do not think they deserve the care we give our own. We balance that thought, however, by recalling that the wagon train will not survive if it does not stick together. Reflection enables us to step aside from our instincts and think beyond the surface.

II

PART TWO. THE PROBLEM OF SELFISH POWER

1. The core problem

We have been "had" by a system that created gross economic inequality, left countless needs unmet, and weakened our country's ability to cope with its threats.

The dimension of the overall problem should guide our response, but people instead usually relax when today's reason for their indignation lifts a little: Health care insurance no longer threatened? Okay, everybody, go home. And what is it now, white supremacy? Hey, come back.

But separate issues may arise from a single source. If you see a cockroach in the living room Monday, the bathroom Tuesday, and the kitchen Wednesday, your problem is not the one and the other. *You have a cockroach problem!*–for us today, the intent of people in power. Those we trusted took advantage of us by their self-interest and distorting public thought (cf. Part Three). When they work for themselves against everyone else, the whole suffers. And when the public tolerates mediocre thinking, systems work poorly, needs languish, mainstream attitudes deteriorate, and frustration rises.

The two problems–selfish power and mediocre thinking–are entangled because the powerful pursue their interests easier when they can generate mediocre thinking among the public, which then is helpless to correct the structure. Unfettered self-interest displaces more worthy needs, depresses collective thinking, and damages civilization's functioning.

The two conditions together have crippled nations throughout history, its details the grit of a narrative people need to know. They can appreciate its impact by relating it to current events and how personal, family, and national history have intersected.

A limit on our assessment of selfish power is that not all the elite are selfish. I have known many to whom I would gladly entrust the direction of the country because they think in terms of values and the whole though beginning in either conservative or liberal premises. They have carved out a constructive niche where they make a contribution while benefiting themselves, doing well by doing good. Many problems today also result from unintended consequences that eventually erupt into our attention.

The strategy detailed here invites activists to assimilate the overall picture well enough that they can explain it to anyone at any length in any setting. Information impotent in print gains force when one person explains it to another. Explosive ideas tend eventually to explode, but we can guide them constructively.

A few points about human nature provide a context.

2. Selecting a lens of change

Align effort with human nature. Social change can be understood through different lenses such as military and police power, political majorities, cultural trends, demographic shifts, economic policies, and legislation. But the narrower the focus of influence, the fewer values it includes. Armed forces, for instance, presume the use of force, though practical conditions constantly press for varied responses.

Social change as we view it here relies on "the lens of nature"– optimal physical, social, and psychological functioning that draws on human strengths. We ask humans to do what they do well, what is natural to them rather than the unfamiliar. The more out of tune they are with a task, the more likely they will fail at it. The bigger the change we ask of them, the more obstacles we can expect, so we do not ask for what grates on ordinary human capabilities.

The lens of nature is a tool of choice because it works everywhere. Leveraging only economic policies, we might overlook leaders lying because we can consult the data instead. But the lens of nature suggests a larger issue. Lying damages the trust a society depends on, so we call out people who lie, and check such behavior through social consequences. We place similar value on keeping agreements and respect for other persons and their property (12).

The methods from the lens of nature are the easy way. Selecting between two roads to a destination, we note that one is paved and straight, and the other rutted dirt with hairpin turns and dropoffs. Which do we take? Cooperating with human nature is the easy, straight road. We are designed to communicate, for instance, so that refusing to talk is the hard road, as are withholding important information and distorting what is shared. Foreseeing conditions on our route that could ruin our trip, we take a different one, and it is the same with humanity. Certain features of the lens of nature are central to our theme.

1. *Humans survive as a group.* While we each care for ourselves with food, water, and rest, we survive better in groups than alone. An African saying advises, "If you want to go fast, go alone. If you want to go far, go together." We need to "go together" because we all experience weakness and vulnerability, and depend on others for prolonged periods—growing up and later declining, and when sick or wounded. 80% of us have a diagnosable psychiatric disorder some time in our lives. Think how quickly a tribe would disappear if its standard were, "From now on, we get rid of anyone who is weak or different." In a few years, all the children, elders, immigrants, and pregnant mothers are gone, and a little later everyone else. We seem designed to face life together.

2. *Group size has increased.* For eons, people survived in small groups often hostile to each other, but many needs now affect large groups. All of us together are changing the climate and causing the sixth extinction of life in the planet's entire history, challenging us to think on a different scale (13). If we attend only to the few in our own tribe, we may miss the larger focus. To promote its economy, an emerging nation may ignore air and water pollution, deplete non-renewable resources, and over-fish

and over-harvest renewable ones, so that needs inevitably become acute. Expanding problems invite different thinking.

3. *Group prosperity depends on unselfishness.* Within our tribe, we alternate between self-care and group-care, but a group of any size does better when everyone in it is committed to its success as a whole. Commentators say about a superb team, "They are unselfish." Communities celebrate citizens who serve them generously, and we applaud leaders whose efforts aid the well-being of their nation. The millions who fought in World War II were "the Greatest Generation" because they gave themselves to an important purpose, many losing their life.

Everywhere in society we can choose short-term self-interest over the good of the whole represented before us at the moment by the needs of our family, community, state, nation, or world. Concerned about others' well-being, we spontaneously think how our action affects them and adjust it accordingly. To endure as a group, enough of us have to take care of others. When our concern is me and mine, we instead push our acquisitiveness as far as it will go.

4. *Individuals can take advantage of group prosperity.* The whole does not inevitably succeed. A few can take advantage of the many to benefit themselves. The Federal Government accumulates reserves as the whole prospers, though individuals may pry away as much as they can for themselves. On a successful sports team, anyone on it might believe they gain by selfishness, might sacrifice the team to show off their individual ability. When others resenting this do the same, the team's effort declines, and the same can occur in government. "Ninety percent of politicians," Henry Kissinger remarked, "give the other ten percent a bad name." Every big issue entails a change of focus, at some point less for me and more for the team.

5. *The essential change is toward a common meaning that warrants shared sacrifice.* People sacrifice willingly for what they believe in. Soldiers of any nation typically are most concerned about not letting down their comrades. With everyone's life in danger, their care for each other has life and death impact, but such thinking should expand

eventually to peaceful goals and the needs of a society. Our organizing challenge is to generate that conviction.

3. How civilizations are overturned

Disintegrating civilizations have left a lesson behind. Throughout history, revolutions occurred as the disempowered gathered sufficient force to overthrow their oppressors: peasants versus kings, plebians versus aristocrats, farm workers versus land owners, slaves versus masters, poor versus rich, barbarians versus civilized, and in our own era, colonists versus Parliament. Their common thread has been protest against unfair treatment. Things go badly when the powerful misuse their power.

The politics of 2016 exposed such a condition here. About half the U.S. electorate, tens of millions from both right and left, made clear their anger at "the establishment" and demanded its wholesale disruption, convinced that it no longer worked for them. Our brief national history does not reassure us that we can avoid an overturning because even a democracy is vulnerable. Autocrats today rule many so-called democracies, and Hitler took power when a German democracy modeled on the U.S. system was ineffective.

The pattern is familiar. The life work of Arnold J. Toynbee, a British historian, was to explain how entire civilizations could fail, such as the Egyptian, Greek, Roman, Persian, Chinese, and Japanese. Each had developed an economic and social system, and solved big problems for centuries or even millennia. They prospered for a time and then succumbed to challenges.

After examining twenty-six of them and many other near-civilizations, Toynbee published his findings, *A Study of History*, in ten volumes about fifty years ago. He explained that everything hinged on what he called a creative minority, the thinkers and leaders who inspired others with good ideas and got them working together. As problems arose, leaders mobilized citizens to face them.

What went wrong was that leaders changed their purpose. From looking out for the good of the whole, they shifted instead to benefiting themselves—our concern today about the establishment. While ordinary people's selfishness may injure society slightly, in powerful leaders its effects multiply. The latter ceased being creative for all and used their position for their own luxury, riding on others' labors, and became simply dominant.

As citizens recognized the unfairness of their system, their loyalty to it weakened, yet troubles or challenges always arise. Resources may peter out, the climate changes, hostile hordes invade, or groups revolt, but without citizens' loyalty to it, the society is vulnerable. The civic virtue faded that for centuries had sustained Rome. It could not cope with new threats, and after ups and downs collapsed (14).

Stepping up to problems. Threats may appear to overwhelm societies, but what matters is the response. In his book *Collapse*, Jared Diamond recounts four kinds: failing either to anticipate a problem or notice it when it comes, or when it does come, not trying to solve it, or trying and failing. He is intrigued most by the third. Why would people not try to resolve a threat? Two of the reasons he explores overlap with Toynbee's findings, the body of public thought and the actions of the powerful.

1. Public thought. The rational step from a later perspective may oppose individuals' interests now. Each losing only a little has low incentive to oppose over-harvesting fish, water, timber, range land, topsoil, and non-renewable resources, leaving an open path for some to use them up. Dispersed mainstream thinking—everyone tending to their own business—fails to check selfish interests. Crowd psychology may lend high status to destructive actions, while boycotts to block them depend on difficult conditions.

2. Powerful individuals. Exploiters often know they will get away with their deeds. Key individuals can swing great benefit to the few, the interests of a decision-making elite may clash with the rest of society, and selfishness may prevail. Mining companies may declare bankruptcy rather than clean up, and loggers cut down rain forests and leave. Diamond observes the same factors today that killed off past civilizations: a majority with little rational discipline, unable to

recognize what ultimately matters to it, and a powerful minority that carries off whatever resources and benefits it can (15).

4. The creative minority turns dominant

The United States is living out the stages of disintegrating civilizations. The first phase of creative effort for the whole began two and a half centuries ago when our Founding Fathers and Mothers, aided at important moments by Indian friends, designed a society to benefit most people. Decade by decade, the new country won the loyalty of its citizens. Individual sacrifices preserved a Union facing Civil War, and we prevailed in two world wars because many gave their lives to do so.

Now however we have completed the second stage Toynbee described, in which a leader-class, the establishment, gains for itself rather than for all the people. The extent of economic inequality is an indisputable indicator (16). Those on the bottom tier did not do it to themselves. It was done to them. If it were only an unintended side effect of positive goals, leaders with good will would alter it at once as conditions came into view. Instead the minority in power has steadily guided economic and political factors to increase its advantage.

The issue is not with gain in principle. Everyone agrees that people can benefit themselves. We want opportunity and success for them. But when they rise by pushing others down and closing doors on those arriving later, fewer find well-being. The biggest threat to the good of the whole is the abuse of it by those who by position or advantage can direct the most resources toward themselves.

This process has gone so far as to change our government from a democracy to an oligarchy—government by a few. A study sponsored by Princeton and Northwestern Universities and echoed by President Jimmy Carter concluded that economic elites determine much policy, and citizen interest groups and average citizens have almost zero effect so that the "majority does not rule" (17). A minority has arranged for American productivity to serve its interests.

We might expect this from a dictatorial government but prior civilizations were not democracies and prospered anyway as leaders looked out for all. When they stopped doing so, their society caved in. Democracy's advance was an attempt at a remedy. People realized that the safest repository of wisdom had to be the collective understanding of everyone together. From all corners of society people would be able to notice, "Over here, this isn't working."

The appearance of democracy can be misleading, however. Our electoral system enables a minority to elect a President, and the U.S. Senate is severely undemocratic with tiny states heavily outweighing New York and California. A Wyoming voter has roughly sixty-six times more influence in the Senate than a California voter, leaving Wyoming's delegation with grossly disproportionate influence over the fate of the nation. But once operating a system at least structurally democratic, how would a creative minority turn dominant anyway and funnel benefits toward itself? How could that occur?

Purposeful changes can happen quietly. American leaders have steadily carried out the strategy Joseph Stalin used to take over Eastern Europe after World War II. "If you're going to steal a salami," Stalin advised, "do it slice by slice." For decades leaders have sliced away the lives of the majority by

    repressive wage levels

    racist treatment of blacks, Asians, and Hispanics

    salary discrimination against women

    regressive tax policy

    anti-union legislation

    shaky pension reserves

    prejudicial housing practices

    discriminatory educational and employment opportunities

    an unjust justice system

Each of these conditions is a tool in the hands of the elite to decrease the power of the common worker. To shift even more power to itself slice by slice, the dominant minority has used two practices—gerrymandering and voter suppression. Many states gerrymander voting districts and also suppress voting by making registration difficult, reducing polling locations, forcing voters to travel distances and wait hours, limiting voting days, scheduling elections on work days people must take off, using prior convictions to deny current voting rights, disqualifying voters, and intimidating them at the polls—practices used increasingly after the violent voter suppression of the Reconstruction Era diminished. Toward the end of the 2016 presidential campaign, media reported on three voter suppression efforts that left no mystery about their aim to strengthen the oligarchy. Republican candidates who received 52% of the vote nationwide in 2016 gained 57% of the seats in the House of Representatives.

Many issues affect the poor disproportionately such as health care for all, job re-training, unemployment compensation, public transportation, disability payments, overtime pay, help for the mentally ill and elderly, consumer protection, voting rights, discriminatory practices, public defenders, unions' bargaining power, and the proposed privatization of Social Security and Medicare.

Ignoring such needs leads to an unequal society where the 'haves' receive even more. Those blocking or manipulating the vote demonstrate that they do not believe in democracy or the rule of law, but rather affirm the dominant minority's exercise of power, a belief Toynbee saw as a fork in the road. Either we are on the side of society collectively, or we favor a minority and leave the health of the whole dangling.

While the majority can be mistaken on a given issue, the point of democracy is that all the people together, on average, judge their needs better than any few among them can. By saying to any person or group, "We can ignore your views," we exclude their report on reality, values, fairness, and direction from the fund of knowledge sustaining society. The more we exclude, the weaker are society's roots in reality. The dominant minority of a decaying country often lived in its own cocoon but sometimes could foresee its impending collapse: "After me, the deluge."

Many want a power-elite to solve their problems, but the Good Judgment Project advises otherwise. It has confirmed a fundamental premise of democracy, that average people's combined perceptions can make better judgments than even experts with inside information (18). In an experiment in 1906, Sir Francis Galton had a dead ox hung up at a fair and invited eight hundred people to estimate its weight. He was amazed to discover that the average of all of them was only one pound from the ox's true weight. Everybody thinks better than anybody if we provide them accurate information, let them develop a considered opinion, and find out what it is—assumptions behind democratic elections. Quiz show audiences are right 90% of the time.

Better thinking can help meet the needs of the working majority.

5. Full employment

In a healthy commercial sector, two legitimate interests compete. The dominant minority wants profits while the majority wants full employment, and leaders decide which determines the other. We achieve the goal by varying the means.

Let us say a downturn hits or a competitor cuts in. If profits guide a company's response, it may fire workers, reduce wages, export factories, file for bankruptcy, cancel pensions, shelter funds in the Bahamas, refuse to pay its bills, or incorporate overseas. The means selected achieve the purpose.

For a goal of full employment at a decent wage, on the other hand, a business would act differently. Profits are a *means* to full employment, which is how society's need differs from that of business. The two are not identical. Business might stretch itself to enhance both its own return and employees' job security by sharing profits and stock, diversifying products, re-training employees, accumulating reserves, and restructuring wages. In a Venn diagram with two overlapping moons, one is labeled "Employee interests" and the other "Owner interests." The oval in the middle where they overlap is "stable, prosperous business," while employees' circle includes "secure, well-paid employment" and owners' circle includes "fair profits."

To the objection that society should leave business alone, society's answer could be: "Every dollar you make uses up the economic system we arrange for you and affects our people so we have a stake in what you do. We want both you and your employees to succeed."

Since full employment depends on profits, the best route to it is *an optimal climate for sustained business success,* which depends in turn on society's tools—physical infrastructure, fair regulation, educated workers, a sound financial structure, and criminal justice reducing crime—conditions aiding both owners and employees. We want workers committed to a business that has a stake in them in a society that enhances profit and security together. Many U.S. companies have discovered a bottom line advantage from such policies but society implements the means only after knowing the goal. Critical outcomes of this arrangement are guaranteeing public support for business success and eliminating hostility. Why argue when both sides prosper?

Finding the optimal balance between these two needs, however, becomes easier when both sides realize that it maximizes their long-term benefit and decide to seek it directly. When the trade-off point only reflects each side's political dominance, it is not likely to have the best effect long term. In the U.S., leverage skewed for decades toward commercial interests has led to severe economic inequality. In France, on the other hand, where labor has had the advantage, business success has been hampered. A strength of democracy should be its ability to draw on the dispersed wisdom of all its people, so that even subtle balance points become clear. A critical decision for society is whether it will accept commercial activity that harms people or the natural environment. In the spirit of "Friends come and go but enemies accumulate," *harm accumulates.*

While employment is affected by the pre-eminence given to business or the employee, the size of business large or small may also be significant. The shift away from family-owned, local business toward large chains and conglomerates hints at influences that could drive inequality:

Do state and federal laws enable large commercial power to obtain near-monopolies, overwhelm local initiative, and leave the small entrepreneur unprotected? Has giant agribusiness all but decimated family farms? As large companies pay only what they must in order to obtain the labor force they need, does this drive wages lower overall and expand the inequality gap? Does their influence keep wages permanently low when many are under-employed or job-hunting?

We assess policies by whether they benefit the whole, so that we must ask how the business sector can prosper while providing security and fair return for working people. For that, do we focus on profits alone—and those for the largest businesses–or on continuous, profitable employment? We want local people confident they can help themselves by insight and hard work, but when the dominant minority aims instead for profit for the biggest and wealthiest, it squeezes the majority slice by slice.

6. How we went wrong

When the Industrial Revolution moved labor from small craft shops to manufacturing plants about 250 years ago, workers faced harrowing conditions such as poisonous air and water, dangerous work, uncompensated injuries, a sixty-hour week, wages as low as they could be forced to go, zero job security, full-time child labor, and no ability to protest and strike. These conditions changed over the decades as workers pressed industries, sometimes with government helping but often opposing them. Power usually lay with wealthy owners as it does today.

Self-interest unchecked by other values depresses society, but seems natural to most. They expect those with connections to marshal their money, friends, lobbyists, and legislators to claim resources meant for all. When Alexis de Tocqueville visited America in the early 1800s, he observed that the main interest everywhere was the pursuit of wealth. When, in the 1987 movie *Wall Street,* Gordon Gecko declared, "Greed is good," Americans by and large were okay with it (19). It did not occur to them that those with power would structure the economy to impoverish those without it, but U.S. society encourages the latter outcome more than do many other countries by valuing personal ahead of group achievement, "getting ahead" rather than contributing to others.

A small change in priorities restores balance. Broad success depends ultimately on cooperation, which presumes fairness. While they know that different abilities bring different returns, people object to unfairness—so basic that it also offends monkeys and dogs. Arguably, it is morally offensive for a full time worker for a wealthy corporation to qualify for welfare payments. People mind it when they feel their work is unjustly compensated because they lack political influence.

The last century saw important trends. After World War II, the country focused on shared prosperity and in the next thirty years gained in living standards, national wealth, education, healthcare, longevity, science, and profits distributed among many. The income of the poorest grew fastest of any group, so that blue collar people *for the first time in history*—not a small achievement–could look forward to secure retirement for themselves and college for their children. When the U.S. acknowledged in the 1960s that many of its people were poor, Great Society programs helped alleviate poverty and made dramatic improvements for the worst off.

But government and management united against labor unions that had been a driving force behind the gains. By limiting the influence of unions, the Taft-Hartley Act, passed over President Truman's veto in 1947, marked a turn away from the collective power workers were obtaining. Many states adopted Right to Work laws, more accurately titled *Right to Work for Less* since desperate, powerless people will work cheaper, steadily reducing labor's share of industry's productivity. Businesses hired people for whatever they could impose so that instead of wages rising as companies prospered, owners kept more for themselves and conceded less to workers. Across the economy, wages were suppressed and benefits slashed even as productivity rose, so that more money flowed to the top and less to the bottom of the economic spectrum.

The minimum wage remained stuck even as inflation reduced its value, and deregulation, import of goods, and globalization undercut pay for American labor. The Vietnam War soaked up resources, and less went to the War on Poverty. Economic growth slowed in the mid-seventies with the remaining advances going to the wealthiest. Government and industry held the line against labor's share, so that profits migrated to the well-off and widened inequality.

In the 1980s President Reagan dismissed mainstream concern about poverty. Despite good things he accomplished in foreign policy, he sold "trickle-down economics" to the nation and cut taxes sharply for top incomes, claiming that benefit for the wealthy would reach others in turn. Comedian Bill Maher explained how this has worked: "Trickle-down economics is like having three dogs and giving one of them a wiener, expecting him to share it with the other two." Congresses enabled companies to evade retirement obligations to their employees while fattening CEOs' pay.

Reagan's worst injury to society was probably his assertion that government was the problem instead of how we solve problems in common. He framed taxes as confiscation from producers to give to non-producers, and dismissed the idea of spreading the benefits of prosperity equitably. Playing on the surface thinking of the public, his priorities undermined the security of the middle and lower classes. Instead of benefits trickling down as promised, they have trickled up. From Reagan's time on, society has steadily become more unequal.

In October 2016, John Stumpf, the CEO of Wells Fargo Bank, quit under pressure due to the bank's creation of unwarranted customer accounts that significantly increased the value of his own stake in the company, while 5,000 employees required to carry out the manipulation were fired. It was announced as a fact of the day, with no moral implications, that he would walk away with $134 million dollars (20).

While we might applaud Mr. Stumpf's business acumen, we could also inquire whether he returned $134 million worth of benefits to society for his use of its economic system. The dominant minority structures the system to benefit itself. Of the four factors Jeffrey Sachs identified as contributing to declining trust in government, two of them overlap with Toynbee–economic inequality and the ability of the rich to disregard the law (21).

If we aim at prosperity for all, the wealthy prosper and the system is strong. If we aim at prosperity only for the wealthy, the majority suffer so much the civilization eventually dies. We have already gone a troubling distance toward disintegration: the wealthiest 1% in the world own more than the remaining 99% of the world's population combined (22).

7. The attack on truth

To sustain the system's inequities, the dominant minority has consistently promoted false information (cf. Part Three). Some do so because they have something to gain, and others label any critical news about them as lies and misrepresentation. Biases developed over generations may saturate some people's thinking, so that they vote against their personal economic interests, are swayed by a candidate's emotions, and allow events to seize upon their fears (23).

Tobin Smith, a 14-year business contributor to Fox News, has explained how a central stream of right-wing opinion developed from a deliberate attack on truth. The channel's founder Roger Ailes designedly distorted the news for twenty years to profit from an audience easily misled. While Smith presents other valuable points, here are highlights:

1. Fox's intended audience–Smith quoting Ailes–were "white guys in mostly Red State counties who sit on their couch with the remote in their hand all day and night." They want to see Fox News contributors "tear those smug condescending know-it-all east coast liberals to pieces…limb by limb…until they jump up out of their LaZboy and scream 'Way to go Toby… you KILLED that libtard."

2. The goal was money-making: "(W)hat mattered most at Fox was to create an entertainment product out of political/military/economic news and opinion."

3. The means was "Visceral gut feelings of outrage relieved by the most powerful emotions of all…the thrill of your tribe's victory over its enemy and the ultimate triumph of good over evil."

4. Fox did not allow actual, principled liberals on its shows but only those willing to talk from a script provided to them. The designated liberal's job was to enrage viewers by reciting standard liberal ideology.

5. Every debate between a supposed liberal and a Fox conservative was scripted and choreographed to the minute: "The outcomes for Fox's 'panel debates' have ALWAYS been carefully fixed by producers so that the home team (i.e. the conservative panelists like me) ALWAYS WON…with a scripted narrative and story line almost exactly like pro wrestling."

6. A reliable Fox contributor always had the "kill" role: "(B)efore I delivered the final rhetorical death blow…the producer of the segment had given me my script 24 hours BEFORE the show started. I know 24-48-hours in ADVANCE how the designated liberal was going to argue his/her point…and more important how I was going to win."

7. For older white males they "created an alternative partisan universe…biggest TV scam ever…a parallel universe silo" (24).

Such deliberate distortion of news is likely to increase as companies promoting an ideology buy up local and national media. Thus:

1. Many people we approach will have a distorted view of the facts, inviting discussion up front about the necessity of and sources for facts and evidence.

2. Face to face contact becomes more important, and delivering as much information as possible that way. People are more likely to believe others they know over impersonal sources.

3. Small-town papers and radio-TV stations often have an open-door policy for citizens to walk in and talk about local issues. This lets us converse directly with editors and producers, discuss shared values, praise features of their services, and then make clear what constitutes a distortion of the news. Though they may seem resistive to feedback (they may be guarded in the face of criticism like most of us), *they need ammunition themselves* so they can say to their corporate bosses, "Hey chief. People here are objecting to what we're running."

4. To counter stone-walling responses, activists might use humor to needle a biased news source. Imagine a one-person stand on a busy

sidewalk at the same time every week under a sign reading "Pinocchio Press: How Your Local Media Distorted News This Week." Have a simple handout detailing how the media slanted the news the prior seven days, compared to the facts. This could stimulate public comment and nudge the media to moderate their misrepresentations.

5. In canvassing, people can be asked, "Did you see the article in the daily paper?" Every manhandling of the news is *locally-relevant ammunition* to use for discussing both an issue and the media's motive for falsifying it.

6. To meet society's constant need to defend truth, Professor Timothy Snyder explained twenty ways aligning with our approach, such as: call attention to treacherous use of patriotic vocabulary, be calm in disastrous times, use language accurately, set an example, believe in truth, investigate, put your body in unfamiliar places, make eye contact and small talk, challenge signs of hate, give to good causes, resist intrusions by the state, learn from others, and be a patriot (25).

8. Impact of racism

Slavery, called America's "original sin," is probably the single most powerful factor accounting for today's economic inequity and stratification. With its worst form behind them, Americans would like to forget it though its influence persists and occasionally bursts into public view as in the Charlottesville conflict in August 2017. In "How the racists of the south have ruled this nation from the very beginning," Susan Grigsby explains:

The Constitution created the problem. Allowing southern states to count each slave as 3/5 of a person but *not letting them vote* increased the states' number of presidential electors and representatives in Congress. This enabled southern whites to block any national legislation against slavery, and to elect a string of early Presidents from the South. After the Civil War, the brief Reconstruction Era attempted to give blacks the vote and other rights, but voter suppression by the KKK exerted powerful resistance. States passed Jim Crow laws, literacy tests, and poll taxes, and encouraged voter intimidation so that states with overwhelming black majorities were permanently run by a white ruling class. Grigsby sums up:

> The Jim Crow laws were more than laws restricting the franchise, they codified a way of life that kept African Americans in virtual slavery, subject to punishments as brutal as what were endured before 600,000 Americans lost their lives deciding the issue of slavery in the South.

In the early 1900s, many blacks migrated to the north and west. They gained little restoration of rights or protection from harm but at least were freed from repressive laws. In the 1930s, however, threats to sink the New Deal led Congress to exclude blacks from many of its programs. Southern politicians blocked any racially sensitive legislation until by 1938 only 4% of blacks could vote in the South.

As a price for their support of crucial federal initiatives, southern Congressmen demanded that state Jim Crow laws not be touched, leaving only jobs in agriculture and domestic service open to blacks. The Taft-Hartley Act undermined the latter's attempts to organize, and while the Civil Rights and Voting Rights acts of 1964-65 appeared to turn a corner, they were soon neutralized by Nixon's Southern Strategy summed up by George McGovern:

> It says to the South: Let the poor stay poor, let your economy trail the nation, forget about decent homes and medical care for all your people, choose officials who will oppose every effort to benefit the many at the expense of the few—and in return, we will try to overlook the rights of the black man, appoint a few southerners to high office, and lift your spirits by attacking the 'eastern establishment' whose bank accounts we are filling with your labor and your industry.

Ever since, Federal housing regulations have quietly segregated whites and blacks. As overt racism became less publicly acceptable, neutral-sounding terms like "forced busing" and "cutting taxes" conveyed the correct stance on policies that disproportionately hurt blacks more than whites–and the South has voted Republican ever since (26). Research has identified 3,959 lynchings of blacks between 1877 and 1950, even while recognizing that not all such events can be accounted for–*four thousand torture-laden murders for having different skin color* (27).

You might check yourself about this topic: Do you remain silent, and edge away from those who make racist remarks? If so, you are part of the problem. You allow something to grow that needs to be challenged. Here are a few steps toward a solution:

1. Face your own tendency to avoid the issue. None of us want to confront others or draw negative feelings toward ourselves. While this is understandable, it is at least arguable that the problem *should* upset people. This life and death issue practically destroyed our society's past and will certainly affect its future. We want one based on constructive values and historical, political, and social truth—a purpose significant enough to warrant putting up with a little discomfort. Recognize and argue down your own stereotypes.

2. Our obvious contribution is to supply objective information. We serve each other poorly when we fail to oppose destructive falsehoods. A movement educates the public in the raw truth of history: *How did we get here?* To prepare, *master at least a five minute answer to that question.* Summarize the historical details noted above, update the theme with relevant current events, and draw from other authors' insights and reports. Practice an evidence-rich five minute talk so it rolls off your tongue smoothly, and be ready to present it at any opportunity.

3. Become a calm, stable, objective, rational presence to people around you. Relate to them constructively about the ordinary issues of life–work, travel, family, children, and interests—and listen to their views. Respect them in their existing condition. While not approving their racism, find a positive element in their life to focus on. They should regard you as someone to whom they can safely say anything. Treat them better than their usual experience communicating with others.

4. For anyone committed to a resistant viewpoint, straight-out assertions tend to strengthen their stand, and we literally cause what we don't want. They code the situation as defending against a perceived attack rather than as an invitation to reflective thought. You want to set it up so they can respond with, "You make an interesting point.

Tell me more about it." This outcome suggests working first around the periphery of their core belief until a path opens to go deeper. The first essential is that they are willing to talk to you at all—a huge step forward. Listen to their family's life history–struggles they faced and how they coped with them.

5. When both of you can explain ideas calmly and listen carefully, to introduce the slightest diversion from the other's stream of thought, *ask permission first.* This sidesteps defensiveness because they realize they have control of what comes toward them. You might say, "Your point reminds me of a detail. Could I throw it in here?" You tell it and turn the focus back to them. Ask permission to introduce angles that "could help our discussion," and with their consent explain and discuss ideas around the edges of racism: the use of evidence in technology and science, the impact of confirmation and desirability bias (cf. Part Three. 4. *Correct thinking*), media distortion of news (cf. Part Two. 7. *The attack on truth*), factors threatening objectivity (cf. Part Three), and how you developed your own ideas about race.

6. To prepare for occasions warranting a longer exchange, learn to discuss the following questions in sequence. See yourself leading the person patiently step by step through a train of thought:

Do you know why the Civil War was fought?

What do you think of slavery?

Do you know what conditions people experienced under it?

What would you feel living under those conditions?

Do you know anyone who defends it now?

Do you know what Jim Crow laws were? Do you know their details?

Do you know what lynching is?

Do you know what a "picnic" was?

Do you know how many blacks were lynched after the Civil War?

Why do you think they were lynched?

Do you know what voter suppression methods are?

Which of them have been used in your state?

Which are used now?

Do you think some blacks have been afraid to vote, campaign,

or speak up?

Why would they be afraid?

Do you think that's acceptable for a democratic society?

Do you value the United States of America?

Do you realize that if the Confederacy had succeeded, *there would be no United States?* Does that change anything?

If you were voting before the Civil War, would you have

voted for slave owners or for those who opposed slavery?

Today, do you vote for those *who would have*

voted for the slave owners?

7. Tell people they are free to believe what they want. This may appear to reverse our direction, but it has been found that people change their opinion more readily when others acknowledge their freedom to think as they please: "You can choose any viewpoint you want about these things, of course. You may feel loyal to your ancestors—I can understand that. You might not want to believe what they did was evil, and you are free to make that choice."

8. When you are about to part from people you will see again, pose a brief question for them to think about. Tell them you will ask them their view about it later, and then leave. Expecting to face you and your question again generates discomfort that encourages them to reflect on their beliefs.

9. We appreciate the problem better by recognizing how deeply people's sense of difference from others may go. In rejecting entire categories of human beings, we play out the most basic bias, *otherism:* "These are not my people" (cf. Part Four, 3. *Orient newcomers*). Once believing that, our brain is likely to continue its implicit bias, often challenging more recently-acquired thinking. Sometimes groups acknowledging their negative views of each other try to overcome them by spending time together, but paradoxically intensify their stereotypes—suggesting they start small and expand success gradually.

10. We must not design society to violate justice and respect. Policies meant to diminish discrimination need the solidity of legislation.

9. Participating in oppression

Understand quiet oppression. You personally might be proud to be in the dominant minority. Early in the Occupy Wall Street effort, a sign appeared in a window there reading, "We are the 1 percent." Pleased that you surpass others, you might still maintain, "but I want the best for all." Dictators can claim positive motives and refuse to acknowledge that they oppress others: "First I get everything I want and maintain the system that supports me. Now what could we do after that?"

While you and I may not have such arbitrary power, *we strengthen an oppressive system by accepting rewards and privileges from it, and not correcting it.* All anti-democratic practices are oppressive, as are leaders' attempts to suppress criticism. Oppression can win for a long time when the oppressed see no way out, so that an apparently stable society may conceal hidden currents.

To its citizens, such a system may seem like a rock wall impossible to breach, yet their non-involvement hands their opponents an easy victory. Governments readily manipulate those willing to ignore how they are governed. Every attempt to exclude individuals, demographic groups, or regions from the electoral process by making their participation harder, longer, or more confusing degrades democracy and leaves a minority in control. Signals of whether candidates want a democracy or a dominant minority are their positions on gerrymandering, barriers to registration, limiting times and means of voting, and tolerating manipulative, distractive, irrational, inappropriate arguments while obfuscating evidence and reasoning. Puzzled people do not correct their system.

We usually think of oppression as an outcome of the coercive force of police and military, yet it accounts only for about fifteen percent of society's stability. Mainstream inertia instead has the larger impact, people accepting familiar conditions. Because they expect interventions in a democracy to be protective and measured, they may not notice how power favors some and disadvantages others.

Voter suppression, for instance, is a coercive use of government power but typically quiet, occurring one slice at a time. Driven by post Civil War racism, many states undertook gradually to squeeze out the electoral influence of blacks (cf. 8. *Impact of racism*), and ever since, voting rights have been an uphill struggle. More than two dozen states instituted new restrictions for the 2016 election and a fresh batch of them were in state legislative pipelines in early 2017. Gerrymandering relies on the same oppressive power.

Our national values show up in who we take care of and who we release to the winds of chance. For whom do we make things easy, and for whom do we make things hard? When we support one economic sector and leave another to scramble, the first steadily does well. Its assured steps enhance its wealth, while stumbles in the second sector leave it consistently further behind. By the 2012 presidential election, Governor Romney, a multi-millionaire, paid a smaller proportion of his income in taxes than did his secretary, a statement of values accepted by the nation.

Gains continue to trickle up. Military spending and money in politics have conferred great wealth on industry while burdening the nation with incomprehensible debt and making the U.S. the most unequal among developed nations. If we aim at prosperity for all, the wealthy prosper and the system is strong. If we aim at prosperity only for the wealthy, the majority suffer so much the civilization eventually dies.

We are built to absorb ideas circulating around us, so that many Americans accept that "Trickle-down economics works," "The marketplace meets social needs," and "Anyone can bootstrap themselves." Assumptions persist despite contrary evidence. But when a community does not protect the weaker, self-interest unchecked has historically left the average person's life "solitary, poor, nasty, brutish, and short" as Thomas Hobbes famously put it. Throughout time, as a minority co-opted its labors, the majority's loyalty waned, and when troubles arose, the wealthy had no allies to count on.

An oppressive but hidden condition explains many people's experience, "Wherever I go the door seems closed." Business and institutions can now use big data for decisions about people. In her book *Weapons of Math Destruction*, Cathy O'Neil recounts how companies are able to combine data from a personality test, police encounters, relatives' contacts with police, drug and alcohol use, zip code, grammar, debt, and credit report to decide if people should catch a break in education, loans, employment, home ownership, court sentence, probation, or interest rate. She notes that if government wished, it could use the same information proactively for allocating resources and services like police and social workers, but the intent now is entirely to exclude (28).

It may seem at first that people everywhere operate by self-interest, seizing the small piece they can, but balancing individual and group needs is trained. We are programmed to catch ourselves spontaneously when we fall, but *learn* to catch others when they fall—which occurred gradually as proto-humans survived better together than alone. But even a view constructive at the tribal level leaves us vulnerable now because so much beyond our sight affects us. Waiting till we physically observe a threat, we are too late. By the time an avalanche rumbles above us, we cannot escape it. The entire system needs constructive change, especially for those in it left behind for the last half century.

10. Who is society for?

Some people's worldview is struggle while for others it is success. As we grow up, our resources or assets dramatically affect our progress, but this may become clear only when we try to enter adult society. Some of us advance quickly from a base in a stable home, an education, a job opportunity, parents who front us a loan or have connections, and a peer group with positive values. Opportunity supplies us an occupation, compensation lets us use society's benefits, and we make confident plans for the future. Assets admit us to a world that works for us.

Many others start off with burdens like joblessness, substance abuse, ill health, poor health services, inadequate diet, family poverty, police encounters, racial discrimination, and substandard education. *Their world does not work.* That it seems always that way diminishes their hope which affects their motivation, and pessimism turns into depression. A conservative TV commentator noted that the hardest job in the country is just being poor.

This matters because policies that meet the needs of the wealthy may offer zero incentive for those less fortunate. In a life of struggle, it is easy to conclude that hopes, dreams, and motivation make no difference.

I grew up in a conservative home where competition was presumed to be so fundamental that government could kill it off. Interfering with it could destroy the nation's productivity, implying that winners and losers were natural to the system rather than a problem to solve, and status levels were inevitable. Some worked for lower wages with more risks and less security, while those with a little more income and influence could assume, "This is about me getting ahead." "Survival of the fittest" seemed to extend beyond animal species to apply to us.

People in the right group knew they were welcome most anywhere. Walk up to the door of a job fair, someone looks you over, smiles, and says, "This is for you." Or you walk into an apartment complex and they smile and say, "This is for you." But enter a tall office building with guards in the lobby, they ask your name, check a list, and say "This is not for you." The people you face may use different words, but their message is that you belong or not, and if you belong, benefits await you.

The same kind of exchange occurs between each person and society in general. In our nation's early history, anyone washed up on the beach might stumble across a sign reading, "Glad you're here. This place is for you." Opportunities would open, starting with former countrymen who arrived earlier.

While many factors affect an individual's entry into society, "a place for you" changes as technology alters employment. Imagine a businessman with ten employees who installs a machine that does the work of all ten. Regretting to do it, he must let them go. The machine lowers the bottom end of the economic spectrum (ten people out of work) and raises the upper end (more profit for the owner). The machine steams on unaware of its success, the ten can add to the economy some other way, and society celebrates the increased efficiency because there is more wealth to distribute. It has more stuff.

But the ten out of work are not celebrating. What will they do? Is society just *about* the owner who fired them, or is it for them too? They look around for a safety net–a scholarship to learn a new trade, unemployment compensation to tide them over, or other work. They have no influence over jobs in their region, so that many at the bottom of society are marginally employed and must choose between remaining in familiar surroundings at an economic disadvantage, or trying to follow work. With voting seemingly irrelevant to the struggles they face, they disconnect from politics and may depend on government programs to survive. Lower middle class voters themselves in financial hardship may resent them, and vote against programs that could help them.

Business cannot resolve this because it dismisses people it no longer needs. It wants to make money efficiently. Pensions and unemployment compensation have limits and do not cover everyone anyway, and if other businesses replace ten with one, employment tightens. Scale up the principle of "more for one and less for ten" to entire industries and a few become wealthy while multitudes are out of work or poorly compensated.

Trend lines in fact are clear: More productivity will come from ever fewer people. Competing for your job next may be a robot who will work for less than you make. An executive whose business studies these things predicted that *in the next ten years technology will eliminate 30% of all jobs,* hitting hardest those with only a high school diploma (29). Any repetitive activity that does not require refined judgment is vulnerable—imagine a single person running an entire warehouse. A problem already big is poised to get worse.

Attempts to resolve the situation often fail to account for all ten workers. The political system and social structure sustain the one who bought the machine by providing the market, bank loan, tax write-off, manufacturing process, and transportation network. That's done. He's taken care of. The question left is, "Does society figure out how the others are going to live?" *Is the fate of the workers as important as the machine that took their jobs?* Look after seven and they vote to keep the system, but the other three are cut loose. While machines may stimulate employment in other zones, the new jobs do not go to those displaced..

The issue is basic. Can society grow efficiently and profitably and still account for everyone? The data do not say. It appears to be a matter of choice. A society has a certain productivity. By its values, it determines how that productivity is shared—so much for this group, so much for that one in money, goods, and services. But the current economic inequality reveals starkly that *a fundamental choice went wrong.* Inequality is not from mute forces on impersonal trend lines but from conscious decisions according to prevailing values, so we wait for values to step up and guide what we will work toward. The U.S. has yet to decide whether individuals' problems matter enough for it to resolve what the individual cannot. If society is *about* competition, producers, people contributing, and those with status and influence, then a built-in bias favors those at the top who, through their influence on the political system design economic policies for their benefit.

The transitions facing society will be hardest, as always, on those with fewest resources. Calls for universal basic income today echo the national college debate topic *sixty years ago* for a guaranteed annual wage. We have long recognized the need for financial stability for ordinary people but have addressed it haphazardly. The *Economist* suggested that to respond to this need, we might examine Denmark's "flexicurity" system that allows businesses to hire and fire people more easily but with government helping individuals through the changes. Much needs to be learned about how to adjust the system (30).

In coming years, two trends will continue. Society will increasingly need better educated workers but business will accrue more profits with fewer of them. These two trends taken together suggest that society tap its surplus to enable every capable but jobless person to advance their education: *pay people to learn.* The result would be: 1) Less would go to the top incomes and more to others, moderating inequality, 2) everyone would be able to participate in the economic system, stabilizing and enhancing it, and 3) the nation would lead the world in all sectors of knowledge.

11. People lose faith in the system

We are now in the third phase of Toynbee's cycle when people lose confidence in their government. Required to bear the burden of leaders' privileges, people suspend loyalty and turn against them. About 70% of U.S. citizens have little faith in the government's ability to solve its problems, three-quarters think their children will be worse off than they are, and only 5% think the system needs no change (31). 45% to 60% may not vote in a given election, most believing it makes no difference. The central theme of the 2016 presidential campaign was the public's rejection of an establishment it perceived as no longer working for them.

Though weak loyalty to the system shows up in shootings and bombings, more dangerous than the violent are those who do not believe in the system but want to run it. Some of the dominant minority have voted to shut down the government, even devastate the international financial system by demanding the U.S. repudiate its debts.

Society invites disintegration as it *fails to solve problems that threaten its fabric,* which today appears to contribute to resentment and discouragement, sabotage against the nation's institutions, terrorist actions against citizens, boycott of the political process, and power to money to skew public opinion. Responses that please one group infuriate another, and they vote then for revolution as they understand it or do the modern equivalent of hoisting pitchforks and torches.

Images of historical violence seem alien, of course. "Oh come on!" we may think. "We've survived everything else and we'll get through this." But optimism stands on realism. A ten-foot ladder does not free us from a twenty-foot hole. People who do not understand a problem often turn passive and look to others to take care of them—exactly the conditions allowing a minority to dominate the system.

Most are oblivious to how their passivity to manipulation nearly generated disaster in the past; how, but for excellent decisions by a few people under great pressure in a brief window of time, our entire financial system could have broken down in 2008, or how a terrible evil saved us from an even worse consequence. At a time when Americans were rigidly isolationist and leaders could not convey geopolitical reality to them, had not Japanese Imperialists attacked the U.S. and taken us into war in 1941, think what was poised to happen: *Germans were working on the atom bomb and jet plane*, and had we not entered that war, would have had both long before we did. What would the world look like now if World War II had reached us by Hitler incinerating London and threatening the same for New York with planes able to down anything we possessed?

The last of Toynbee's stages sees the effects of people's declining loyalty to their society. It no longer unites people to face challenges that gradually overwhelm it. Problems are in every direction: the dominant minority controlling elections, manipulation of public opinion, economic inequality, an unfair justice system, and struggles with immigration and education. We need to sort among candidates and address how a movement succeeds, the world our children will inherit, money in politics, technology-driven unemployment, ill health, poverty, water and air pollution, and conflict between classes, religions, and races.

The world is under stress as well. It faces global warming, species' extinction, rainforest destruction, ocean acidification, millions fleeing turmoil, sectarian war, ignorance, oppression, and unstable government. World arsenals contain around 15,000 nuclear bombs in varying degrees of availability (half of them in the U.S.), and lesser weapons are everywhere while diminishing trust between the dominant minority and the majority worldwide weakens society's ability to cope. We use up non-renewable resources, migration is contentious, and violence strikes randomly. When the dominant minority is preoccupied with self-interest, problems remain unaddressed and trend lines do not self-correct.

Those who presume society will continue to solve its problems should remember that *every civilization approaching breakup probably thought so too.* Solving the same problems for centuries means we will continue to do so, right? Right. Until we don't. And then it's too late because the structure within which change can occur is gone.

We are more vulnerable than most realize. We know already that a handful taking over an airplane can kill thousands, but poisons from a single laboratory could kill millions, a few with a dirty nuclear device could make a big city unlivable, and a single terrorist can create havoc. Many countries ignore the vulnerability of their infrastructure until disaster hits, like Japan's nuclear reactors before the 2011 earthquake, or the U.S. Gulf oil spill in 2010, the worst in America's history.

A signal of decay easily overlooked is a gap rather than an event–that issues do not find their way onto the agendas of hearings and committee meetings. The missing item means the responsible body tolerates the problem and prefers to ignore it. When lead-lined pipe poisons your people and you refuse to discuss it, you let disintegration proceed; similarly with bridges weakening, pipelines eroding, highways pockmarked, jails inhuman, the mentally ill warehoused, schools bereft of resources, viruses unchecked, and so on.

Responsibility is the critical intangible. Many have not grasped Grandma's Rule: *Chores first and then go play.* Grandma knew that the rule assured the most well-being for the longest time. A wealthy man I knew credited his success to his motto: "Do what you have to do as soon as you can so you can do what you want to do as long as you can." Personally and nationally, we tend to skip the first part of the sentence and go right to the last, enjoying ourselves as long as we can. We demonstrate responsibility instead by how we address obvious needs. About pollution, for instance, even baby birds quickly learn from parents not to soil their nest, and relieve themselves over its side. On many issues we could rise at least to the intelligence of a bird.

The question, "Who is society for?" is a civilization-determining point. If it is for everyone affected by problems, everyone has a role and is considered. If not, if society uses up people for the designs of the dominant minority, civilization's life shortens. We first decide who is in and who is out, who to plan for, who benefits–a simple choice placing us somewhere between selfish and unselfish. From that determination, policies follow on immigration, employment, the safety net, health care, education, housing, and other issues. We show we value everyone or a few. Is society for winners and not losers, me if I get there first and not those who come later, the healthy and not the sick, the rich and not the poor, white people and not everyone else, a few or all? We can reasonably debate how to express care by our mix of social features and prioritizing the responsibilities of levels of government, but first we figure out who to include, a choice foreshadowing whether a civilization survives.

12. Meritocracy and advantage discriminate

The U.S.'s handling of merit has expanded inequality and the privileges of the dominant minority.

For decades we have assumed worthiness in people because they have money, connections, and power, which justifies giving them more opportunity in finance, loans, tax breaks, government favors, health services, insurance, education, and opportunity (32). Because their children are healthier, look better, sound better, and know more, they seem to deserve more breaks, early hiring, and faster advancement.

Another child might be an ethnic minority. Their single parent may work two jobs, and they may be more unruly, sicker, and talk less with adults. They may perform worse and receive poorer grades overall so that they are shoehorned through school till dropping out early, and work for lower wages with less stability.

But why should society decide that the first child merits its concern and the second child not? Parents of the latter may have been poor to begin with, hit by illness or injury, translating from a foreign language, excluded from a "get started" loan, and struggling to find employment, but still hungering for education and willing to work. A decades-old book offering "secrets" to starting your own business advised hiring people born in a foreign country because, it maintained, overall they would be more honest, work harder, and take nothing for granted. If expending effort is the equalizer and our system wishes to reward it, why not do that? Rules ostensibly fair can evade the point. Anatole France, for instance, called out the French government: "In its majestic equality the law forbids rich and poor alike to steal loaves of bread and sleep under bridges." The issue to address is why people are stealing loaves of bread and sleeping under bridges.

Meritocracy lays a devastating rule on those who lose in its system: "Because you are behind, we can give up on you," allowing pre-existing conditions to rule so that many more whites attend college proportionately than do African-Americans, American Indians, and Hispanics. With minimums to the poor, foreign, criminal, disabled, uneducated, politically non-influential, and socially marginalized, they are less likely to find a place in society. If we value students' willingness to work, we should reward it wherever it occurs so that those of any ability can help themselves by fresh effort.

And we cease viewing money as the indisputable signal of worthiness. A humane government does not further unbalance an unbalanced economy, but redirects some upper class wealth into adequate wages, education, health care, and a safety net for all. All children deserve to be healthy and have straight teeth, adequate nutrition, a safe environment, superior education, and a marketable competence. Wages should enable working adults to parent their children, and we should guarantee everyone at least fourteen years of cost-free quality education. Each one discarded is a tally mark toward civilization's disintegration, and the more of them there are, the larger is the army ready for revolution.

An influence that parallels meritocracy is advantage, leveraging any gain for more gain: "Because you have power, the rest of us give you more power," or "Because you have money, we give you more money," or "Because you have influence over legislation, we give you more influence. Name any advantage you have, let us know, we will give you more of it, hope things turn out well, and Godspeed to you!" This thinking cannot fail to split society into haves and have-nots.

Society works instead when one person's progress does not hinder another's, which distinguishes advantage from benefit. The former means progress not by skill or competence but by starting up a ladder two rungs ahead so that one's advantage directly handicaps another; easier for one is automatically harder for the other. Benefit, on the other hand, does not imply unfairness. Each takes their next step without handicapping someone else, everyone has their own ladder and can move themselves up it.

Advantage multiplies in a subtle way, however. Consider two 4-year-olds in preschool. One has a stay-at-home mom who can coach him so that he knows all his numbers upon entering kindergarten while another with a single working mom and a sibling does not get the help. At every point afterward, the first child uses more fully the help available and accelerates a little more compared to the other. The result is that *each one's knowledge of arithmetic on leaving preschool predicts his high school graduation*—the first one likely, the second one not. Uneven resources at the start affect every step later when all later steps depend on the prior. If we want children to prosper, we use every means we have to bring them up to speed early.

Every newborn has an investment in society, and society in the child. We account for all even though we can still encourage talent, reward effort, and build on capabilities. Some lifeboats may have cushions and others planks, but everyone survives.

13. Market forces can unbalance the system

The Industrial Revolution gave free play to market forces that resisted in every possible way–politically, economically, and often with violence—nearly every change in pay and working conditions that would eventually make the system humane. Power able to impose its values typically widens the gulf between strong and weak. When it accumulates in one place, only equivalent power can stand against it. Sometimes churches have been a civilizing force, sometimes government. But the latter can be controlled by organized crime, drug dealers, a culture of bribery, or commercial interests as now.

People have traded since the start of communal life, so trade is not the problem, and by encouraging ingenuity and initiative, free enterprise has contributed wealth to society. The problem lies in a kind of trade where one side steadily loses. Many proponents of our market system assume that for the greatest benefit, *some have to suffer*; that maximum profit is essential even though others lose their job, pension, and health coverage; are reduced to generational poverty, endure a toxic physical environment, or others' control of their lives matches historic slavery. We underestimate the danger in market forces when we encourage unlimited self-interest.

To balance that picture, we acknowledge first that the structure of free enterprise stands separate from social needs that do not turn a profit, and hence can unwittingly damage non-monetary values. A healthy economic system instead weighs all impacts by their long-term good, focuses steadily on the good of the whole that in turn sustains individual benefit and adds to the nation's resources. It is only due to society's productivity overall that people can seek help from the Federal Government, which has no independent fund from which to distribute endless benefits. Our manner of seeking gain must enable society to weather its challenges and enhance the well-being of all, or some of us may be digging roots in a forest for food.

To proceed toward the good of the whole, we need to limit the pervasive damage from mediocre thinking.

III

PART THREE. THE PROBLEM OF MEDIOCRE THINKING

1. Don't do stupid stuff

The policy of the Obama presidency which could have the most lasting impact is, "Don't do stupid stuff." While the public at large has not yet embraced this historic axiom and may await a cottage industry that can explicate its complexities, an astute observer of American culture explained what the President was driving at:

"Life is hard," said John Wayne. "It's harder if you're stupid." Stupid exceeds ignorant by implying that we do not use even obvious facts before us. Immersed in dull thought processes, we create tides of problems.

This can happen to any of us due to a natural limit on human awareness. We are each confined to a stream of thought, a narrow focus, that we can appreciate from three angles.

Imagine being turned loose among the millions of books in the Library of Congress but with the lights off, and required to read one sentence at a time with a penlight. This condition might seem disabling, but substitute **single-focus mind** for penlight and we get actual experience. We all think by channeling our attention, with the downside of needing to count on other people to handle absolutely everything else while we do so. But we court stupidity by discarding entire sectors of knowledge with no thought for their significance just because we own the one thing we are looking at.

A second characteristic of mind leaves us even more vulnerable. We have no innate check against **believing something completely false.** We do not automatically assess evidence objectively due to the brain's ability to exaggerate and minimize data, a skill that undoubtedly aided mankind's early survival. Hearing an unfamiliar noise in the brush behind us, every resource in us tenses up, trying to understand it. Imagination, scouring all possibilities, may declare a simple assumption to be certainly true.

We carry this flexible capacity today. Our brain can balloon a few points so they overwhelm our awareness, shrink others to pebbles easily kicked aside, and entirely dismiss the remainder—all from our creative control of our attention. Any deep concern can collapse our focus around a tiny facet that dominates our inner world and separates us from the real world around us.

A third problem is how our brain generates a unique knot of perceptions it believes affect its well-being that **for us is reality.** We may accept logically that a larger reality exists outside us but fail to notice how we distort the picture of our corner of it.

We can appreciate this internal reality by noting its opposite. If someone said to us, "My inner experience feels unreal to me," we would have them examined for mental illness. We can instead declare any picture *is us* that is actually but one of many we could have chosen. It is as though we scrolled a list of a thousand movies, said "I think I'll take this one," *and conformed our life to that story.* But rather than drawing a completed life-model from such a list, most of us scoop up pieces here and there almost randomly and patch them together. But noticing that our story is a composite of pictures we claimed, we gain freedom by realizing we can choose others.

These three conditions—the narrow scope of our attention, our easy dismissal of evidence, and the presumed reality of our version of the world–can leave massive gaps in our thinking. In a sense, we are all idiots immersed in our own fantasies. Lift us out of our niche and drop us anywhere in the world, and suddenly we can be club-footed, making dumb mistakes and maybe not surviving. The Peter Principle applies. Looking in the mirror after a blunder, we may tell ourselves,

"You have just run your store of knowledge as far as it will go." The three conditions are important also as reasons not to blame others for their different views, and not to be angry at their apparent obstinacy. The conditions are a structural basis for the limitations in all of us and warrant our compassion and understanding rather than blame.

We escape this personally-unique, misshapen picture by connecting with the world outside us, and estimate mental illness by the degree to which people's concepts distort it. The path diverging from evidence ends eventually in ideas that do not work, and we regain rationality by re-aligning ourselves with external reality. Imagine being in a boating accident in a dense fog but in shallow water. Our little world becomes the few feet we can see in each direction. We do not know if a deep chasm is below us, or if we are being swept out to sea, or are within reach of safety, but then our foot touches a sandbar. Linking to objective reality outside us relieves our panic and restores us to the larger world.

We may assume that the physical world we share aligns us automatically with others, that we all "come our senses" using our eyes and ears upon it, but this reorientation is not automatic. *We can dismiss all of it, and even knowing about others' versions, can assert our own as the operating one,* and let others modify it only guardedly.

Through exchanging sensory evidence, we try to extract each other from the quicksand of our personal, narrow, mental configuration. To make workable plans, we have to get each other to pause long enough upon a grounding in the real world. There, our connections establish in our minds a picture we can enhance together. If we refuse to exchange personal, sensory data, *we each are left presuming that our own picture is the real one* when it may only multiply our fears and primitive emotions, and be completely false.

Below we look at specific uses of mind that can damage society; how emotional fixity gathers strength, works against us, and misleads us into believing our ideas are solid; and how for many group achievements we must help each other toward more comprehensive thinking. Understanding pitfalls, we skirt them better.

2. How mediocre thinking is a problem

Mediocre thinking does not work. It makes too many mistakes, is incomplete, emotionalized, misapplied, or simply false, and has bad outcomes. Our founders foresaw the problem for an infant nation, and tried to limit it by distributing power among branches of government to add to the stabilizing influence of churches, media, business, state laws, foreign governments, and intelligence services.

We might guess their concerns. From their respect for George Washington, many were ready to make him king, though he declined. So then, a President. But from their problems with kings in England, it would occur to them that they should not trust the judgment even of a good President, and devised a House of Representatives, parallel to England's Parliament. But constant turmoil between an autocratic king and a volatile Parliament suggested they should not trust even that so they added a Senate that should be more stable, and a Supreme Court to settle disputes. If all four entities together could not solve a problem, the people could exercise their power eventually to replace occupants of the four branches.

In grade school I was reassured that our founders figured out how to head off disputes, but their solution has actually presented only a minor hurdle to those manipulating government. Thinking turns mediocre when we concentrate on a single narrow value like power while excluding other important values, which has been happening here for over a half-century.

In 1956, C. Wright Mills in *The Power Elite* described a growing class of managers, the wealthy, and the powerful who were determining society's direction (33). Mills saw the structure visibly ceding ground to many people's drive to increase their influence. Five years later, President Eisenhower warned Congress of an accumulation of power that could threaten democracy:

In the councils of government, we must guard against the acquisition of unwarranted influence, whether sought or unsought, by the military industrial complex. The potential for the disastrous rise of misplaced power exists and will persist (34).

"Unwarranted influence" by national leaders, like Toynbee's findings about dominant minorities, could lead even to disaster. An early draft of Eisenhower's speech included the word "military industrial *scientific* complex." His staff induced him to remove the third word, yet his warning has come true as scientific knowledge has turned into technological power affecting every corner of national life. We have had his prescient insight for over a half-century and ignored it.

Thinking based on "misplaced power" took us into the Vietnam War. Ignoring rational ideas cost 58,000 American and over a million Vietnamese lives. U.S. officials spurned invitations to talk with the North Vietnamese, did not discover till too late that they were not friends with the Chinese and that no domino chain of nations was about to fall to Communism. Robert McNamara, Secretary of Defense then, reflected later on lessons missed that could have changed history, such as:

> Empathize with your enemy. Rationality will not save us. There's something beyond oneself. Maximize efficiency. Proportionality should be a guideline in war. Get the data. Be prepared to reexamine your reasoning. Surface the fundamental issue for debate (35).

We cannot assume that we have remedied mediocre thinking just because we can look over our shoulder at what went wrong. Polarized public attitudes in 2016 suggested poor thinking spread widely. Seeing neighborhood children *unable to talk to each other,* we would exclaim, "How childish!" and wonder how they would function in society. But "childish" just means mediocre thinking. What applies to them applies to us. It is childish to be unable to communicate with people who disagree with us.

And while candidate Trump could gain national support apparently by offending people, some elements of his appeal encouraged polarization. The most common way people change, for instance, is when three things occur at once. *They join a group, adopt its values, and participate in its actions* (cf. Part Four. 3. *Orient newcomers*). When we share time and activity with others holding similar values, we readily absorb their viewpoint, and might notice that happen when we enter a church, a team, or a classroom, but negative feelings intensify the conditions this way:

Operating a society depends on our willingness to restrain negative feelings so we can exchange products and services. Most of us probably bear an upsetting condition in some corner of our life, but it would not work for us to vent our frustrations to the cashier at the grocery store. Meeting our present need outweighs unloading our burdens, so we keep a lid on them.

But imagine that everyone in our family dislikes Albanians, though we do not talk about it much because we all accept it. Then one day we happen upon a group where *everyone* hates Albanians, and in fact come together to make life hard for them. Just being in the group encourages us to vent our suppressed feelings. We are accepted completely when we do so, and think, "I've finally found *my* people!" This acceptance attracts others who suppress the same feelings, and unhappiness of any kind can have the same bonding effect.

But joining the group against Albanians also influences our standards. To a degree, our group takes over our neural identification with ourselves, spurring our brain to answer differently to the question, "Who am I?" Our normal thought, "I am doing this" is partly displaced by "*We are doing this*" according to the group's norms. Group think displaces personal responsibility, encouraging the group to carry out its hateful agenda.

This phenomenon may play out in a courtroom as an attorney pleads, "A good kid got carried away with bad people," claiming a temporary change in neural identification as a defense (36). Similarly in an angry crowd, normally law-abiding citizens may surprise themselves by breaking windows. Because neural identification with our group affects our attitudes and values so pervasively, *the group we join can be the most life-altering choice we ever make.*

Mediocre thinking supplies poor strategies for our lives anyway, but worsens them by rationalizing negative feelings and allowing them greater scope and expression. Our mind does not spontaneously compensate for this lapse but awaits our conscious will to change

3. Sources of mediocre thinking

Weigh your group's thinking against the following influences. Effective thinking determines plans, and plans determine outcomes. Mediocre thinking means mediocre plans and outcomes. A movement needs to develop constructive thought deliberately, convey the standards to everyone, practice as a group to call out each other about them, and apply them to public issues.

The points below describe common reasons people may not think well. To appreciate how they might affect judgment, pick out a problem in society that concerns you. As you read each influence, imagine how it could degrade thinking about the problem or has already done so, and what a balancing perspective might be.

Absolutes. We ruin useful ideas by pushing them too far. Better to act today on the step we understand and agree on, and weigh where our effort should go next. Absolutes interfere with this observant activity by assuring us we can ignore evidence, conversation, or compromise. Unless we can appreciate divergent ideas, old viewpoints restrict our thinking.

Principles we regard even as absolute truths are not adequate by themselves, but rather check each other. Democracy, but when and how? Responsibility, when and how? Tradeoffs are inevitable. Columnist George Will suggested three valuable words for politics, "…to a point." Any principle may be helpful but only to a point. How exactly do we weigh justice for the injured against mercy for the offender? Or about freedom, all agree that government should use "can't" and "must" sparingly, that freedom depends on personal responsibility; that problems should be solved if they can without government or at its lowest levels, that happiness cannot be guaranteed but its pursuit can be made easier, that people have an innate drive to enhance themselves and provide for their loved ones, and that we want self-interest to operate fruitfully while preserving fairness. Such outcomes depend on degrees of freedom.

But other values are at stake in attorney-client privilege, regulating commerce, incarceration without charges, electronic eavesdropping, jail for inability to pay, the need for security, mail monitoring, hate speech, library searches, stalking, Internet bullying, private behavior, and holding witnesses. When we fail to grasp where balance lies, we may abdicate effort in one area and over-control in another. Much social webbing concerns who is responsible for what. Levels of government may pre-empt some problems and avoid others—conflicts with no single resolution. Each issue implies balancing an array of values.

Yet we do not leave all our ideas soft. We are not like the member of the British Parliament described by a peer: "Lord X resembles a chair that retains the shape of the last person who sat upon it." We adopt goodness and responsibility as firm principles, but negotiate the conditions that apply them.

Automaticity. Most of our actions are automatic. We barely have to think about them because our prepared response arises spontaneously. We label sensory data milliseconds after it reaches us, our brain supplying us what worked before. By the time we think consciously, our mind has reasserted habits and ignored new evidence like a king passing through a village by train at night. Citizens slumber through the royal presence, which for us is any transforming idea right at hand that we fail to notice.

Personal assumptions dominate our awareness. We spontaneously carry out the action they imply, but this narrow attention works against group success, limiting our thoughts and displacing a universe of alternatives. An action repeated many times becomes our standard response, often embedded in a familiar feeling. Increasing the difficulty is that most of our habits started when we were immature. At eight years old we adopted an eight-year-old's perspective seldom optimal decades later.

Bringing automatic thought under conscious control affects everything. We resist an unthinking return to what we did before so that the versatile in us corrects the patterned. We remain conscious of our thought-stream, catch our reaction before expressing it, soften comments that could come out harshly, and attend to details we are about to dismiss. We restrain our instincts long enough to steer them toward balance. Slowing them just five percent per day, in a month we can eliminate any negative tone. We de-automatize what we want to change by pausing it enough that we can think about it.

Bandwagon. Great bargain ideas draw us into them. A friend who was a teenager in Germany in the 1930s remarked at how appealing were the mass rallies, songs, and torchlit parades. Hitler's crowd psychology influenced even the intellectuals, who assumed they could out-think the propaganda. But with their moral understanding rationalized, average Germans either cooperated when Jews were picked up or stayed quiet.

With our thinking manipulated, we tend to relinquish personal responsibility and then blame others for using the power we gave them. Failing to notice how we are led, we may even sacrifice our lives for a poor idea. Subduing a foreign country that never threatened their own, soldiers required to stand aside from politics say, "I'm defending my country."

Assumptions fuel bandwagons better than do facts because they are malleable, and sometimes we realize only later that we were bamboozled. General Smedley Butler, awarded two Congressional Medals of Honor during the early 1900 wars on foreign soil, wrote later that our interventions generated substantial commerce and were really for profit. He offered a corrective: When the country mobilized, industry leaders should be mobilized also and receive the same $30 a month pay that Army privates did then, posing a question: Why is sacrifice asked, who is asking, and who is sacrificing (37)?

A bandwagon's influence can be alluring because we are surrounded by people who agree with us. When they confirm what we say, we have set up group think to reinforce our assumptions. Self-selected feedback filters out challenge and amplifies our blind spots. Hearing a bandwagon approach, we need to check our wallet. The one who understands recruits the one who does not.

Beliefs. We instinctively limit ourselves by drawing the bulk of our thinking from those around us, so that entire nations tend to believe the same. Born in one country, we will certainly be Moslem; in another, Catholic; in another, Protestant, and so on. The power of beliefs to spread locally reminds us of a cautionary question: "Why should inherited certainties be allowed to threaten human connections?" Rational considerations should slow us down: "Wait a minute. Those people are my enemies *only because I was born here.*"

Countries and people act according to their dominant beliefs so that we often can reason backward from the action to the belief that must have impelled it. A belief precedes one person shooting another. Beliefs that sustain suspicion, hostility, fear, or uncertainty can influence bank loan officers, voting administrators, hiring managers, housing agents, scholarship committees, and judges. Each refers to what for them is the central belief of the moment, but it can be whatever they wish.

Beliefs powerfully affect how people apply rules: "I have to bribe this clerk for him to help me," "I can't sell him this house because he's black," "He's at the end of the line for the job because he's Moslem," "I can't promote her because she's female," "Let's go easy on him in court. He's rich and I'm sure he won't do it again," "I know they broke the law, but they are important people." High rollers almost took down the U.S. economy but avoided consequences themselves. Shared beliefs tell us what to tolerate and what to hold out for, but different sectors of society tend to have their own.

Better communication between the six major systems could help change America's direction. The critical understanding is that despite the positive contribution each can make–religion, transformationals, corporations, governing, media, and the disempowered—each also inherently poses a threat to society if not carefully guided to remain in balance (38).

Consistency. Besides our immersion in present time, we overgeneralize what we think we know, correctly or not. A parallel is the blind spot created by the lack of photo receptors in the eye where the optic nerve takes off for the brain. Locate it by facing a blank wall and closing your right eye. Hold a pencil before you at arm's length with the tip at eye level. Continue to look straight ahead at the wall with your left eye, and slowly move the extended pencil to the left in your peripheral vision. In about eight inches *it disappears* as it enters your blind spot. Your visual field does not show a black hole because your brain fills in, drawing on the adjacent texture.

What we see supplies for what we do not see, just as with our knowledge. Our brain constantly jumps the gaps in our thinking in order to harmonize its contents. Blind spots are as invisible to it as the pencil tip is to our eyes, and may lead us to ignore scores of meanings crowding upon us, like a robin poised on a lawn listening for the sound of a crawling worm and oblivious to cars rumbling past. Absorbed in our personal version of the world, we make our thinking vulnerable to whoever wishes to manipulate it. Only deliberate restraint counteracts over-generalizing.

Another way to grasp this tendency is to remember a time you ignored good advice about a problem you faced. You were committed more to your existing thinking than to the possibility of improving it. You over-estimated the value of your prior knowledge and suffered from its limitations. If you ever decided, "I'm going to make all the mistakes I want and don't try to stop me," you align your current thinking with past thinking. You are consistent. You own yourself. But you also reveal that you would rather endure suffering you cause yourself than accept good solutions from another.

Entitlement. This problem often has early roots. Parents lead children to believe that they personally are special *and therefore should receive special treatment,* opportunities, and advancement. While all of us want to encourage our children, we do them no favor by failing to teach them the balance between individual and group. The larger world then becomes populated with self-centered people. When others do not cooperate with their expectations, they first experience disappointment and eventually anger, resentment, and blame toward others. Retaining this attitude into adulthood is a natural basis for an oligarchy: "We are special and deserve more, so we can design society that way."

Ignorance. All of us are more ignorant than we realize. To appreciate this, on a large piece of paper draw a big circle representing all the knowledge in the world. Inside it, make a smaller one that shows the extent of your knowledge compared to the total. You might do so before reading on....

How does the size of your dot compare to the large circle? *The area outside your dot is your zone of ignorance.* You are already wrong about it when you declare a viewpoint. Each of us is in the same fix, but ignorant people especially do not appreciate their ignorance. Dunning and Kruger, two researchers, found that the less people know, the more certain they are about their ideas; "the incompetent person is too incompetent to understand their own incompetence" (39).

Even experts frequently overestimate their knowledge, a problem made worse by people's tendency to defer to those who appear sure of themselves. A study of scientists—committed professionally to objectivity–found paradoxically that those most sure of their own objectivity were proportionately more prone to bias while those less sure of their objectivity were more likely to try to verify their ideas. *No single criterion tells us whether we are objective or not,* making self-checking important. We each have an independent responsibility to grasp reality.

Indifference. We become irrational by not caring whether we are or not and then deciding we know enough. We say, "I've seen a lot in my years" and call it good, ignoring how tiny is the mental box we fill. Viewing the Taj Mahal in Agra, India, one person says, "Nice work" while another experiences a life-changing inspiration. We remain as we are until we realize there is more to assimilate.

Because a movement's purpose is to convey ideas, it must matter to us that other people grasp what we say. We do not talk into the wind. If overcoming our limitations is not important to us, when we get to the end of our ability we are presumptious and naive. So watching those in power do foolish things, we need not feel superior. The spotlight has not yet turned on us. Short of the summit of our ability we appear smarter, that we know what we are doing. To grow in understanding, we presume that we are constantly searchers, hobbled by errors we do not recognize. Seizing our deficits speeds us toward competence.

Personal motivations are the energy of the movement. Love, responsibility, and unselfishness fuel common purpose, so we check ourselves: What are you about? Our deeper mind shrugs and awaits an answer arising from our action, and our doing resolves the ambiguity. We may note in ourselves a well-intentioned laziness, quick to promise but slow to follow through, that we expect our co-workers to make allowances for us, that we are touchy when corrected. It should matter to us that others have something to offer, especially truth from opponents.

Quick answers to challenges or criticisms may reveal our hidden feelings, but we want to shift to our best answers, our thoughtful second response. We develop character as we change from our first reaction to a better one, but we learn from the first. When someone offers us a critique, we need to examine their words to grasp our flaw. If we are defensive and hurt, protecting our ego is our priority. With low self-awareness we are more likely to be blindsided. New influences touch our perceptions delicately so we need to seize them when they arrive.

Locality. The action of people elsewhere used to concern us less. Primitive mankind could dismiss them because everything was local. Yet if everyone attends to local, no one handles elsewhere. We cannot assume now that those beyond the horizon spontaneously do their part. Needs there may languish and thresholds pass before we even learn about them. Small local improvements can relax people's sense of urgency, so they often need help even to notice a global perspective.

During the 1930s, Americans adhered tenaciously to isolation, and tried to ignore Europe and Asia, but with Pearl Harbor the world linked up overnight. Had we not entered the war, Germany or the Soviet Union would have won the war in Europe, either outcome altering civilization. The attacks that cost over 3,000 lives on September 11, 2001, reminded us once more of our link to the world.

Recall the shock of understanding how DDT was poisoning the earth, the ozone hole admitted lethal radiation, and acid rain affected plant life. In the latter case, New Englanders were puzzled to see their trees starving, foliage dropping, and seedlings not sprouting, and traced the source to coal burning factories hundreds of miles away. Today, distant people affect many of our needs but can promote their own interests instead. Because society everywhere has insisted on local thinking, the moving Antarctic ice shelf and melting Greenland ice cap are projected eventually to flood coastal cities.

Unless we deliberately pay attention to it, *everything is out of sight.* Anything we think about rarely we turn over to those who think about it continually. Immersed in our own interests we release systemic issues to people who bend them for their own gain. Understanding what we are up against, we need to **think local, global, total, and vocal.**

Moral confusion. This arises from readiness to distort reality for one's gain. Joseph Heller summed it up as a strategy in *Catch-22:*

> It was miraculous. It was almost no trick at all, he saw, to turn vice into virtue and slander into truth, impotence into abstinence, arrogance into humility, plunder into philanthropy, thievery into honor, blasphemy into wisdom, brutality into patriotism, and sadism into justice. Anybody could do it; it required no brains at all. It merely required no character (40).

Few of us even consider morality in our daily activity. Our actions were okay yesterday and should be today. We prefer not to debate their implications, or weigh them against right and wrong. But in discounting them, we remain in willful ignorance and are likely eventually to injure others. A movement addresses the morality of society's operations.

During the last several years, for example, a curious facet of the mainstream discussion about inequality has been its missing moral character. Media portray the distress of millions of people with the same objectivity as on interplanetary exploration. Should anyone want to mention morality, it's up to them. We never hear that anyone *caused injury due to selfish intent;* as though the condition dropped out of the sky, mute forces momentarily bending the economics of society, so that no one can be held responsible. But in fact these circumstances are loaded with damage for some and benefit for others, and are not morally neutral.

Sometimes Americans pay attention to right and wrong and

sometimes not. During World War II, Allied forces did not coerce prisoners but instead obtained substantial information by treating them humanely, and later tried Japanese as war criminals for waterboarding U.S. prisoners. Yet when our government sought intelligence after 9-11, to avoid scrutiny it outsourced "enhanced interrogation," torture, to countries that employed waterboarding. Our nation's highest officials authorized their agents to do what we had already called a war crime, and the public let them evade this challenge to conscience. Another such issue is solitary confinement: Since when is is it not cruel and unusual punishment endured at length by over 65,000 men and women nationwide?

Moral concerns involve an emphasis more than evidence. We can snarl at each other like animals or assert a human value. Doing the right thing may depend on subtle thought, noticing something more carefully. The financial instruments widely used before 2008 involved deception that was willfully ignored, as were the conditions of our entry into the Iraq war. Because we become destructive unobtrusively, we need vigilance. Even suspecting a lesser quality in our deed, we should delay it in order to think it through. America's intermittent indifference to such issues reflects on its leaders and the media. The former may do as they please and the latter transmit the former's propaganda uncritically (41).

Ourselves as baseline. Many believe that if they personally succeed anyone can, but they discount their luck and exaggerate the value of their personal experience. Many winners barely notice that the economic system is built for them to win, and success reinforces their presumptions.

The error becomes clearer as we obtain for ourselves a resource that belongs to all. Arriving first we congratulate ourselves, but limited resources mean the rest fail. In musical chairs, each round offers one chair fewer than people, so someone is eliminated—a no-win situation. The emotional impact of this is apparent in watching small children play the game, with those bumped out crying on the sidelines. Asserting "He could have fought harder for a chair" presumes a society in which the powerful oppress the powerless and minor differences at the start are progressively magnified.

We utilize ourselves better as baseline when it helps us understand others, which is The Golden Rule, "Do unto others as you would have them do unto you." We are to think carefully about what we want and apply it to them. Taken too literally the rule limps because people want different things, but its deeper invitation is valid: *Get outside yourself.* How others see their life is as important as how you see yours. The effort is toward unselfishness.

Pain and stress. Physical exercise draws blood from the brain into the muscles, rendering our thinking less efficient and our mind somewhat untethered until blood flow regularizes. Other circumstances can have a similar effect. When upset we may notice our mind stuck and uncomprehending. In a situation similar to a prior stressing event, our brain may resurrect the same fogginess as before.

Judgment wavers also when we are immersed in hurt or fear. To elicit another's worst thinking, we need only attack or reject them. Our anger closes down their flexible thought and thrusts them into the grip of their lowest instincts. Even just telling ethnic groups their test scores represent their race stresses them so much they test worse. *Thinking* about being shamed or embarrassed depresses people's mental ability measurably. Physical pain, emotional hurt, and fear rigidify their naturally flexible intelligence. Knowing this alerts us to mellow out our stress before asking too much from our judgment, and to notice how others' emotional state affects them.

Polarization shows up at the national level in name-calling, false accusation, exaggeration, distortion of the facts, outright lying, and passionate but ill-considered stances. Ill will impairs cooperation on urgent issues, leading some to sabotage a constructive step just because opponents are involved, even at the cost of ignoring national needs.

To solve problems in this climate, people need to know how to set aside their own polarizing tendencies and help to moderate others'. We each have skills for getting along with people and other skills for creating distance. A reason for using the former is that when we make someone feel worse, *they find it harder to do better*. When they feel better, they more easily do better. Worse feelings typically lead to worse behavior (42).

We can appreciate this by watching our thought stream when someone is angry at us. We think first of defending our self-image, ideas, and feelings. But because defensiveness narrows us, it collapses the range of values, positive thoughts, and actions at our disposal, and we become less intelligent.

A small, easy, personal step toward social change is giving up anger. Being angry at people we want to influence is even foolish. We may think we have more impact that way and assume it gives us more control, but usually it narrows the thinking of both ourselves and others, and drives others away. They become defensive, and we don't get what we want from them. Medieval advice about relating to a king was, "If the king is angry with you, do not be angry in return. He will forget his anger, but will not forget yours."

We can consider our inability to change the king's mind as our own limitation to overcome by means other than anger, many of which we discuss below. If the feeling seems to invade us, we can channel it into constructive effort on the issue at hand. Passionate determination is more likely to achieve our goals.

Pressure. We want to engage others by reasons that fit their life. Some may not. Dependence on us, for example, influences people to conform to our views. As we loom larger in their world, their commitment to our purpose is less free. And in mass settings, people feel more anonymous and less likely to be caught doing wrong, so that the group's morals somewhat displace people's neural identification with their own morals as we noted above. And being raised to expect simple explanations for complex problems, having limited information, wanting to imitate leaders, being with others making commitments, and associating with the like-minded all reduce their freedom.

Yet legitimate energy may be present despite such conditions. The potential for good or ill challenges our integrity and obliges us to alert people to influences on them, and help them understand their tendency to defer power even to us. We affect them only with their consent, and try to preserve their freedom by telling them, "This situation may change your thinking. You are free to disagree, but if you join us, do so with open eyes."

We demonstrate our actual values by ranking others' well-being ahead of their service to our purpose, and *do not want them* joining us when the circumstances of their life do not fit. We do not "use people up" but rather enhance their lives by helping them align with the highest principles available to them.

Quality of effort. If our co-workers are unreliable, backbiting, or controlling, our belief in our common purpose may compensate awhile for their deficiencies. We persevere even if they make foolish decisions, claim higher knowledge because they were there first, and leave us confused about expectations. But once noticing efforts poorly run, we soon skip a meeting, let the phone ring, get busier in other parts of our life, and finally tell the secretary just to keep us on the list. Because defects sabotage effort, we recognize a problem about quality early and deal with it.

Organizers especially need to notice what is constructive for the group and corral those who wander too far off. After a meeting, a leader catches a member. "Mike," he says, "could we discuss your comment a few minutes ago?" Everyone needs to welcome feedback and make reasonable adjustments.

Resentment. When signals tell us, "Nobody is minding the shop," people become discouraged, and their unhappy feelings fester. Let down by their leaders, promised much but receiving little, they are resentful, a feeling that combines anger and a type of burden.

Anger may serve a human need by increasing the power we project and helping us move others temporarily to comply with our demand. The other part of resentment is the sense of enduring an unjustified burden, offense, or pressure. The thought "Others take advantage of me" combines with anger to produce resentment. It is more threatening than anger alone because "I'm taken advantage of" may solidify into a habitual attitude and even encourage paranoia in some. New occasions may replay old resentful feelings.

Because resentment overwhelms positive emotions, it can generate random violence and prevent people even from remembering kindness and other values. Upon deciding that the economic system treats them unfairly, they lose faith in it, refuse to contribute to it, and the most severely frustrated try to destroy it. In April 2013, a power substation near San Jose was fired upon, a fiber-optic cable cut, and transformers disabled by people who had nothing to gain. They apparently resented the system so completely that they only wanted to inflict damage–like the 9-11 attacks and the 1995 Federal Building bombing in Oklahoma City. Resentful attitudes can feed racism, inter-group hostility, and violence.

Roles. In adopting a role, we accept ready-made patterns of thought. By saying "I am a…," we take on role-based thinking, don clothing that fits it, and take on its mind-set–a policeman, soldier, judge, laborer, mailman, nurse, or citizen of a particular country. Our language and apparel tell others what to expect of us, but a role also can reduce our desire to learn. We may fix ourselves more tightly to what we know, over-learn and misapply it, develop trained incapacity, and become comfortable only when thinking within our label while dismissing continents of information. We overlook what lies outside our orbit, and do not recognize our isolation because our role excuses us from the effort.

Over a century ago Naval gunnery illustrated the danger. Before 1898, gunners estimated the distance to a target, guessed an angle for their cannons, waited for the ship to roll, and fired. Aim was so bad they could practice all day without hitting anything. A British officer noticed a gunner getting more hits one day, however, by trying to aim continuously with the cannon's clumsy elevating mechanism. When mechanical changes made spectacular improvements, an American ship applied them with similar results.

The Navy did not seize upon the method, however. Resistance was so strong that only President Theodore Roosevelt's personal intervention secured the change. Studying it later, a social scientist found the problem in how seamen identified with their work. Some liked handling the familiar gear and discounted its limitations. Others objected to changing their way of life, while some were just rebellious. Resistance had nothing to do with results but only with attitudes (43).

Maybe you do not see this in yourself, but I do. Do I love my tools and how I use them? *I hated selling my old car and releasing my old typewriter.* Do I enjoy my life pattern? *Only an earthquake could alter my routine.* Do I resist anyone telling me what to do? *How dare others criticize me?* My modest request of life is to use the tools I master, maintain my habits, and not be ordered about. Is that too much to ask?

Identity politics today can present an obstacle similar to role-based thought. It facilitated advances in the past when no better means of change were available, but many goals now can be achieved only by altering the system as a whole. An identity group, furthermore, carries with it an unavoidable obstacle: *People tend to discount appeals from those wanting to benefit themselves.* United effort should achieve benefits for all—LGBTQ efforts to benefit blacks, blacks' effort to benefit Moslems, Moslems' effort to benefit the poor, and so on. An inclusive message all agree on gains credibility.

Role-based thinking can lead to disaster when reality changes and the role does not. Groups can turn into enclaves holding out against an evolving world. Institutions with noble purposes can become obsolete, repeating old forms while insisting that circumstances change. Because a role stabilizes daily activity, for a time conditions answer to its direction, but retained too long it freezes progress. Ancient wisdom warns: *Ducunt fata volentem. Nolentem trahunt* (Destiny leads the willing. It drags the unwilling). Circumstances we fail to master destroy us.

Selfishness. Concern for individual gain diverts us from the flaws in our system, and directs us to make our problems all about ourselves, about how their narrowest form affects us. We look after our well-being day by day for survival, and broadening that emphasis just a little we easily picture the entire world revolving around us. Mark Twain proposed an infinite number of axes to the world, one through every village and hamlet.

Our challenge is forgetting ourselves enough to attend directly to the good of the whole. This change from self to others, from small to large, is so important because only the quality of our collective ideas connects us to the reality we must deal with together.

Stability. Our makeup is our tool kit and tends to be stable because we use it continually to cope with our challenges. Even if we act poorly, our identity reminds us, "This is what we do." Once managing our surroundings, we are wary of drastic changes. Sensing how circumstances could upset us nudges us to keep to the proven, not to question habits that meet our perceived needs, yet doing so can mean tolerating the same conditions for generations. We are each partly captured in a system of thought we share with those around us, and though we assume we can change, many of our qualities stay the same year to year, even decade to decade, unless we have deliberately altered them. Think how predictable are people you have known a long time. Chunks of their thought and attitude persist.

Stability can also turn a population passive when conditions appear impervious to influence. A stable society may even believe it has every problem solved, but Toynbee found a common stage of civilization to be a universal state that brought everything under control usually not long before its collapse. When we think we manage all the variables, we are more vulnerable than we realize.

Tendencies. In countless ways, our physical/mental system is programmed with a preferred response changed only by conscious thought. When we notice a tendency nudging us, we restore freedom by using our brain to decide if it is a good idea. For instance, we tend to distort any new knowledge just by focusing on it intently so that it looms up to become disproportionately huge. We become more objective by asking, "What's the larger context? What's behind my thinking about this? What could balance my reaction?"

Accusing another of a flaw engages familiar tendencies. We dismiss empathy for him, remove his unique humanity from our estimation, and treat him as an adversary. Hearing a novel point, we tend first to label it friend or foe. Does it fit what we already think or must we defend against it?

We also often assume that our present understanding is enough. But if our group knows more than any individual, our thinking is only a piece. Knowing we think incompletely, we refuse to finalize a plan while any of it remains unassimilated, cease believing that our understanding can settle our mind against further change, or that others should think as we do.

Habits established when we were young can be strong but we cannot rely on childhood patterns to solve adult problems. Politics can worsen our distorting tendencies of thought, like children inventing what they wish were real and exaggerating reactions to events. Only conscious reflection corrects our tendencies. We release ego attachment and limit our opinions to the available evidence; submit our ideas humbly to the group and purify our combined thinking as best we can. The group together thinks better than any single person in it.

Time envelope. Our physiology can sabotage our understanding by planting us within a brief time envelope. Embodied where we are, immersed in the circumstances of the moment, we can fail to notice causality unfolding. The future evades direct awareness, and from the past we consciously keep just a few pictures here and there.

Compare your experience now to your impression of life several years ago. Doesn't much of it collapse into random images? Going back a few months we lose chunks of time, can recall only scraps of what happened, and soon mistake even the year in which events occurred. Entire periods could be excised from the narrative of our life without affecting who we are.

Yet in all those times, our experience felt as central as today's does now. This day is the real one but we cannot hang onto it. An irresistible tomorrow pushes it aside and it joins an evaporating cloud of unimportant yesterdays. The wave of significance, the crest of which is this moment, heightens, fades, and moves on. Our awareness puffs up the impression of the moment while keeping only a tiny slice of it, gathering in everything and discarding almost all of it, thousands of moments of experience per day.

We depend on limited tools to learn from the past and project plans for the future. Our senses send yesterday's valuable and useless to the same guillotine. To build on prior knowledge, we need to try resolutely to hold onto it or else our physical processes spontaneously cancel it. Wisdom knocks on our door, waits a moment to be invited in, and proceeds on past. If we do not save it, it is gone, maybe forever.

Views. Of two general sources for our thinking, one is reality-oriented based on evidence. Civilizations progress mainly as parties settle their differences by facts all can inspect. The other source is the zone of intangibles. Some are values that describe qualities important to human society such as love and responsibility while other intangibles may be views, interpretations, and preferences that stretch beyond the evidence. Out of pride, religious conviction, self-promotion, fear of appearing ignorant, or creativity, people may adopt a stance with little objective foundation. When ego prevails, they may assert such beliefs against the evidence or dismiss it as unnecessary. Stating their view may be how they assume they obtain respect. They declare their opinion and others think they are *someone*, but if others threaten their ego by telling them they are wrong, they refuse to acknowledge it and double down on their error.

Knowledge honors the objective world of phenomena, while views can gradually distort our mind. For years I posted on the door of my counseling office a point made by Paul Twitchell: "There is no need to seek truth. Just stop having views." Doing only that, we cease giving energy to our distortions of reality, we stop creating pressure over issues still uncertain. Errors drop away one by one, and what is left over is truth.

Even acknowledging their limitations, people may still find change difficult for many reasons: Current experience can drive out long-term concerns, false memories support the conclusions they want, they discard others' ideas before hearing them, their opinions turn into ideology, overusing their strengths causes damage, fears narrow their perspective, they organize thinking around their dominant feeling, and they oversimplify.

Violence. Violence emerges especially when people feel vulnerable and assume that more force is their answer. A handful of terrorists attacked Paris in November 2015, reminding the population how vulnerable they were. In response, police raided hundreds of Moslem homes to little avail while tips from the Moslem community helped them instead. Trust between it and the Paris police enhanced everyone's safety, while blunt-edged raids had the opposite effect.

Americans' sense of injury after the 9-11 attacks fueled a desire for retribution that helped propel the U.S. into the Iraq war. People feeling threatened by crime are more prone to "Jail them all and throw away the key," which has not reduced crime. We restore balance by noticing whether our activity achieves what we want.

About individual terrorist attacks, it has been found that family and peers usually know ahead of time, and we wonder why they do not speak up. But recall the Unabomber who between 1978 and 1995 targeted people involved in technology, mailing exploding parcels to them. Despite the largest manhunt in FBI history, he was not arrested until his brother and sister-in-law turned him in. To his family, preserving lives outweighed personal bonds.

So think about it. Why shouldn't the lives of innocent people everywhere be motive enough for anyone to speak up? Here's why: When you see the world run by others for their own benefit, and you yourself feel disrespected, ignored, and pressed from every direction, society as a whole holds no substance within you. Loyalty needs to be two-way. *To turn in a family member, people must commit to the values of a society that values them.* If society is not for everyone—some are in and some are out—then everyone watches their own back and protects those close to them, and we do not get the timely call to the police.

The world has not assimilated the lesson of South Africa; as apartheid ended in the early 1990s, how it averted civil war through apology, forgiveness, and reconciliation. Respecting individuals, pursuing justice, and having a place for everyone forestall violence. Encountering deeds the human race cries out against, we go first to our integrity and start with the most goodness available to us regardless of the evil in another. We seize the other if we can, hold him still, confront him with the meaning of his actions, and remember that he is not cured by being broken, demeaned, and ignored.

4. Correct thinking

Question whether your previous ideas still apply. Early times were simpler because we could see a whole problem–catch the fish, harvest the nuts, prepare for the winter, and so on. Hands-on experience enables us to absorb reality directly. We connect to the activity with our fiber, and allow it to touch our feelings. The effect is partly physiological. Neurons in us evidently fire spontaneously to mirror what we notice others do, which helps explain why good models are so important (44). Presence broadcasts subtle qualities, touches invisible receptivity, aids our empathy, and expands our ability to understand others' inner state, so we tend to rely on it.

But civilization altered the usefulness of immediate experience as personal survival came to depend on decisions occurring in systems far beyond our influence. The present and surface seizing our attention may be little help on problems far away. Remote origins escape our sight. That our air is a trifle gray does not inform us adequately about degraded air quality threatening children with asthma. People who believe only what they see may dismiss others who process numbers, but since we cannot directly watch ourselves kill the last sea turtle and coral reef, we have to gather field-related evidence; analyze the environmental stressors that will result in cancers a hundred years from now, endocrine disruption from chemicals loosed into earth and sky, and die-offs from many causes. About dispersed problems, we often lack the whole story and mistake the meaning of scattered circumstances.

It is no solution to give up thinking and rely on others. Rational people try deliberately to correct their thinking. Among all living creatures we are peculiarly dependent on good ideas. We possess tendencies and instincts similar to lower animals as we noted above, but ours are vaguely focused whereas animals pop from the womb or egg knowing just what to do with minimal guidance. They can rely on their instincts to survive, but we cannot. Our higher brain, the neocortex that makes us human, must learn about our circumstances from scratch even though inherited tendencies may insist they know perfectly well what to do. Anger, fear, hunger, and sex drives–wired in for personal and species' survival–tell us straightaway that they have the situation figured out and we should run, fight, eat, or whatever despite incomplete information.

Our usual way to correct thinking is by consulting the evidence, but this may not help due to confirmation bias–seeking information that affirms our beliefs—or desirability bias affirming our wishes (45).

My wife and I listened to a radio news summary about the imminent 2016 presidential election. "So who is going to win?" she said at its conclusion.

I noted that an array of polls had the Democrat in the lead.

"No, they were saying that the Republican can win," she countered, *and I heard nothing in the report suggesting that conclusion.*

We listened to the same broadcast but were affected more by what supported our assumptions, and less by points that could modify them. Corrective evidence lacks the power we would expect because we would rather affirm our existing beliefs and wants than neutralize them.

Consider the reasoning: If I wish to increase my confidence about something I want, I logically collect that kind of evidence. Gathering equal amounts of pro versus con information presumes I have no skin in the game, that either outcome is fine with me. But being creative and intentional, I choose the values I want to apply. To develop the certainty I prefer, from a pile of evidence I pick the nuggets that fit my purpose.

In this way, studying the same stream of evidence can move disputing parties further apart as each applies a different criterion for what to draw from it. Each creatively builds the conclusion they expect or want. As each day's news separates them further, after a year of following their unconscious bias, people may barely be able to talk politics in civil tones across a dinner table.

Evidence unites us *only when we both want the most rational conclusion even if it contradicts us*—a high bar. When it is critical that we work with an opponent to obtain the best idea, we should establish at the start that neither of us want to support what might turn out to be a mistake. Giving in to our preference instead, we inevitably limit our judgment. And though we choose to distort reality, reality eventually catches up. Presuming good weather does not prevent bad weather. Reality wins, but the longer we oppose it, the more painful its victory likely will be.

Aside from the many aberrations of thinking we note here, two basic clues alert us to the quality of our thoughts. One is our intention, the first cause of our thinking. What do we want to accomplish? Its quality may tell us to stop right there because it may do more harm than good ("I really want to start a war"). The other sign is the idea's outcome. If a leader says, "Doing this avoids war" and war comes, the thinking was flawed.

Mediocre thinking is more damaging when turned into formal policies. Even ideas substantially correct can be captured in boxes that degrade their quality like roles, stereotypes, ideologies, surface impressions, selective memory, a desire for power, dependence, ignorance, overuse of strengths, and false consistency. We need to rein in our mind's tendency to misread reality.

5. Acting on ideas

Examine every idea for its implied action. The refusal of Congress to act on global warming over a half-century ago demonstrated that facts are not enough. Scientists could not move Congressmen whose interests were elsewhere. The influence of their other priorities, however, helps us understand the role of a movement. *It applies information to cause change.* The picture we "paint and color in" reconfigures social conditions.

Certain physiological functions operate. As we act, the idea currently in our attention guides our behavior and is usually the one to which we have given the most recent interest and energy (46). Intending to act in a certain way, we immerse in its thought stream, so that engaged with ideas connected to our goal, we find the right action clear. Our human way of improving our action is by improving the picture we act on.

The significance of this is that action constantly refers back to the realism and clarity of ideas. *To guide people whose thoughts may carom randomly anywhere in human experience, we must help them hold onto the reasons for and means of action.* Failure at this largely explains organizational breakdown. Thought did not match purpose. If we want people to value a policy, register, vote, and persuade their friends, the price is to help them think that way. If we want them to resist manipulation of their interests, we help them identify and counteract it. To help them supply their community with productive ideas, we bond with them and stimulate their conversation. A movement not only offers ideas to guide actions, *but sustains them in people's minds until they are acted upon.*

For some goals, our knowledge is ready for implementation. For others, we lack the necessary breadth of perspective. Passionate intensity does not certify our plans. We may need to improve the quality of our understanding before lifting a finger to apply it. And besides possessing a good idea, we need it to unite us, and do not achieve this spontaneously. We do not possess swarm intelligence but rely on consciously absorbing the same idea. Lacking one from education or social policy, we open to people whose beliefs attract us, clustering with the like-minded. Compassionate people value our compassion and the competitive our competitiveness. Any demographic label could constitute our initial bond, but identifying with too narrow a group can make it harder for us to think with a larger.

6. A change narrative

Master a narrative about the urgency of change. We rouse people from their complacency with an urgent picture, and select its details according to their interests and receptivity.

What picture do we want to paint in general? For ourselves, we need a comprehensive and accurate grasp of conditions so we can make good plans. But the mediocre thinking described above is so pervasive that, unless we are careful, we can collectively make big mistakes. Any problem has its basket of details. To solve the problem, we need to know what is in the basket. About economic inequality, for instance, we could begin by updating details like these:

A half dozen heirs of Walmart own $90 billion, more wealth than the bottom 30% of the U.S. population, 130 million people (47). Between 2009 and 2012 as the country slowly emerged from its financial crisis, 95% of the income gains went to the top 1%, to those who needed them least. The system protected the well-off and continues to do so (48). 47 million people receive help with food stamps, 40% of them white (49). 63% of the population don't have enough savings to meet an unexpected $500 car repair bill (50), and two-thirds of the public do not consider themselves financially secure (51).

Such points taken together paint a picture. We invite others to assist change by explaining it, and constantly connect what we learn with what can be done about it, tailoring our message for the people we will meet. To some, climate issues may stand out, or refugees fleeing violence, or hostility between countries, demographic groups, or religions. They may suffer from an economic system that excludes them, worry about losing health insurance, or focus on disappearing non-renewable resources or immigrants who seem alien to them. To make our responses easy to remember, we give it a "sticky" form if we can, presenting it as a story that is simple, unexpected, concrete, from a reliable source, and that enlists emotion (52).

To prepare, we could make it a group project *to find a compelling anecdote from an authoritative source about each of the top twenty issues of the current campaign.* Everyone learns them by heart, and the group continues to add provocative and appealing ideas.

A movement could assign to individual members a study of potential challenges to society: A solar flare could cause widespread damage, the west coast of the U.S. is vulnerable to earthquake and tsunami,

Yellowstone may erupt and cover western U.S. with ash, a comet could strike, and we can count on more hurricanes, broken pipelines, floods, droughts, and earthquakes to inflict misery. What do we need to know ahead of time about each threat?

Then there are man-made problems: a financial system more fragile than we thought, national debt barely manageable, economic inequality severe enough to threaten the social compact, a worsening opioid epidemic, depletion of fresh water, destruction of arable land, degradation of irreplaceable natural environments, and so on. These issues deserve society's attention. And what do we need to know in order to stand against those who would underfund education, increase pollution, deregulate the financial sector, dismiss hunger and poverty, let infrastructure decay, militarize international relations, and funnel to themselves the fruits of American productivity? Specific change relies on specific knowledge.

Jared Diamond notes physical problems threatening the world that rarely appear on political agendas: Loss of species, genetic diversity, and natural habitat is accelerating. Toxic chemicals pollute the biosphere causing endocrine disruption and a declining human sperm count. Alien species can devastate a region, and gases warm the planet and deplete ozone. The world's major energy sources now are non-renewable—oil, gas, and coal—though use of renewables is increasing. Freshwater aquifers worldwide are dropping. The earth's ability to grow crops and wild plants is more limited than previously realized, and human activity reduces it. Wind and erosion strip farm soil faster than it is created. Two billion people depend on the oceans for their protein but declining stocks are managed erratically. Citizens of the U.S., Western Europe, and Japan consume thirty-two times more resources like fossil fuels and produce that much more waste than do those living in the Third World. Diamond concludes that we are on a collision course and must resolve these problems by planning or by war, genocide, starvation, epidemics, and social collapse (53).

Details of such issues together feed a general sense of urgency and lend substance to election debates and assessment of candidates. When the opportunity opens, a movement can deliver key information to hearings and committees where it can make a difference.

7. Align with evidence

Design your thinking around what is known. For ourselves we need a commitment to evidence, a group standard that subordinates opinions to data. With so much of the latter available, we start *by applying the evidence already pounding on our door.* What is the obvious reality affirmed by objective people?

Social policy may seem like an unfitting venue for exact thinking. We may instead presume we can invent whatever we prefer, and count on society's operation despite its problems. The standards of today's omnipresent technology, however, could benefit social policy: *total accuracy, zero defects.* A single mistake guiding a system can have earth-altering consequences. The more we leverage a shaky fact, the greater the disaster if it is wrong. A spacecraft sent out with a one percent navigational error goes billions of miles off course.

Errors seemingly small can affect social policy the same way. One almost indistinguishable at the start but carried out over generations multiplies like compound interest, such as occurred with economic inequality. A couple generations ago, no government committee said, "Let's set up a system where in a few years one percent of the people have most of the wealth, okay?"

There were no approving shouts, "A great idea, yes, let's do it." The move went practically unnoticed yet society awakes to find itself far off course.

How could this happen? A few may have foreseen the outcome and worked to obtain it, but most had no clue as minor influences accumulated. When they could, leaders laid hold of a benefit here and there. That some would pay a few dollars less in taxes and others receive a few less for schools was not a problem big enough to bring people into the streets. But small errors once made, banked, and taken for granted can expand for decades. Though they eventually become gargantuan and the public senses things go awry, it cannot pin down causes because details taken alone seem insignificant.

Successful systems accomplish their goals differently. When NASA sends a spacecraft one percent off course, does it say, "Too bad. Lost that one," and go on to the next? Or, "Get it back on course!"? NASA lives by its ability to recognize mistakes quickly and fix them.

The bottleneck for solving social problems is not whether people will work together to do that—a concern arising well after the road has begun. Before that, we must first agree to rely on evidence and information, and balance among constructive values. Since a controlling minority does not accept even this much, we first try to insure that those given power to guide society *at least believe in evidence*. We remove debate from ideological assumptions and historical antagonism, and advance by patiently addressing the facts of citizens' well-being.

Analytic tools. We make evidence useful by how we elicit and apply its implications:

1. CAUSE and EFFECT. What determines or affects what? Do we mistake sequence or proximity for causality? Four causal influences impacting a situation may be physical objects and conditions, purposes, ideas, and the agents driving it.

2. CERTAINTY. How certain are we? Healthy self-doubt helps free us from past mistakes: "I may not see this fully." We welcome challenge to our thinking.

3. COMPARE and CONTRAST. How is one thing the same as or different from another? A condition may not be what we expected.

4. EVENTS. Several causes may converge in an event. Is it predictable or unexpected? How does it connect to other events past, present, or future?

5. FACT. Is it based in fact or opinion, true or false? Resolved by gathering data or weighing competing interpretations?

6. IMAGINATION. How can this be visualized? Can we picture it differently or from another angle? Make a story out of it?

7. IMPORTANCE. What scale do we use to judge it and where does it stand on that scale?

8. MATERIALS. What are its components or parts? What can be seen, touched, heard, shaped, or handled? How do physical qualities influence outcomes?

9. MEANING. We gather the meaning of an author's words from their frame of reference found in other writing. We apply our own meaning to them by integrating them with our other knowledge.

10. MOTIVATION. What moved the people who brought it about? How did they appeal to others? What influences were major and minor?

11. ORIGIN. The first cause of something often determines its quality. What is the source of it? What is behind it?

12. PART and WHOLE. How is this part of something larger? What are the smallest units of it? How can it be structured or divided?

13. PATTERN. How is this ordered? Is a pattern intended, accidental, or changeable?

14. PEOPLE. Who participates, benefits, or is affected? What are their concerns?

15. PROCESS. Is this a "how to do" something, steps in a sequence? Where does it begin and end?

16. PURPOSE. Who intended this for what purpose? What outcome can be inferred from its conditions?

17. REASONS. Is this evidence supporting something else? What supports it? Is evidence assembled or awaiting collection?

18. RULES. Is this a rule for understanding or doing something? Is it used rationally or arbitrarily?

19. SOURCES. Are the sources of information reliable or do they have an ulterior motive? How can we tell?

20. STEREOTYPES. What general labels are applied? What shreds of truth do they contain, and how can others remedy their gaps?

21. SUBJECTIVE and OBJECTIVE. Is this created in someone's mind, in their view of the world, or does it exist in external reality?

22. SUBSTANCE and QUALITY. What is the basic, permanent nature, and what temporary qualities does it possess?

23. VALUES. What intangibles are affected or expressed? How would

a spiritual viewpoint differ from a practical or material one? What are the priorities?

24. VISIBILITY. Is this hidden or obvious? Do appearances differ from fact? How do we distinguish surface from substance about an issue (54)?

A task force studying a regional criminal justice system might draw on such factors in its investigation: the causes and reasons for criminal activity, events of public concern, stereotypes impeding the system, who gains and loses from possible changes, the desired outcomes of imprisonment, the processes of rehabilitation, the values and views of the major players, comparison to other countries, the validity of the founding principles of the system, improving parts independently, evidence to gather, imagining differently from the ground up, and novel solutions proposed (55).

8. The appeal to churches

Find common ground with churches. Churches exist for the sake of enduring values that aspire to the summit of Maslow's need scale and the optimal functioning of human nature, while trying to account for consequences even beyond the grave. Critics of religion might balance its perceived drawbacks–narrowness and dogmatism–against two important factors: 1) Church goals directed toward this world parallel a movement's aim that people experience love and well-being, and 2) church membership implies a values-guided life. In joining one, people express willingness *to restrain their weaknesses in order to follow a principle*, an attitude basic to a movement.

The church-affiliated who are more politically than spiritually motivated, on the other hand, have been a problem for society from the ancient past to the present, which we discuss in the next section. The persistence of this tendency recalls a study done long ago about the attitudes of clergymen and a conclusion from it that prompted my own self-examination: *they were more interested in power than were others.*

Appealing to the positive values of church members is personal for me. During my time as a Catholic priest, my favorite reading after the Bible was lives of the saints. These were men and women who usually began life in ordinary ways, but upon certain personal events grasped that they lived also in a spiritual world. Organizing their life around it, they developed its features of faith, love, humility, unselfishness, and service, posing a standard for the rest of us: *these are the things to aim for*–immersing in the spiritual reality and applying its meaning in the world.

Speaking to Christians, I know you recognize these two essentials. Inspired by the first and living the second, your support powerfully aided the Civil Rights Movement and on countless fronts you have defended the needs of the most vulnerable. You may regard many in your church as saints from their service to others, and your congregation may be a last resort for people in need. In Genesis, God handed the good and completed cosmos over to humans for their use and management, so you may feel called to be a good steward.

Because others manage most of the world, you need to figure out how to work within limitations, but Jesus urges you not to give up: "You are the light of the world. A town built on a hill cannot be hidden. Neither do people light a lamp and put it under a bowl. Instead they put it on its stand, and it gives light to everyone in the house. In the same way, let your light shine before others, that they may see your good deeds and glorify your Father in heaven" (Matthew 5:14-16).

He wants you to be accessible to others and offer them light and service; tells you even to invite others to watch how you apply your beliefs so they can be encouraged by it, "See, folks, this is how you do it."

You are free to choose your focus, of course. The array of needs is vast and all values invite attention, but controversial issues could obscure your light. Non-believers turn defensive when you preach at them or try to control their lives. You may decide to act less on issues that separate people and more where all can cooperate.

Jesus suggested just such an emphasis. We appreciate it first by noting what his followers expected. They resented Roman rule, believed the

Messiah would free them from it, and thought Jesus would step up. He appeared to do so as he called out Jewish leaders for their lack of compassion and burdening people, but he avoided comment on the worst aspects of Roman society, such as its brutality, infanticide, slavery, and crucifixions. Confronted even with the woman caught in adultery—a deed universally condemned—he told followers to leave it alone. They should not even judge her. If anyone was to do judging, he would take care of it (Jn. 8: 1-11).

And about judging itself, he could have provided succeeding centuries with rules of conduct covering every human failing, dictated precise standards, told his followers to lay them on everyone, and designed an insulated society around them. But he did not and even forbade them to make judgments of each other, warning that what they put out toward others would strike back at themselves (Mt. 7: 1-3). After he was gone, his followers did not address even the brutality of Rome, and focused instead on the spiritual needs of their own assemblies. Why?

Asking why suggests an unknown, a context missing from our assumptions, a question we have not yet asked ourselves, so we need to think carefully. The question checks our tendency to elaborate instantly what we assume we already understand. Context matters because, oddly again, early Christians ignored the brutality, torture, infanticide, slavery, and crucifixions they confronted in daily life. Why would these issues be overlooked when they had universally expected the Messiah to clean out all the oppression, sin, and materialism they lived with?

Jesus' emphasis puzzled his followers at first, and they did not get clear on it until after he was gone. *His point was not about correcting human behavior.* That would change as people changed inwardly. Forcing it only on their actions would not work, and trying this in later centuries they created societies more terrifying than the Roman (cf. next section). He intended instead to introduce them to a different reality. Three ideas describe it, the second and third aligned with our objectives:

1. Live in the spiritual dimension I open for you. Get right
with God.
2. Stop trying to control other people.

3. Take care of their needs.

About the first idea, he distinguished a materialistic from a spiritual life. Sin kept them on the material level, and particularly they were to avoid love of riches, which proposed today from a pulpit would be taken as anti-American. But in saying, "You cannot serve God and money" (Mt. 6:24), he presented the two as masters competing for influence over a believer. Money could rule you, a condition so contra-spiritual that he compared a camel's difficulty passing through the eye of a needle to a rich man entering heaven (Mk. 10:25). And in a vivid tale, he described two men dying and facing different fates, a rich man into torment and a poor man into bliss, yet the rich man was not described as cruel and had not caused the poor man's lot but was only indifferent to his suffering (Luke 16:21-27). His point, hammered upon throughout the Old Testament and New, was that *the path to God involved loving others unselfishly.*

About controlling people, the second point, we hear not a peep from him or his apostles that they should hunger and thirst for social dominance or force others into their beliefs. He scolded James and John for wanting to bring fire on those who refused his message (Lk 9:54-55), *and pointed out that they lacked an essential understanding of themselves.* They were to accept people as they found them, win them over by their own goodness. Inviting them into a spiritual reality and then coercing their lives would have contradicted and overwhelmed the picture he presented. Politics, the art of controlling one's environment, means controlling people (56). Political motives can gut spirituality while co-opting its language.

About the third idea above, to make sure they would face squarely their own spiritual condition, Jesus described the ultimate assessment of their lives in the most practical terms possible so they would make no mistake: If they cared for even the lowliest with food, water, clothing, shelter, and help as needed, they did it for him with lasting spiritual consequences. He even predicted the excuses they would make when he confronted them at their Last Judgment and the fateful answer he would give them (Mt. 25:31-46), a scene suggesting a dialog to open with a Bible-literate Christian:

"Do you think that when you die, you go to your own final judgment?

"Do you believe Jesus will conduct it?

"Are you familiar with the Bible passage where he describes what will happen then? Could we look it up?

"Do you think that only believing Christians will 'pass' that judgment?

"Okay, so help me understand something. He sends people into eternal fire who did not give drink to the thirsty, take in strangers, clothe them, and minister to their needs, but these people object. They don't think this is fair. They protest in verse 44 that they never recognized him as needing these things: 'We didn't get the word about this.' But he says whether they got the word or not, '…as you did not do it to one of the least of these, you did not do it to me.'

"How do you read this? The Son of God must have known that this would all be printed out in the Bible and taught to all Christians, right? Right. **No Christian could say,** 'No one told me about the standard' because they've got it right there in black and white, and he knows they know that.

"So Christians are not going to answer that way, which means he is judging everyone, Christian or not, by the same criterion. He is saying that he raises up those who do what he asks, even if they don't realize its spiritual importance nor its connection to him. People who do these simple things, whether 'believing in him' or not, go with him. Isn't that the obvious sense of the passage? I'd really like to understand how you could reach any different conclusion."

The concerns Jesus enumerates (and all human needs by implication) are visible work Christians can accomplish hand-in-hand with non-believers, Jesus says nothing is more important, and the message is relevant to society. So how can Christians agitate over issues he ignored, "hunger and thirst" for political control, and ignore issues he explicitly declared are most important to him? Can a Christian dismiss the condition of the poor? Government programs that benefit each of us reveal our values. Saying, "I'm lucky the government provides for me, but the poor should go to private charities" is hypocritical, supporting a system that takes care of us but not others. Jesus leaves no doubt about his message to a wealthy nation (57).

Your faith means that you grasp the meaning of a spiritual heart, that you love good things, are not consumed with opposition and conflict and condemnation but are filled with gentleness, honesty, and compassion for those who are different. If Jesus' instructions are unsettling, you can use your spiritual tools: Pray for guidance. Bringing a spiritual heart to social change, you can lift others. Rules are not enough. Jewish leaders back then believed they followed all the rules but they were oppressors. Today also, some people follow rules while burdening others, and oppressive leaders still pray for the poor. The wealthy shred the safety net and oppose even food stamps while obtaining lower taxes for themselves.

You personally may find the change suggested here to be mysteriously difficult, even somewhat alien, but the reason for the difficulty is likely to be entirely apart from your religious/spiritual beliefs and rooted instead in basic human traits. Growing up, most of us are guided to focus intently on ourselves. Messages saturate our brain daily that feed our personal focus: my abilities, my family, my creativity, my effort, my learning, my work, my attractiveness, my fame, my future, my life. Even in Christian homes, the attitude Jesus pictures as determining our spiritual fate can become but a good idea added on the side, like a small chocolate on our plate after a five course meal. The messages we continually consume return us steadily to ourselves, a flood of self-preoccupation we must counteract in order to be of service. To take our next step, we have to change that way of thinking.

A movement team might suggest collaborating with a congregation on a series of public seminars about the policy implications of each verse of the Sermon on the Mount (Mt. 5-7), which for those unfamiliar with the Bible is an excellent summary of Jesus' most provocative teachings that apply to daily life. Participants could learn to talk each other's language, Christians could decide if they want society to take seriously Jesus' emphatic teachings, and all could focus together on being good stewards of the world.

9. Religion without control

Help church members balance their priorities. Religion can co-opt secular influences and vice versa. A ruler flexing military power might ally with religion for two unspiritual reasons: His assertions become incontestible, and doing so historically has justified extremes of violence. In the Middle Ages princes led devout armies against each other, but the tendency is not just medieval. Everybody's God goes with their army. With a wry smile, an elderly veteran of the World War I German Army showed me his old uniform's belt buckle stamped with the words, *Got Mit Uns* (God With Us). An NRA member today sports a bumper sticker: "My god can beat up your god," casting religion like mixed martial arts. We determine which of us is stronger, and stronger is better.

But that gods even appear to compete is an error in reasoning. Imagine two lines of ships emerging from a fog bank. Captains of the first in each line are certain about what is back beyond the fog bank, but they tell different stories. Both could be wrong, but if they contradict, both cannot be right. Those listening to the captains pick the version they like and declare it true.

Many aspects of religion are available to the physical senses. Prayer, a sense of being guided, being uplifted by worship, gaining peace through repentance and forgiveness, growing in strength by virtue, having needs met providentially, and receiving "a personal miracle" are like the line of ships clearing the fog bank. Experiences may leave one no doubt of their contact with the divine, but the more distant field they connect to—what lies beyond the fog bank–escapes their inspection. While they may trust people who describe what is there, others with their own confirming experiences may be just as certain about a different picture.

This leaves reasoning beyond the fog bank vulnerable to both legitimate differences and catastrophic error, such as certainty that God's voice tells us to exert power over others. A wound in our psyche evidently awaits an empowering force, a worst that can rule our best when we seek social control, and no simple criterion identifies the source of the voices that seem to speak within us. Rather, we are all directed to notice how our actions affect the observable well-being of others.

Throughout history, people's desire to rule has led them to disregard even the moderating influences in their own cherished beliefs. During the Thirty Years War in the 1600s, merely for different dogma, Catholics and Protestants tortured each other in ways so grisly they wrench the stomach to hear of (58). Death for disbelief—often after torture–occurred between Jews and Moslems; Catholic Croats, Orthodox Serbs, and Bosnian Moslems; and Shiite and Sunni Moslems. Old Testament Jews killed off the nomads they encountered, the Crusades and Inquisition made almost a joy out of murdering others, confident churchmen executed tens of thousands of supposed witches, devout armies cut their way through Mayans, Aztecs, and Incas, and many countries still persecute their own citizens lacking mainstream beliefs.

No spiritual rationale justifies these atrocities. Those caught up in aggression appear instead to lose their grasp of humans' spiritual nature and the values that should guide them, a state the Bible sums up tersely as "hardness of heart." An enduring thread of European history has been political motives co-opting religious language, while spirituality depends on perception of God's activity.

But if negative beliefs can dominate so thoroughly, it must be at least possible for positive ones to motivate, and our American experiment has offered a way. It was the first modern attempt (after Iceland 800 years earlier) to design society around rationality and common experience while rejecting religious control. It is familiar that the Pilgrims, and many like them, came here for freedom to practice their religion and prosper materially, but often overlooked is their desire to escape persecution *by religion.* Before the mounting emigration to America, Europe had been a religious blood-bath. Not seizing this clue quickly, colonists argued vehemently from the start about a formal role for religion in the new country. But hoping finally that it was at least possible for government not to be repressive, they designed the Constitution for freedom from other people's beliefs.

So if our national pastime is not to yoke others to our religion, what else can we do? If we cannot apply revealed sources to everyone, what remains? The alternative is grounding social experience in the concrete reality available to all. We develop our proposals from the common activity of humanity, and implement values we agree on. This is not, as the saying goes, rocket science.

We can encourage churches' flexibility at this by understanding detail and field. Details are within our power, but their context, their field, is not. We drive our car, but negotiate unpredictable traffic. We state our view, but others debate whether to accept it. *We manage only part of the field we wish to influence.*

Religion can be seen as a system of details, a world of its own, defining itself by tenets of belief, personal practices, and group worship. But in the society where it is placed, conditions shift constantly. To enter this changing public square with its message, a church must relax rigid patterns in order to participate at all.

Adapting in this way, church activity may parallel or join with a movement to offer a message. Together we might help someone change their opinion by knocking on their door and offering them an idea. All our lives we may never have done that, but we do it because we care enough, understand why, and the means are open to us. To move toward our goal, we may need to release what we do well in order to master an unfamiliar field.

To collaborate with others, we bind with the goodness in them and suspend our attitude about differing beliefs. If Mother Teresa's shelter for the homeless had been in our city, we would say, "I see goodness there." And if the Dalai Lama knocked on our door asking, "Would you help me with this?", we at least would not hold his Buddhist beliefs against him. We focus on the quality of our effort, release struggle over details defined differently, and move out of our well-managed corner into the common but variable field where all can cooperate (59).

In the story of the Good Samaritan, Jesus pictured how people who to us have wrong ideas can still have a spiritual heart, and that we need not draw the most polarizing implications from differences (Lk.10:25-37). Anyone can see, for instance, that daily the sun goes around the earth, right? Right. The sun *obviously* goes around the earth east west east west no change day after day. So does that mean we must threaten death to someone who is sure the earth goes around the sun instead? And is it possible for someone believing human evolution lasted millions of years to ally with another who is sure it all started six thousand years ago? Does their difference in belief mean they cannot each grab the arm of a homeless person and together see that he gets a meal and place to sleep?

10. Use resources wisely

Conversing with a friend working in an energy company, I expressed concern about the depletion of non-renewable resources facing coming generations. He laughed and tried to reassure me. "They'll just do something different," he said, confident of industry's ability to work around any limitation.

Innovation advancing civilization endlessly is an attractive prospect, but an aspect of it warrants attention—that we can use up anything we can lay hands on, assured that those coming later will just "do something different." The idea is not sustainable. If whoever gets to it first takes it, we are left standing eventually on a square foot of bare, parched, sterile land with everything else gone.

The problem arises from a limitation in human consciousness. Our perceptual system inflates the significance of what we directly sense at the expense of the long-term. A primitive tribe occasionally harvesting a mammoth goes after the one at the end of the valley but does not instinctively take account of the fewer now than in granddad's time. We meet current needs by habit, but for those in the future must use our imagination. How could European settlers expanding west in the 1800s, for example, not realize how valuable the bison were, that they should not be destroyed? But the future accessible only to imagination was overwhelmed by the bisons' seemingly inexhaustible abundance open to their weapons.

The "tragedy of the commons" illustrated the danger of unboundaried acquisition. Back when each family might have a few farm animals, a town fenced in a grazing area where everyone's livestock could feed. But when someone increased their herd, others receiving less complained, and more stock added to the commons made them unworkable. The idea, "I can use everyone's resources for myself," quietly replaced fair use for all.

The challenge of fair use applies today to water, radio bands, Internet broad band, arable land, fish, wild animals, and non-renewable minerals. We can even ruin air. And when I worked in an Alaska fishing town, an old fisherman told me he and his peers called a fishery "economic" if it were profitable until all that kind of fish were gone. Some eagerly use up what others need.

We want a collaborative picture of human life. When a majority is preoccupied just with resisting others' greed, a positive design lacks the attention it deserves.

11. Convey a group perspective

Teach group thinking. Even a tiny society survives by teaching everyone how to operate it: "Let's all work together to collect these clams"–pick the berries, dry the fish, track down the moose, and so on. A society's division of labor expresses its values. All of us start off as self-absorbed babies and only gradually learn how group effort helps everyone. A story illustrates:

Once upon a time, a mother gave an end-of-school party for her son's friends but wanted them to practice responsibility. After they had played outside for a time, she walked out to talk to them.

"It's time for the cake," she said, "Please form a line at the table inside. One at a time, cut a piece for yourself and leave some for others."

The biggest ran to the front of the line and took large pieces, but when the line was half through, the cake was two-thirds gone. Those still in line looked at each other nervously, but even as they took smaller pieces, the last was a quarter the size of the first. Since the cake was delicious, the final child looked at the mother mournfully and stuck out his lower lip. The next year when the mother offered another party, her son insisted they serve the cake like his grandmother did: cut equal pieces and distribute them herself.

As they enter society, children presume that rules they already know still apply. If they never adjusted to others' needs, they expect the same privileges later. Because we all tend to start with mother's indulgence (take everything you like) and only gradually appreciate grandmother's rules (be fair to all), we tend to need grandmother figures running our lives until we learn to balance our own with group needs.

Some never get it and will always need someone else to apply grandmother's rules to them—cut the cake, restrain them within what is fair, and educate them about how they survive together. Greed will take what it wants unless others check it. A society can let things turn badly, can allot resources of food, health, education, income, and opportunity by any criterion at all such as "the farther ahead you start, the more you receive," or by parentage, connections, height, weight, or skin color. Advance those labeled "advantaged" with more access to resources and provide the others as little as possible. Celebrate the winners and shame the losers so they both think they deserve what they get. (Skin color as a criterion for identifying winners quickly, we might note, *is so last century*. For full disclosure, I am certain society would benefit greatly by steering advantages instead to tall people like me.)

Everyone's innate valuing process helps them benefit themselves, but we need ideas to grasp our relationship to others. A two year old on a playground carefully makes a pile of sand, and as I watch, another two year old comes by and thoughtfully steps on it. Images flash past my mind—adults trying patiently for years to help the latter child learn how to live in the world. Either we communicate about the design we want, or accidents of power, impulse, and advantage pit people against each other. *We establish social norms by choice or by default.*

Core values discussion. We can begin by posing a question such as the meaning of fairness in a healthy society, listen carefully to people's answers, and follow a train of thought with them:

"Hey Kim, I've been thinking a lot about what's going on in the country, and I wanted to get your views." Ask a question, listen to Kim's answer, and discuss it piece by piece:

"So let's say that our nation produces goods and services, okay? Let's say you lost your job and income and couldn't buy food. In your values system, would you want society—other people—to step in and help so you didn't starve, or would you starving just be an inevitable downside of your system?

"And if positions were reversed, would you want to help other people so they didn't starve?

"If we don't want people starving, does that imply that they deserve a share of society's productivity? Children, the elderly, the sick, the out-of-work, and the downsized?

"Does your reason for them not starving come from a basic value of responsibility for others? Or is it just a gesture today that you might not feel like tomorrow, just a passing impulse?

"Does that imply that you don't want to design our economic system to leave some people destitute?"

"If we defend those who can't defend themselves, how does it benefit society?

"Does a working society provide tools to people to help them participate?

"What tools have helped you in your life? Did someone else provide them at first?

"Do you sometimes feel caring toward others who are down and out?

"When you feel that way, do you think government programs might help?

"Sometimes do you want to cut off government aid for the down and out? If so, why?

"Do you have children? Do you teach them to be good team players or to get everything they can for themselves?"

Answers to these questions may be obvious, but people take society downhill by resisting the obvious.

12. Change negative attitudes

Help people choose the better. Attitude, a combination of thought and feeling, matters because it is the first cause of much of what people do. A negative one tends to persist day to day. When people give it fresh energy on awakening, it colors their activity, interfering with social functioning at all levels.

Many aspects of society cope with the tendency to worse. We have armies, wars, refugees, violence, greed, and crime because of what James Madison referred to as "a degree of depravity in mankind." We may encounter some of it in ourselves and even blame others for it: "I could do better with this, but because you do worse, I'll do worse too."

A well-documented human tendency *is once we start into the bad, the bad becomes worse.* Illegal and immoral actions multiply because the restraint from our conscience diminishes over time as our mind becomes accustomed to a repeated stimulus. When the admonition "I shouldn't do this" surfaces in our awareness, our mind recalls facing it before, remembers "That wasn't so bad," and *normalizes* it: "Oh, that again. I can skip it." The mind dismisses the cautionary note ever faster, so that dishonest behavior tends to escalate (60). Lawbreakers caught for one crime may admit to hundreds of others.

This makes it important for a movement with positive aims also to check the negative. Those who use their position to lie, cheat, or steal need to be brought to account quickly *with the small stuff,* like the "broken windows" principle in law enforcement. We need to correct departures from the lens of nature at once. When leaders get away with small lies, they go to bigger ones, and from antagonism to hate, and from hate to violence. The public may eventually accept this slide as normal, but this tolerance has a powerful consequence. *It teaches people to ignore the difference between good and evil* so that soon they are easily misled even about which is which (cf. Part Three. 3. *Sources of mediocre thinking,* subsection *Moral Confusion.*)

As we try to remove moral failings from social patterns, some people may object to being held to what they call the "politically correct," asserting that no actual moral issue is involved but only a minor departure from someone's artificial rule. Use of the phrase, however, could occasion a helpful discussion:

> You say you refuse to be 'politically correct,' so could we just look at what you do mean to convey? People who object to "political correctness" may actually have hostile feelings toward blacks, women, gays, or foreigners but express it with insinuations or in backhanded ways. Is that what you're telling me, that you have feelings you don't think you are allowed to express openly?

What matters is whether their comment portends injury, like the top of an iceberg warning ships to stay away. People who harbor resentful feelings about other races or classes may be unwilling to examine their thought processes, but we can invite them to try.

We are concerned most about living by our own values. Exchanging opinions is a bonus. In the face of a disagreement, we focus first on valuing the individual, place ourselves in their shoes and think how we would wish to be treated—be heard, argued with, debated, etc. This stance enables us to be creative and appreciate how some values limit other values. We may rank our own opinion ahead of theirs, but our respect for them guides how we act on the differences.

Collective survival requires seeking the better together though no default mechanism protects us from worse. We are vulnerable to mainstream attitudes. As the positive functions of civilization break down, worse can take over and the human race could return to the Stone Age in a generation. So when we see large numbers of people who regard resentment, fear, and hostility as normal, we know that we have not grasped how to proceed constructively as a nation.

If we expect to change others' attitudes, a positive beginning is changing our own–a lesson I was presented when very young.

"Snap out of it!" my father would say to me, mildly annoyed. I needed to face the attitude in my complaining, crying, moping, whining, sulking, feeling sorry for myself, procrastinating, or protesting.

"You know better than that!" my mother might admonish.

I did not grasp that I "knew better than that," did not realize choice was possible, that I could hold onto an attitude or not and might change it even quickly. My feelings were my reality. When you are young, you lack an alternate perspective but eventually try to grasp what your father is talking about.

The lesson "Snap out of it" applies broadly. Business expert Rick Shefren explained it as critical for commercial success, "the realization that you see the world through a particular lens." Upon noticing our view is only one lens, we gain freedom to change it. People resist change instead by fixing their views immutably to their identity. But saying, "I am a Republican," we might acknowledge that there is more to us than that. Realizing we are intrinsically independent of our labels lets us explore options. We need not cement ourselves into a single picture because the universe will steadily expand our boundaries if we allow it.

13. The necessity of limitation

We limit our thinking first by conscious choice. Having identified an issue of concern, we pursue a narrow trail of information about it, avoid what we consider irrelevant, and limit ourselves to what we think is important.

During the development of the atom bomb, one of its architects, Nobel Prize winner Richard Feynman, gained a reputation as the smartest man in the world. He had a prodigious grasp of scientific and mathematical details he had mastered by constant effort, yet in college tested at the 5th percentile in cultural knowledge. He tuned out everyone else's central concerns, selected his focus narrowly, and we do the same when we master a body of knowledge. Our mind seeks efficiency by giving less space to information we judge to be less important.

This has enormous implications. We narrow ourselves around what we think helps us achieve our goals, which becomes a feedback signal. We know we change our goal by how we change our thinking. Does today's thought stream lead to the goal we say we want? If the two angle apart, our goal is really just a wish. We fail to match thought to purpose.

A second important limitation is the impact of our emotions on our thoughts. Any of us can appreciate a common experience: We carry on our life day to day and then make a mistake—socially, financially, maritally, occupationally, or vehicular. The appropriate correction of the mistake may be clear and we do it, *but we also chew on it.* It circulates in our head seemingly by its own momentum, intruding into our thoughts, and we find ourselves unable to release it maybe for days, weeks, or even years.

But what could possibly be more important than that we made a mistake? How about this: *We want the full resources of our mind available for all the other values in our life.* As long as we are preoccupied with our mistake, our mind is not free for anything else.

A third issue is a belief most people carry that worsens any problem they encounter. They use others' mistakes as an excuse to lower their own standards: *"I see a flaw in you. It bothers me* and gives me an excuse to do it myself."

Counteracting gossip. Others' flaws bothering us can give rise to corrosive gossip that can be approached from several angles:

1. Assume first that gossip may be "the canary in the mine," a clue that something going wrong in the organization needs to be addressed: "You make an interesting point. Maybe we should bring it up at the next meeting and talk it out."

2. It could signal a key individual's resistance to feedback: "Maybe you and I could sit him down and get to the bottom of this."

3. People may fail to understand organizational principles: "We need to grab hold when something affects our progress. If you think this matters, we should bring it up to the planning team."

4. Individuals may need to talk out their feelings and experience with the group: "So you're feeling frustrated that…."

5. People may project their own insecure feelings onto others ("Someone here has a problem, *and it can't be me!"*). Their supervisor

may need to listen to them at length to discover the real issue, and then conduct the problem-solving steps described below.

Connecting with another—likely also to be a flawed human being–should not be hard. We can presume that most of the time people's thinking makes sense to them. Economist Beardsley Ruml declared that "Reasonable people always agree when they understand what the other person is talking about." Our stance toward them could be, "Oh! Given that you want to accomplish *that*, I understand where you are coming from." Or that you have experienced *that*, or joined *that*, or fear *that*, or believe in *that*. You have put together a field of thought that makes sense to you, given everything that has affected you. You have constructed an inner world enabling you to cope with your outer world.

To appreciate others' thinking that way, we need a certain selflessness, a willingness to grasp their views and present no barrier to their attempt to color their ideas, pose no needless obstacle to their expression of it, nor meet their negative attitude with one of our own. To help them change their thinking, we first understand it as they do.

This does not mean we deny objective information, turn passive, or ignore negative qualities. Instead we acknowledge a sequence in the change process: 1) Understand, 2) enable the other to realize we understand, 3) establish back and forth communication, 4) gain the other's permission to problem-solve, and finally 5) problem-solve. Believing another's view is flawed, we proceed by steps and do not waste time with heated assertions. Though their limitation may present us a barrier, we refuse to use it as an excuse to upset ourselves. Our unhappy feelings display our ignorance, our failure to understand how to assist change. We demonstrate this when we tell ourselves, "If you're frustrated, just get upset, okay? Then others are sure to accept your ideas better!" As is quickly obvious, this attitude is foolish.

It is disarming to admit our limitations: "Let me tell you my gaps about this issue. I realize I don't have all the details. You've studied aspects I haven't, so I'll count on you to fill me in." Acknowledging our limitations helps us welcome new information. If we say we lack details, we then listen carefully, assimilate points the other supplies, verify their accuracy, and combine them with our knowledge. When we do this, others realize, "This is someone I can work with."

Admitting our limitations (and hoping others forgive them) makes it easier to understand others' limitations and forgive them also. If they wish to prove their personal worth by asserting themselves, we do not blame them for this tendency, but accept all their ideas we can and express them accurately so the other knows we receive them. We find the edge of goodwill, competence, insight, or energy in them we can cooperate with.

It helps a working relationship to get our respective limitations into the open so that no one feels they must defend themselves. We want the fact of limitation accepted up front. A teacher of a marriage counseling class illustrated how this could occur when a student asked if any brief questions could identify a good prospect for a relationship. The teacher replied:

> Ask them, 'Are you crazy?' They should answer 'Of course.' Then ask them *'How* are you crazy?' and they should be able to explain how they see their weaknesses. Then ask them, 'Could I tell you how I am crazy?' This reveals their receptivity to others' viewpoints and limitations, and their openness to you.

A technique referred to earlier (and noted again later in another context) helps to skirt limitations. Opening a conversation with someone immersed in a negative attitude, we begin with any question at all, listen carefully to what they say, *and ask them a question about the least negative part of it.* If they are ranting about a family car trip where they ran into bad weather, least negative choices might be lessons the family learned, destinations, interesting foods, other experiences on the trip, coping efforts, and so on. A legislator discussing a bill with an opponent might focus on the other's intended outcome, relations with constituents, a committee that worked together, or a family member's experience on the topic. Think in terms of the issue's periphery.

We do not begin by contesting details but remember sequence–first aim for just positive exchange, a simple intent. Accomplishing that kindergarten step, we may later aim higher.

14. Use power carefully

Understand the human drive for power. Power is the ability to change one's environment, to generate desired outcomes. It manifests on a long gradient from a baby's helplessness at one end to adults who govern their own lives and those of others.

The impulse behind the gradient accounts for both our gains and our problem. From birth, we use all our resources till we hit a barrier. We crawl, rise to our feet, toddle ahead, and master our world. Our impulse whispers "More!" but as we grow, we must learn what to aim for–protect more children and feed more of the hungry, or attack more enemies and subsidize more friends. We plot our power by our ability to manage our own lives, the people we influence, and changes we generate.

While people's effort for gain advances their life, no natural stopping point marks where it becomes counter-productive. Some regard possessions as scores in a game of status. Having more draws others' esteem, so they presume they should obtain more yet. But if they do not know when to ease up, their acquisitive drive can distort their judgment. The more power they have, the more blind they may be to its fairness and less likely to question it. The more advantage a system gives them, the greater is their ethical test in weighing it. In an effort they view as competitive, where advantage is a conscious aim, people are more likely to cheat and hence require more exacting rules, while in the same effort without competition they do not (61). Thus, *even framing politics as "races" encourages people to cheat.*

Society adds to the problem by rewarding people for blinding themselves to fairness. Endowing them with more when they already have much reinforces the presumption that more for them and less for others is right. When California growers opposed farm workers organizing in the sixties, a sample were questioned about their attitude toward workers' needs. The more subsidy the grower himself received, it turned out, the more intensely he opposed welfare for the poor. Suggesting they themselves have taken more than their share enrages some people, but ironically the more they have, the less they can weigh its legitimacy. Those killing off an Indian tribe to take its land would not call it injustice but rather victory. Upton Sinclair described succinctly the tension between gain and objectivity: "It is difficult to get a man to understand something when his salary depends on him not understanding it" (62).

As power expands, it is more vulnerable to misuse. Lord Acton's aphorism, "Power corrupts. Absolute power corrupts absolutely" may exaggerate the effect while Lincoln observed more accurately, "Any man can stand adversity. If you want to know his true character, give him power." It provides us scope to reveal our qualities so that exceptional power can manifest exceptional mistakes. Napoleon, feeling invincible from all he had conquered, decided to take his army to Moscow, and Hitler, ignoring Napoleon's experience, did the same.

Since the power to enhance our lives is essential even for our survival, disempowered individuals weaken their society, providing us an incentive to remedy their needs: "These over here are not pulling on their oar because they read below fifth grade, so let's get them up to speed. Now what else? These need financing to start a business, now what else? Those need a dentist so they are not in constant pain. Now what else?"

Most Americans probably think little about how their society empowers some over others. They respect "producing," and tend to dismiss any downside to ability and wealth, do not see strength as even related to, much less a cause of, weakness. Yet history warns of the tendency of power to ignore the rights and needs of those who lack it. In our brief national memory, we have supported slavery, accepted terrible post-Civil War oppression and discrimination against blacks, felt justified in seizing the entire continent from its Indian inhabitants and lying to, displacing, robbing, and killing millions of them. Presuming our use of power was right led to defeat in Vietnam and chaos in Iraq.

Desire for power soaks up energy we need for understanding the world. Used against the weak, it results in oppression and alienation. The more power we have, the more care we need in balancing our values, a responsibility especially incumbent on the United States. At this writing, it remains the most powerful country in the world, but its very sense of its power makes *hubris* a temptation.

15. Learn from emotions

Read accurately the message in your feelings. Our thoughts are our main tool for confronting problems, but thoughts may come and go randomly until emotions provide a context, flooding our awareness with the essence of the situation. Do we face gratitude, love, worry, sadness, frustration, anger or what?

Our central emotion informs us what kind of situation we encounter. We absorb an experience, decide what is important about it, color it with that kind of feeling, and the feeling circulates in us until we use its information to cope with the experience. We need not vent nor suppress the emotional charge, but listen to its message, balance it with what else we know, and let go of it when it no longer serves a useful purpose.

We do not extinguish emotion completely because that can render us neutral, distant, and cold, and inhibit our appreciation of values. Positive emotion gives wings to an idea, multiplying its impact and helping us sort out meaning. Others' emotions can stimulate our own and add worth and connection to a group atmosphere.

Judgment suffers most, however, when emotions go out of balance. While they may provide valuable information, they are not designed to describe the whole situation accurately. Rather, they tend to produce a singular kind of impact, negative or positive, and hence do not serve well in complex situations. Think of the effects created by these emotion-infused traits:

If I'm angry, I drive others away.

If I underrate myself, I fail at the task needed from me.

If I'm sensitive to criticism, I exaggerate opposition.

If I'm hesitant, I do not roll into timely action.

If I'm indecisive, I over-analyze and confuse others.

If I'm dominating, I diminish others' ideas.

If I'm controlling, others cannot lead.

If I'm passive, I deprive the group of energy.

If I'm reactive, I don't think things through carefully.

If I'm possessive, I claim my turf rigidly.

If I'm loyal to only a few values, I do not treat other values
fairly.

If I'm self-interested, I commit less to others' needs.

The stronger our feeling about an issue, the more it narrows our thinking. It may not make our idea incorrect but does place boundaries on our perceptions. Frustrations commonly arise as we encounter difficulties, but these just signal something we do not yet manage. We worsen this familiar experience by locking onto the surface message of our emotions, like our little dog fearing distant thunder. He runs for someone's lap shivering, unable to realize he is safe. When we cannot direct something as we wish, we may upset ourselves needlessly and even add to it *by feeling bad about feeling bad.*

Instead of bouncing from one feeling to another, we can act on the information it conveys. Remember that our brain is trying to do us a favor by keeping us focused on what it assumes is the most important element. Fear, for example, tells us to keep running while we check whether a threat is real, loneliness invites us to reach out to friends and make connections, frustration calls us to assess our means to our goals, indignation tells us to unite our efforts for change, jealousy aims at removing a rival, anxiety suggests we scope out threat, uncertainty directs us to verify our ideas, and so on. Each feeling-driven meaning is incomplete, however, until our rational observations supply a larger context. Until we grasp the context in a way that resolves the situation, we accept the feeling's presence.

As we combine the feeling-sensation in our body with our understanding about it, the two elements create an ongoing attitude. Saying, "She's always trying to get attention" or "He always has a chip on his shoulder" describe a fusion of feeling and thought that can expand. Angry people move more easily to violence when their thought processes justify their anger. And when an angry person shares his view of a situation, another assumes he too should be angry. Enmity can continue for generations as people insist that the emotional meaning they apply to it remains true. Relief arrives only when a different meaning recasts the situation.

We are hindered by having our emotional life begin long before our mental life is equipped to guide it. Whatever a child feels appears certifiably true just because they feel it that way, *a child's response we can carry into adulthood.* And once we are certain our emotion accurately describes reality, we resist contrary information. If I am angry at an opponent, I have absolutely no doubt why. My mind in fact helps me along by exaggerating evidence that supports my anger, and shrinking contradictory evidence as we noted earlier– "Even if your point is true, I declare it insignificant." Our feelings become our subjective reality and the creative palette of information we use to paint our world.

As valuable as our emotions may be, by allowing them to govern our thinking, we invite the outcome noted at the beginning of Part Three, *believing something patently untrue.* People do not match the depth of their belief to the extent of their evidence, but instead make up whatever they want and assert it as fact. Many are so convinced of their version of the invisible worlds that they will shed their own or others' blood to promote it. Others, like it or not, must agree with their picture of the unseen or they have no right to live. Emotion-driven beliefs only slightly less aggressive can break down governments, separate demographic groups into hostile camps, exclude some, and oppress others.

Almost any belief system can acquire emotional force. 70% of those questioned in mid-2016 said the year's election campaign brought out the worst in people while 7% lost a friend over it. Probably none of the latter calmly sat down to examine evidence together and reason their way through differences, but instead retreated into emotional rigidity that drove others away. *A big task awaits just to free important decisions about society from the grip of emotional presumptions and ground them upon the rational assessment of evidence.*

We want to help people realize they have arbitrarily adopted a viewpoint—looked at life through a limited lens—and can release its hold if they wish. The contents of their mind are like options a football team can employ creatively. Opponents would crush a team that used the same play over and over, but stalemated problems tell us we re-run obsolete plays. Representative democracy is an idea *and any idea can be overwhelmed by an emotion or subverted by another idea.* Voting affords only a slight advantage. Almost a century ago, one of the most educated democracies in the world with international leaders in culture, science, and technology elected Hitler. A democracy laced with anger and inter-group hostility can be co-opted by special interests and perpetrate injustice; can leave essential needs unmet, its structure uncorrected, and its public in factions.

While we easily recognize the social impact of such emotional patterns, we need to own their main implication for us personally. The critical point is *realizing that the immediate meaning our emotion applies to our experience is limited and is inadequate for making decisions.* We instead acknowledge that two voices vie for prominence in us: "I realize that I'm feeling really disappointed right now that …. didn't turn out as I hoped. But I can look at the larger picture, remember other factors working in my favor, know that time will bring me new options, and not allow the disappointment to govern me and weaken my sense of direction. I can reclaim my good feelings about what I'm doing and proceed." In this vein, we can inquire of others: "So that's what you're feeling. And how about your thinking?"

Collective survival requires seeking the better together though no default mechanism protects us from worse. We are vulnerable to mainstream attitudes. As the positive functions of civilization break down, worse can take over and the human race could return to the Stone Age in a generation. So when we see large numbers of people who regard resentment, fear, and hostility as normal, we know that we have not grasped how to proceed constructively as a nation.

Emotional entrainment affects much of the mediocre thinking described in section 3. above, snagging individuals and groups. When reason governs, we appeal to it with evidence and work out problems directly, but instead frequently encounter emotion-laden rigidity.

Absolutes often come from a fear of loss of control.

Automaticity gains force when emotion cancels alternative considerations, confining people to their past habits.

Bandwagon generates an unwarranted sense of trust.

Beliefs tell feelings which alternatives to adhere to.

Consistency organizes all considerations around their service to primary feelings.

Entitlement generates acquisitiveness for undeserved benefits.

Ignorance may prompt self-blame, though the mind may compensate by declaring learning unneeded or overestimating the value of current knowledge.

Indifference may result from feelings of emptiness, a lack of positive meaning, which diminishes the value of everything around us.

Locality attaches constructively to the mainstream thinking of a place, but by a small step can narrow one's view of reality and reject parallel values in other regions.

Moral confusion dismisses positive emotions toward others, negates their needs and rights, and excuses destructive behavior.

Ourselves as baseline amounts to vanity, seeing all the world as a satellite of ourselves as center.

Pain and stress make emotions less resilient, balanced, and reason-directed.

Polarization enlists emotions of hostility and defensiveness.

Pressure bends our feelings to align us with people important in our lives.

Quality of effort reflects how our feelings sustain and energize our efforts toward our values.

Resentment expresses frustrations we may direct at others who are not to blame for our circumstances.

Roles absorb our time, attention, and emotions in routines that excuse us from considering other issues.

Selfishness can arise from fear of loss, attaching to material goods as a substitute for interior happiness.

Stability in the structure of our lives reassures us, but as its own purpose can blind us to changes needed.

Tendencies provide us a spontaneous, often emotion-driven response to conditions we face but can easily exceed due proportion and appropriateness.

Time envelope emphasizes the reality of our present feelings and immediate experience, making it hard for us to think well about our future and learn from the past.

Views express emotion-driven opinions for which we lack evidence, placing us in a self-affirming mental construct where we feel we know everything we need to know.

Violence is often the last outward expression of unhappy emotions, frustrations, resentments, and polarizations.

In Part Four, we examine ways to work with the emotional quality others direct toward us. For ourselves, we skirt countless problems by recalling that *our emotions mislead us in making a guess about our situation and presuming that the guess is appropriate and true.* They become useful only when guided by the broader perspective our good thinking can supply. Too often standing alone they are dumb.

IV

PART FOUR. THE PROBLEM OF ORGANIZATION

1. Movement inward and outward

We achieve the good of the whole as we identify the levers of change and accumulate enough influence to move them, but may work together with different degrees of integration. An organization's internal cohesion enables it to manage its activities directly and train employees: "Learn this in order to do your job." In a movement, on the other hand, numbers pursue a common direction more independently, allowing greater scope for initiative and adaptation to local conditions, and conveying skills by persuasion and agreement rather than by paycheck and control.

As they begin, people's connections and activity together must assure them they are on the right track and sustain them until their effort begins to achieve external objectives. In a coherent strategy, mutually supportive elements multiply the overall effect, inviting us to identify and perfect the pieces that must come together. A particular sequence, for example, guides whether individual members are likely to continue to attract others and build their numbers:

1. High quality **personal contact** invites a new person into the group.

2. By participating, they experience the group's **support** and learning.

3. Group support enables them to assimilate its **vision**.

4. Implementing the vision guides the group's **action** in society.

5. Action in society produces **accomplishment.**

6. Accomplishment keeps people **motivated** to maintain the group.

7. To maintain the group, members continue the **personal contact** that initiated the process, and the group expands.

The four problems in the book title that await people's efforts are the need for a meaning to unite them, the good of the whole; a specific target for change, selfish power; the need to think well about everything they do, mediocre thinking; and how to carry out their effort effectively.

While these general purposes have lasting implications, time will constantly present fresh targets for a movement, so we explain the conditions enabling it to succeed for any goal it chooses. We need to be consistent with essentials while welcoming innovation and energy everywhere else.

This fourth part describes creating the active force, *people doing something.* We look at how the group applies learning, vision, action, and mutual support; how internal communication, inter-personal bonds, problem-solving, planning, and personal development strengthen and guide the movement's activity.

2. Four ways to start

A movement begins as people gather face to face about an idea.

Invitation. One person may invite another. If our theme were "Raise the minimum wage," a solid beginning is to double our number. Someone needs to cooperate with us like our friend Evan:

"Evan, could I talk to you about why we should raise the minimum wage?"

If we have guessed his interest accurately, he answers, "Sure."

Like a salesman pitching a product, we notice what he is ready to hear, and explain to him the importance and urgency of the issue and how personal action could help. We have a plan and incorporate Evan into it, but two of us agreeing do not comprise a movement. 85% of the country may already favor a policy Congress refuses to enact. We become a movement by deliberately increasing our numbers to achieve a purpose, so we ask a second question: "Could you talk to someone in your family about this?"

"Yes," he says. "My brother would like to know," representing intentional movement, an idea passing on.

Anyone can make the request. A high school student can start a movement. An arthritic home-bound senior can say, "We need a meeting on this street!" She goes on the phone, jars a few friends who bring others, and thirty people show up. The beginning is an invitation and a reason. Anyone willing to step in front of it can awaken such activity by explaining why change is needed and how action together could accomplish it.

A friend named Jack lives not far away. If he came to me fired up about something, I would think about it because he is thoughtful and credible. He could offer me a personal connection and involve me in an action because I respect him. If he were turned on to something, I might be also.

"Tonight there's a meeting at Barry's about that issue you and I discussed," he might say. "It should be interesting. Can you come with me?"

He arouses my curiosity, and I am on track to follow his invitation as far as he can lead. At the meeting, I hear ideas, offer my views, and perhaps tell my own experience. When they divide up activity for the week, they offer some to me. Leaving the meeting together, Jack and I discuss it. I think more about it, and focus on my upcoming responsibility perhaps to march, visit the newspaper, make placards, man phones, research an idea, or distribute door hangers and talk to people. My action follows from my personal connection with Jack. He leads me, I do the same for others, and more follow from us.

Transmitting an idea. Perhaps you have only yourself and an idea. Others can bond with you through it.

A parallel is the miracle in an acorn. Think how it grips the plan of the tree it becomes. *The molecular design in the acorn instructs it in how to organize all the resources arriving from outside to make that particular kind of tree,* just like your plan for changing the world arranges the resources reaching you.

Your plan must address substance. Let us say you obtain a limited hold on Evan's interest, engage him in a brief activity, and now you are each back home. When he wakes up tomorrow, his former life beckons, twenty-four hours already portioned out to his interests, but here you are, standing beside his bed, asking him to join you. He may feel self-conscious and uncertain, may not *get all that* as unfamiliar impressions crowd his mind, and may feel awkward and out of his element.

This discomfort is common in new activity. We all approach novel situations guardedly when we risk incompetence or embarrassment. Before expecting new people to make unfamiliar judgments, we prepare them with the thoughts and feelings they will draw on, and resolve their concerns by clear plans and personal support.

Evan's needs on the second day are like what a company offers to new employees. They receive a work location, task training, a supervisor to solve their problems, ways to monitor progress, tools for feedback and assistance, and a salary for motivation. *Day one on the job they receive a detailed picture of how the company achieves its objectives.* Evan also awaits such a picture because his rewards at first are only his tentative belief in the activity and his bond with you. As you two reach out to others, he relies on your mastery of details in order to believe in his own effort. Transmitting the plan to your friend Evan, you double your number.

Direct action. We could explain to our friends why our idea is important, and they might nod in agreement, but that alone will not lift it past their other priorities. We do not act on an idea *because* it is important but rather *to make it* important. Engaging our physical nature converts it from theoretical to real.

The principle applies broadly. We give people a tool to engage others, place them where that will happen, and it happens. Throw a football to a boy and he throws it back. Toss a soccer ball to a group of children and they kick it back and forth. For us, the tool we set out *is an idea people can express*. They act on an idea about society mainly by explaining it, and doing so where others can challenge it helps them understand and assimilate it. You might invite Evan to accompany you.

"Evan," you say, "Saturday noon I'm going downtown to pass out information about Sunday night's talk, and I could really use someone with me. Could you help me with this for an hour?" Evan is glad to go with you, so you pick him up (assuring follow-through), distribute the information together, and the situation does the rest. As he talks to people, new ideas circulate in his mind. Next week you and he write out a statement, stand on a street corner, hand it to passers-by, and they take aim at you.

"What is this all about?" they ask.

Spurred by questions, Evan quickly learns the points he explains, but more importantly crosses a watershed. From ideas being like random clouds in the sky, *they appear real to him* and form the content of connections he develops. Sharing ideas alerts him to the limits of his knowledge, and opens him to learning more so he can have more to say. Putting concepts into specific words, he firms them up, claims them, and comes to understand that acting on ideas is the force transforming society.

Interest group. People who already know each other may share values, want similar change, and begin easily. They get together, notice their common views, express ideas they want to apply, and proceed directly to action. They could announce an organizing meeting, contact all their friends and acquaintances, have a stimulating presentation, follow with small-group discussion, project toward specific activities, and begin to apply the organizing features explained below.

3. Orient newcomers

Recruits at a boot camp or rookies on a football team welcome being pushed to exhaustion because they are certain they want in. Social issues inflaming people's indignation may enable them to accept an intense mobilization for a time, and a movement then seeks to develop their temporary feelings into long-term commitment. Below we explain how.

Millions are available, however, during calmer periods. They worry about society, are willing to help, and wait to be led, but we engage them within the motivation they possess. Trying to land a 10 pound trout with a 2 pound test line, we do not just reel it in but must coax it, not challenge its resistance directly but guide it gradually.

Need for welcome. Once underway, we arrange a "come and see" public meeting where we remove our edges—our signs of status, cliques, and turf control—and focus on newcomers' needs.

Some feel self-conscious and isolated. Needs left over from childhood may emerge as they recall previous rejections and do not want to attract others' attention ("Just checking things out," they say). Unobtrusive signals like meeting their eyes, our quiet nod, or a brief smile reassure them. We let them mingle as they wish and become comfortable at their own pace. We introduce ourselves, comment on the current occasion, inquire about their interest, listen carefully, respond deferentially, and draw out their ideas: "What are your concerns?"

With those who seem tentative or uncertain, we listen first. For people already interested, we may add, "Great! Do you know anyone else who feels this way?" or "Would you like to get started?" Some are ready for a next step, and others make up their mind carefully. We respond to differences.

After receiving initial attention, they wonder next if they have a place in our group: "Are these folks my kind, or am I too different?" They sense whether personal bonds are likely, which are a strong reason people continue in social action. Hired into a new job, they look for common ground as they learn about each others' families and interests. As connections deepen, they stay longer. A study of what makes people happy found a prime factor to be the esteem received from peers, an influence that operates everywhere (63). People are deeply affected by what they think of each other.

Our emphasis is personal. We would like to send ten thousand Twitter messages to roll directly into action, but behavior change usually needs individual contact because engaging deeper mental strata. We seldom develop new traits via mass-distributed one-sentence bites.

We presume any newcomer can be a resource for change but to achieve this we must think about them individually. What do they need to learn? We can supply it. What action will engage them? We can supply it. What support and guidance connect them to the group? We can supply it. We can provide the teamwork, encouragement, feedback, inspiration, and accomplishment they need to change from a passive observer to a leader, and we believe everyone can become one—noticing needs, identifying the appropriate response, and pointing the way toward it.

Personal warmth is important from the first but easily overridden when activity seems a higher priority than the people doing it. An impersonal atmosphere depresses a group. While everyone finds this stressful, ethnic minorities suffer from it more acutely so that they may need extra reassurance. Warmth can be offered easily. We first let ourselves *like* others. Are we glad to see them? Our smiles, nods, receptive comments, respectful questions, and handshakes let others know they are welcome. The most helpful kind of warmth is conveyed less in expressive bursts and more as a pervasive condition that enables other good things to happen (64).

Three conditions. Inviting people to meet briefly, we explain what we're about: "We want to start a movement of people who believe change is urgent." We outline what it might do and how they could help.

This simple beginning supplies three conditions that solve the mystery of how people change, as we noted briefly above. They 1) join with others who 2) share a common value, and 3) act on it together. They associate with people whose thinking they agree with, take up activity offered to them, and change as a result: group + values + action = change. While this is easy to observe, say, in an exercise group, the crux of it for our purpose is the last of the three conditions. *People do not change until they act with the group,* so that a specific involvement is essential for them to assimilate the group's values.

The three factors help explain students' often-puzzling resistance to school. Like adults, when joining a group they expect to adopt its values and activities but instead may find classroom rules to be alien, regimenting them, isolating them from the support of their friends, and lacking a satisfying outcome for their effort. Pressure may compel them to obey without touching their heart or enlisting their willingness or interest. They need to discover appealing activity already at work so they can quickly adopt its perspective. Teachers and coaches encourage learning by creating meaning students can engage with and claim for their own (65).

Bridging differences. To welcome people into a group, we bridge across sameness and difference.

With sameness we are safe, perhaps with those already at our elbow. At the refreshment table after a meeting, we notice the person next to us, taking in hair style, clothing, and physical movement, and listening for code words. We hear voice modulation and pace, and how murmurs, nods, and gestures synchronize with our own. Matching categories mark us as the same sort of people, eligible to connect.

The other condition is difference that leaves us uncertain, facing distance we must overcome and resolving to create a bridge anyway. We seek out similarities, look past appearances, and inquire about the other's life and concerns. Labels we assign to people tend to push them away, so our frame of reference needs to connect us.

Two attitudes help. The first is that this person is valuable. If we do not remind ourselves of this, we may appear to rank our ideas ahead of our listener, yet the person is primary. We stay grounded in the value of every individual.

A second attitude is curiosity about their views. We take interest in how they form their mind. We actually do not get how they do this, so we convert our uncertainty into wonder at how they look at everything, how they reconcile beliefs and data we might not.

We follow their words patiently, absorbing what they say—"Tell me how you look at this, how you put it all together," understanding rather than challenging. When they pause, we express in our own words what we hear and check it with them: "You're saying…. Is that how it looks to you? Did I leave out anything?" A position appearing extreme to us was warranted for them. What led them to believe as they do?

We modify our words as they suggest until they are satisfied we understand them. Our careful listening face to face encourages their careful speaking. Our moderation and reason elicit the same from them, and on exchanging positive feelings we each may take in ideas we otherwise would not. We would like to think big, but our tools are little—our personal contact in this particular minute.

Reaching out to a nation and world, we welcome the full spectrum of personal qualities and realize we can bond with anyone. The care we offer to all is the substance of our movement, and addressing their needs expresses our solidarity with them. We can correct what separates us, and seek out harmony behind differences; reach beyond our natural constituency to those different in age, interests, occupation, location, class, income, or religion. Consider:

He's an immigrant, barely speaks English. He can take these ideas to a whole new population.

He has a different skin color. Great! He and I can show how people of different ethnicity can work together.

He's a night owl, seldom see him during the day. He connects with people we never encounter and can continue the work while the rest of us sleep.

He's had a military career. Has experienced team planning and group projects. He can remind us about focus and discipline.

He's a pacifist. We will listen to him especially about values and compassion.

He's wealthy. He has access to resources. Some will hear him who will not hear us.

She runs a business. She understands how society works, how things get done, how to draw on community enterprise.

She's unemployed. She has a feel for people who struggle.

She's older. Probably has dealt with aging and family, and has had illusions corrected.

She's immature. We can help her develop traits she will use for life, and we like her enthusiasm.

She has strong opinions. I'm not sure we can work together. She needs other strong people who can steer her. If we get her pointed, she will go forever.

She's capable but wants status. We can respect her ability and show how we offer status to everyone.

His values seem so different from everyone else's. We talk out how to work together toward a common purpose, or shake hands and go our own way.

He's Republican (Democrat, Religious, Secular, Asian, Black, Hispanic, Liberal, Conservative, Hindu, Moslem, Christian, Labor, Corporate, Gay, Straight). He may have a different take on issues, and can help us connect with others who believe as he does. If we can bond with him, he can carry our message into places we could not.

The common theme is acceptance across differences, a principle that counteracts *otherism*, the primitive belief that safety and meaning lie in sameness. Animals apply it to their survival, wondering "Does that kind of thing eat my kind of thing?" and we humans do the same in our own way. In seconds we figure out what distinguishes us from others and decide whether we belong in the same world. Facing variances of culture, people may assume their own counts more, and apply otherism to define entire populations as alien. Familiar otherisms separate people by wealth, social status, nationality, culture, race, sex, gender identification, and age. They worsen social problems by erecting arbitrary barriers.

Because otherism is a survival factor, we may have a natural propensity toward it, but to unite our effort with others who seem different, we must decide consciously to counteract it. Instincts direct us to be in-group and tribal, while world problems today beg us to focus on the whole and its systems. The omnipresence of otherism suggests that we prepare to face and explain the problem itself as we reach out to others:

"Because we survive through our bonds with other people, we

naturally look for safety among the people we call our own and instinctively turn toward those who are like us. But when our own group cannot supply us with everything, we need to expand our boundaries deliberately and link up with people who seem different. Doesn't that make sense for the world we live in now, that staying just inside our own tribe will eventually fracture the whole?"

A movement cannot be broad-based if it appeals only to one segment of society, so we need to agree together 1) to expect differences, 2) remember that they can divide us, and 3) decide on a meaning that unites us instead.

It matters that we realize our common humanity because aliens are more readily lied to, taken advantage of, oppressed, imprisoned, and killed. Concluding that others do not deserve the consideration we give our own, we treat them as we please. Had our ancestors regarded Native and African Americans as deserving, they would not have enslaved and murdered them. An inclusive society presumes that regardless of differences, we should value each other because we are people, but some cannot think that way. Their world includes a few others they label as theirs, and they dismiss everyone else, ranking their dog ahead of any human being.

Mounting evidence from DNA, however, is that none of us are pure anything. We can cheerfully say, "Hey, we all like to be with people more or less like us, but wouldn't it be fun for you and I to check where we actually came from? Would you like to find out? Ancestry.com offers an inexpensive DNA kit we could share."

4. Ask for a response

Get people into low-stress action. Many are ready to be active but need to know their effort counts. Accomplishment is their best encouragement. Saying "We did it!" affirms pride in their effort and prepares them for a next step. Our perennial question is what to ask them to do.

A group forms as people sustain the same idea. Hour by hour we all follow the idea that hangs in our mind, so that a repeated thought guides a repeated activity. Think what has to happen in this case: In one photo, a man raises a sign with a message on it and in a later photo, ten thousand pack the National Mall holding the same sign. Between the two pictures, many had to come to think similarly. Activists had to convey that thought person to person to person.

But what thought stands out? People agree with many ideas they do not act on, and ignore those settled already or that others handle. The thousands of available ideas challenge us *to make a single one spring into view* that people will make their own. We do not just talk *at* them because that leaves them passive, and once they begin saying "No" inwardly, they easily say it again. To engage them we might comment on an issue, and ask them a question about it (more on that later). But we especially want to know how to turn their initial willingness into thought processes they can follow on their own, help their thinking become active resolve.

Leaders may assume incorrectly that others know how to become active and so ask nothing of them, leaving them to find out by themselves how to use their capacities. The problem with this is that people limit their aspirations to the scope of their thinking. They may not be able to recognize even a lifetime opportunity handed to them for free, so we use persuasion to engage them in activity that launches them on further development. When we encourage our child to jump in the pool, they say, "Would you hold onto me? Then I can do it." The older and wiser are caretakers of beginners' first steps, so we choose carefully the initial focus for connecting them to the movement.

Since expressing ideas is our prime activity, we want to make it easy to do. Two challenges are involved, **The Approach** and **The Message.** With the first we exert a little initiative to reach out to someone else, while the second can entail assimilating many ideas over time. We want to help everyone get past the first one quickly to raise their confidence and readiness for more action, so we ask for it up front without any pressure for a particular outcome: They identify someone they already know who disagrees or even *might* disagree with them, open a conversation, stand or sit physically close enough to be a substantial presence (e.g. between three and four feet), draw out the other's thinking about values, social concerns, and national policies, and find out all they can about the person's frame of reference. To minimize stress, we ask them not to challenge what they hear but instead listen attentively and invite the other to expand on their ideas.

This activity opens the door that eventually leads to a changed society, so we want it to happen as early, often, and easily as possible. Returning to the next meeting, people will describe their attempts, explain what they learned about the listening process, laugh a little, and look forward to carrying out *The Approach* often.

Their confidence at it increases their interest in mastering *The Message* related to the group's goals. Many starting points for this goal are workable depending on people's readiness, issues of the day, and the direction the group adopts. One is to ask people at their first meeting *to memorize the opening lines of the Preamble to the Constitution* (cf. Preface and Appendix II), and discuss the meaning of each phrase with a partner right there. In a few minutes they will refresh their grasp of our ancestors' vision for us, and realize that they have acquired ammunition for discussing the direction of the country and criteria for estimating progress.

Once people are meeting to pursue a common purpose, a few need to give deeper thought to its direction. For this they choose planners.

5. Choose planners

Implement features that strengthen your group. We need to consider numbers from several angles.

Public protests engaging even hundreds of thousands may at first seem unstoppable. But because they occur so far from decisions that structure society, they typically dissolve before generating remedies (66). Community groups may continue for years with small numbers. An experienced organizer who had guided several local political campaigns told me after one of them, "It always seems to come down to six people."

Yet an enormous reservoir of good will waits to be tapped. *A quarter of American adults volunteer in some way,* and Greg Baldwin, President of VolunteerMatch services, believes that the main reason more do not is the lack of leaders to invite them. Our aim then is not just to gather numbers but to generate a leader attitude that steadily increases them.

A natural transition can occur from a public event. After attending a presentation, people might agree to meet a couple more times to develop a common perspective and direction for action. The group structure they adopt, however, affects their progress. One too large can feel impersonal and unsupportive. Wandering about in an anonymous crowd many experience anxiety, but a group too small may seem too limited to accomplish much. Interest appears sustained best in a middle-size group where everyone can know each other but large enough to accommodate diversity, learning, and action, suggesting they aim for a size between twenty and a hundred and fifty (67). A group can join with other groups for mass action, divide into smaller teams for specific purposes, and as numbers expand can decide when to split into two or more groups.

Because clear roles help people accept responsibility, a planning team needs to coordinate, which also influences group size. *Planners need to know personally the people to whom they offer tasks.* An active bond between the two is like a blood vessel transmitting energy between parts of a body. Knowing members individually, planners can recognize what they need to learn for their development, and the action that suits them best. Upon completing an action, people return to the bond to confirm the significance of their effort.

Having leaders they trust motivates people, so those who carry out the plans should choose the planners. They cooperate better with leaders they select, and implement plans faster that they help design, but a common problem with leader selection is some wanting the job out of ego (68). Those who show up first may expect to control turf, and others attracted to power may put on their best face and say what people want to hear. Losing an election may cause some to leave the group.

To find leaders less affected by ego, we do not wait for them to put themselves forward because they may never do so. Small groups that know each other well may regard leader roles as a service and take turns at them, but elections and turn-taking are limited in expanding leadership.

Nominating (like the Pope is chosen) instead of electing, and having a team instead of an individual lead the group can minimize the impact of ego, encourage collaboration, and advance leaders with the most representative thinking. While an organization might still operate effectively with different features (such as might emerge directly from a public event or a candidate's campaign), those described here help sustain people's motivation. If the group employs different ones, it should monitor their effect carefully.

Selecting the PT. Once people are acquainted, someone explains the role of a PT: Personal contact with members gives planners an intimate grasp of the purposes of the group. They select specific targets, design activities that keep the group functioning, assign organizational roles, work out details of campaigns, choose learning material to aid group development, manage funds, establish a formal legal identity if desired, and coordinate with other groups on regional and state issues. They support members by weighing their ideas and offering them tasks that fit them.

At a nominating meeting, everyone writes down the names of the five (or seven for a larger group) they would like as their planning team. An odd number seems to aid group process. An independent visitor might collect the nominations, tabulate results, and identify those named most without revealing the count for each. With a tie for last place, the team can either expand by one (for a larger group) but return to the prior number when anyone leaves, or flip a coin. The planning team then in the same way nominates a chairperson from among it who leads meetings of the PT and the larger group, and focuses particularly on maintaining the quality of the group's efforts.

A group may reconstitute its PT every three to six months or annually—more often to incorporate new faces or during fast-paced activity. A renominated PT usually retains some and adds new members, providing continuity with change.

The PT may propose plans the group can affirm, alter, or defer, or may present options: "Our conversations with members have turned up two directions that seem to interest people. We could either jump into X which has a short time frame, or take on Y that would be longer. What do you think?" Obtaining people's direct approval of a plan spurs them to carry out their role: "For the plan you wanted, here's what we would like you to do." Some projects may engage many members with other assignments individual.

If the larger group often requires lengthy discussion of a PT proposal, the PT might examine why. It may not have thought through its plan or connected adequately with members' ideas beforehand. Resolving complex problems by frequent large group discussion can lead some to over-talk while boring others, and discourage people from attending. Members are more likely to want large group time spent on small group discussion or inspirational, educational, or action-oriented activity. For weighing an issue in detail, the PT can appoint a committee to develop a recommendation for the larger group.

6. Functions of the planning team

Bring high quality thought to PT decisions. A PT's judgment is the first cause of the group's success or failure. The PT elicits members' ideas, meets apart from the larger group to design its goals and activities, and sorts out what to do.

A single constant question before it affects everything in real time, and no simple criteria resolve it: *What is most important to focus on?* In short, continual prioritizing. The answer often is unclear because of competing needs. The PT must address long-term planning, short-term organizing, selecting activity toward society, practical housekeeping, generating a message, conflict resolution, individuals' needs, group support, directions for learning, and working smoothly as a team.

A helpful perspective is to think backward from our goal to specify what must happen before something else can. Multiple elements of preparation do not occur all at once. Some depend on completing prior ones, *and laying this out visually* helps clarify the necessary sequence. To improve at this planners might search the Internet for instruction on Critical Path Method (CPM) and Program Evaluation and Review Technique (PERT). The key insight is that when some steps depend on others before them, *following the sequence* assures the smoothest, most effective action.

A priority for planners' attention that offers few external checkpoints is balancing individual members' learning with their involvement in action. To make learning most valuable, planners need actually to notice members personally, and think, "What basic misconceptions do I hear?" and "What unhelpful assumptions are they buying into?" and "What's the next step that would help most to fill in their understanding or increase their confidence?" Often public action invites specific learning: "We want everyone able to explain the ideas on this handout." We help people learn what best sustains their activity.

The balance between action and learning, however, affects members' development at a different level. Continued learning infuses action with meaning that feeds our self-motivation. Without learning, our efforts more readily become routine and rely more on external motives others provide us. When people together in a group grasp the significance of an idea, they are more likely to apply its meaning even to a lifetime of commitment and effort. We assimilate deeply the learning we integrate with our group activity. Through our action, we realize that we ourselves become better, and it inspires and motivates us to persevere with it instead of it depleting and draining us.

The issue for planners, then, is how to sustain and broaden members' comprehension of the meaning of what they do, even as they undertake varied activities. To meet this need, we discuss below a group and an individual approach to learning.

In focusing on a campaign or a long-term activity, it is helpful for planners to think like Eisenhower preparing for D-Day: *Is my army equipped for what I am asking it to do?* Three criteria inform us:

1. Do they have a sense of purpose? Do they know what they are going

to do, and have an intense desire to do it that gives energy to everything else?

2. Do they have the means, the tools, the skills? Some means for us are physical resources like fliers, phone, map, signs, contact information, laptop, etc. Other means are people's mastery of the ideas they will explain and skills at listening and connecting they will draw on.

3. Are they optimistic? This does not mean they pin hope on outcomes that may or may not happen, but rather that they bring a beam of positive expectation into any circumstances they encounter.

These three conditions do not happen by accident but result from the tasks and learning the planning team arranges. The group as a whole may need to think through general priorities: Is now the time to increase membership quietly while working on local needs and contacts? Or should we get everyone really confident with our message? Is now the time for us to go public boldly? Is targeted political action begging for attention?

Unanimity. For important decisions, the PT and group should seek unanimity rather than majority rule. People often join voluntary organizations to advocate their views, and may feel obliged to promote them aggressively. But while a particular view may be correct, it can also narrow a group's focus. Instead of relying on assertive voices, the PT needs to regard the group's entire thinking as a resource. If the group has talked out values and goals in small group discussion (cf. below), appreciated each one's contribution, maintained strong person-to-person bonds, and worked together in large group meetings, activities, and campaigns, people will already align on 90% of their goals. Examining the remainder together, they take each objection as part of the group's intelligence and resolve conflicts carefully. Hearing a novel angle, the chairperson arranges access: "Sounds interesting. Could you go over it with Aaron (planning team member) so the team can consider it? Thanks."

We want each thing done to be effective, with speed secondary. Delaying an activity briefly to weigh a suggestion can result in big gains over time at slight cost, although when a deadline looms, the group can agree to a majority vote. If an imminent event warrants thorough examination, PT members might each lead a sub-group discussion and afterward integrate what they learn.

The PT's meetings should be open to members except perhaps when it settles conflicts or discusses members' abilities for particular assignments. When individuals have personal knowledge about an issue the team is weighing, it can invite them to attend and share their views. If members wish to listen in on a discussion, the PT can set chairs around the outside in fishbowl fashion.

When its role is clear and it enjoys the group's confidence, its members invest more time and attention. If instead those not members of the PT drop by as they please and insert their comments at random, they can dilute the PT's sense of responsibility. Members who welcome more involvement might instead be offered a project they can lead independently.

Five steps translate ideas into action, with 1, 2, 4, and 5 below comprising the total planning effort. One organizer suggested spending three-quarters of the time preparing the plan and one-quarter carrying it out:

1. Plan. We think through how everything goes together, arranging objectives, time, effort, and resources into an overall picture.

2. Organize. We translate the picture into specific assignments, who does what, each responsible for a part. We avoid problems with a *pre-mortem*, imagining ourselves looking back later at something that went wrong. What could it have been? Then looking ahead, we determine how we can forestall every possible "what if…."

3. Act. Each of us carries out the role we agreed to.

4. Monitor. We gather information on how the action fulfilled the plan.

5. Correct. We do a *post-mortem*. How did our foresight work out? We use the data collected to correct the next phase, and repeat the five steps.

With hindsight the planning team learns what the group should do to improve its foresight for the next event. If even knowing the results of our actions we cannot figure out what to do differently, we repeat mistakes. Common sense tells us at least, "Let's make sure we don't do *that* again." As the group takes on more members and issues, it can assign project groups with their own planning team.

We cannot expect to organize society if we cannot organize group activity. With muddled effort, we offer muddled ideas to society and allow those in power to do as they please. A corrective voice needs to be clear enough to fend off distractions. With its biggest hindrance a limited viewpoint, the group continually asks, "What can help us think better about this?"

A rule for samurais was, "First defeat your enemy in your own mind." We foresee how our plan will produce the results we want. If we cannot do that much, our actual effort has little hope.

7. Communications for planning

The quality of communication affects planning. No group acts beyond its thinking, and planning is the group's brain.

Slogans of past revolutions have typically been brief, like "No taxation without representation," or "Off with their heads!" Theorists of revolution may have complex ideas, but ideas that move large numbers tend to be blunt. We cannot ask people to make careful distinctions when their driving force is rage and their action plan is "Kill."

But because the world has undergone a quantum shift in complexity, every venue of society needs people thinking more carefully. A movement only gets the outcomes it can understand, making it a priority to gather information and elicit people's best thinking.

Planning in this way, however, departs from common experience. In most of our interactions, we say something and another responds. Facing one person, we each expect to speak and listen, but often in a group we speak and no one listens. Someone else wants to be heard, and our voices overlap. A third person wants in, and three voices compete.

What is happening? A key is that *dominance precedes reasoning.* People first want to be assured of their influence, and may decide they have enough of it only when others accept their idea—others who may have the same need. The attitude has a certain logic. We cannot expect others to appreciate our idea unless we can direct their attention to it. But when the conversation is not one-to-one, we need a wider range of responses, and a particular tool can help.

Communications checklist. While it may appear to limit spontaneity, a checklist introduces critical behaviors easily overlooked. Its use became more accepted in the 1930s when the U.S. was developing a heavy bomber. The problem was that planes' increasing complexity meant ever more extensive pilot training. In 1935, a test design that would eventually become the B-17 was taken up by the most experienced pilot available, Major Ployer "Pete" Hill, but crashed soon due to wind locks not released. Designers realized that no amount of training could remedy such a need, and turned to a different approach. With a checklist for all important details, even average pilots could learn quickly how to fly the B-17 that later aided the war effort.

Using a communication skills checklist in classrooms, I found that even second graders could begin to assess themselves against several skills. Fourth graders and older enjoy rating themselves against a dozen skills following an interactive experience, or rating another student or the teacher. Every time children compare their behavior to a standard, they learn the standard better (69).

A checklist can help adults. In the early 1970s when my wife then and I were doing personal development workshops, a church group in a distant state engaged us for two weeks of growth experiences. They cautioned us that the church was about to dissolve due to conflicts, but agreed to try to settle their differences with our help.

The day we arrived to begin we were invited to sit in on a meeting of the church's Board of Directors. The meeting was so courteous, constructive, and well-run, however, that I was baffled and at the end drew a director aside.

"How can your group be having problems with a meeting like that?" I asked.

She handed me a sheet of paper she was holding, a list of communication skills for a meeting that I had mailed to them several weeks before. "We all put this in front of us and follow it during the meeting," she said with a smile.

The list below is slightly expanded from that one. Duplicate a copy for everyone in any meeting where decisions are weighed. Go over it when first introducing it, and discuss participants' experiences when the skills were used or ignored. Midway in a meeting, everyone might review how they have applied the skills, and afterward give feedback on each other's use of them. Their unifying theme is, "Anyone can talk who wants to, and everyone who talks gets listened to":

1. *Check your inner activity.* Notice others' desire to speak, feel respect and consideration, wait your turn, and focus on the one speaking.

2. *Allow a brief silence* after each comment to let everyone think about it and decide if they want to speak next.

3. *Use short messages* instead of long. Weave together many people's short messages like a tapestry.

4. *Summarize* the previous comment and the speaker's feeling about it before offering your own. Referring to others' names, thoughts, and words aids continuity.

5. *Check your guesses* about others' thoughts and feelings. If you do not understand what a speaker says, ask someone else to clarify and let the speaker verify or correct it.

6. *Appreciate* and thank people, give compliments, and tell what helped you. Feelings have priority over thoughts.

7. *Complete a theme.* Get group consent to switch topics. Review the progress of the discussion from time to time. Point out similarities and differences and do not minimize the latter.

8. *Include everyone.* Get everyone's viewpoint and feelings, and treat them respectfully even if you disagree with them. Everyone has a right to their opinion. Draw in the hesitant.

9. *Welcome correction.* Accept challenges and corrections

gracefully. Each needs to be able to say what they really think but also be open to feedback about it.

10. *Share leadership.* People develop confidence as they contribute to and initiate group thought.

Release tension. While the skills help a group deal with open issues, tension or suppressed feelings may signal a hidden one. A leader might sense this and ask, "Is there anything about this we've not addressed? Have we covered all our bases?" and look from one person to another.

A friend who attended Quaker meetings noted that if even a single person objected to a decision the group was considering, they would delay it until everyone agreed—exhibiting a group value of respect for each one's elusive ideas.

A consultant who worked with Indian tribes years ago told me how meetings could go for days circling a conclusion that to an outsider seemed inevitable. Anyone could introduce a tangent the body might pursue for hours. But this apparent randomness, he realized, removed any tension in the group. Everyone's good feeling about the eventual decision was the best sign it would work.

An agent visiting Eskimo villages about government services found that he might need to look up the village leader on his front porch, sit next to him silently and watch the landscape and weather for a day without talking business. With harmony established, discussion could open.

A quality that improves the outcomes of meetings in general is just that people laugh. Everyone can help lift the atmosphere of a meeting, but leaders might think how to do this consistently. People like a job where the atmosphere is so upbeat that they look forward to going to work. We want the same for movement activities.

8. The key role of supervision

Make each individual's activity important. Once welcomed into the group, people wonder, "What will I do?"

How the group answers distinguishes a movement from political campaigning. Politics focuses on electing a candidate, and a worker's motivation, doubts, stresses, and skills are secondary: just get the job done. A movement's focus on the long-term, instead, means watching *how every current task builds endurance.* We want to know what activity today helps the member do it tomorrow and afterward. Many will give themselves steadily to a good purpose, but someone else needs to believe in them, understand them, and know how to encourage them.

To help meet this need we can connect each member with their own supervisor-coach-support-friend who understands their interests and readiness and helps involve them in activity, or who may lead a project that includes them. While we refer to it as supervision, it emphasizes a personal connection that the group can name anything it wants. It is important for *maintaining the significance* of members' activities. We want more than exhaustive effort on one occasion. We want members to know that what they do is valuable and can have meaning far into the future.

Planners might divide supervision among them at first, each taking several members to work with, or select supervisors from the membership, or utilize Contact groups (cf. below) if the group retains that form of organization. Each planner also has their own supervisor to report to for their individual work or can make their contribution to the PT as their report. However it may be structured, the value at stake is that presenting the results of our effort to someone else validates it.

Through their assignment, people apply their values, contribute to the group's goals, merit its respect and acceptance, and experience a sense of accomplishment. Reporting back, they receive appreciation, approval, and warmth: "Thanks for getting that done." We give a compliment, or note the effect of their help: "You really saved us some time," "You got it done before the deadline," "That's exactly the data we need!" We express how we notice people individually. Timely aid for their activity also can matter to them. Particularly in fast-paced periods, people appreciate a hand.

Particular qualities enhance the interaction between supervisor and member:

1. Rapport. The supervisor's attitude is, "Glad you're here. We appreciate your interest. We'll take care of you. Whatever you are willing to do or learn, we have your back and are ready to support you." The two become comfortable talking out concerns, but for a deeper connection, the supervisor *enters the member's frame of reference* by adopting cues such as the same vocabulary; speaking with the same pace, tone, and quantity of speech; and with similar physical position, gestures, and movement. Such similarities increase people's sense of safety because unconsciously coded as evidence that the two match each other (70).

Since deliberately moving into rapport with someone means changing our habits, we might easily think, "I'm just going to be myself instead." If it does not matter to us whether we connect or not, then of course "being ourselves" is fine. But thinking that way means we do not care if we make another uncomfortable, and we leave it entirely on them to adapt to us. If our goal instead is to connect, we make it easy for that to happen.

Identity politics suffers from a parallel problem. If I must remind you *how separate and distinct* I am from you, then you have to overcome the distance I create before we can even work together. Instead, our combined effort needs to displace my identity as our focus (cf. Part Three. 3. *Sources of mediocre thinking,* subsection *Roles). Messages that convey "I want to connect with you" between supervisor and member affect the tensile strength of the movement. People seldom remain in a group lacking emotional bonds.*

2. Action. The two explore the new member's skills and interests to uncover the latter's best focus. People are more likely to succeed at what they already do well than by struggling with what is difficult for them, and at one level we fit the task to the individual. A computer programmer may build a website, organizers design events, the crafts-oriented make signs, the sociable do phoning, abstract thinkers formulate position papers, researchers gather campaign material, and the

innovative stage a flash mob. Some who have natural ease in approaching strangers concentrate on it and bring new people to others who further their learning and action.

Some are more inclined to bursts of public effort and others to the predictable and steady, but any style can help. And while the movement may draw on personal capabilities, all can do some things together, like bringing movement ideas to the public in a demonstration or canvassing. In our contact with every voter, official, or media person we think also what exchange now will make every later one easier and more aligned with our purpose. How could this person's interest and receptivity add to the strength of the movement?

3. Assignment. The supervisor may offer the PT's suggestion or accept the member's preference. The assignment is put in writing–what, how, and when to return with the task done. Being accountable for specific details reassures people and aids reliability. During an assignment, the supervisor may check in with the member to inquire whether they need help. At the agreed time, the supervisor (or PT together) receives the report, expresses thanks and appreciation, and finds out anything the member learned that could aid future activity. Failing to receive a report implies a discount of the effort.

4. Progress indicators. Tallying results encourages people. Elections are feedback on long-range effort, but progress by any measure adds interest: "How many new people did all of us contact this week?" or "Let's keep track of those who are passing on ideas." Voters registered and information distributed afford tangible numbers.

The single measure that correlates best with the group's effectiveness, however, is *the time members spend explaining ideas face to face* (cf. *21. Face to face needs*, subsection *Social action as sales*). At every meeting, members could turn in their personal minutes at this since the last meeting, and post their combined weekly total on a wall chart. A flat line would show their effort coasting while with an upward line they gather momentum, and each new person accelerates it. Besides tracking the group's impact, the chart's greater value is *reinforcing the critical activity that builds the movement.*

Visible scoring meets a pervasive human need, with the entire field of sports one demonstration of it. When results from our effort matter to us, we instinctively plot our progress and are pleased at seeing it happen ("Okay, I'm halfway there" or "Hey, everyone, hump day today," or "Profitability is up 3%" or "We're ahead 27 to 24"). And while we cannot directly measure our impact on others, **we can know precisely how much of the key effort we expend.** Counting up and displaying our time at it keeps us realistic about group effectiveness.

5. Work at a distance. Face-to-face connections help sustain motivation but many interested cannot participate due to distance or personal circumstances. They have the same needs as others for vision, action, learning, and mutual support but we meet their needs via telephone or other means. We can 1) arrange a weekly conference call with dispersed allies, 2) find out each one's preferred activity, 3) help them decide on individual assignments, 4) receive their report on their effort, 5) encourage their outreach to others, 6) help them build their own network from the ground up, and 7) provide support and direction as we can. While discussion of issues may raise interest on these calls (i.e. what is happening somewhere else), the movement-building elements concern what people themselves are doing.

To orient individual efforts to the group's plan, supervisors should meet regularly with the PT to match members' readiness and skills to group goals, and PT members of all groups in a region can coordinate their efforts via conference calls or meetings.

The value of challenge. All of us appreciate teachers and coaches who "got the best out of us" by pointing us to our next step. We grew as we undertook these efforts yet also needed the assurance of repeating what we already did well. A PT monitors how action challenges members' skills.

Many might appreciate two assignments—a routine one that still advances the movement's goals, and another that taxes their ability. Acts of courage particularly give structure to character and help people master fear. Positive qualities flower that cannot while fear rules. Anxiousness at public speaking, for instance, may seem a minor personal limitation yet expressing ideas is the central work of a movement. Thousands applauding a speaker may have little impact until they learn how to explain ideas themselves. Organizations with millions on their mailing lists may be ineffective because not guiding their members to reach beyond their natural constituency. We cannot change the system if we talk only to people who already agree with us.

Challenge helps people own their capability. Napoleon, asked why he was so hard on his troops, replied, "If you make everything hard, the truly hard things become easy." Doing the hard things till they become easy, in fact, is how we gain any skill at all. We want to make clear to people the stakes involved and suggest actions that arouse excitement, advance a goal, and stretch competence: "If something is difficult, it doesn't mean not to try. It just means to try harder."

A frontier of difficulty exists where members draw on their convictions. Handing out fliers where they attract opposition helps them understand the influences arrayed against them and can strengthen their resolve, while doing the same in a sympathetic location may turn up more new members. When we continually direct strong individuals into easy tasks, they may be unable to match their identity with our purpose so that the group attracts the less serious. Determined people are glad to expend energy for a goal.

The value of sacrifice. We can understand challenge also in terms of sacrifice, which done for a value is an important motive. People expect a match between a value and its price. We are not surprised when great sacrifice leads to great achievement, but the connection is broader. *The fact of our sacrifice affirms the significance of our purpose.* "If this weren't valuable," we think, "I wouldn't be doing it." Sacrifice lets us tell ourselves we have taken hold of a worthy goal.

The same thought stream feeds inertia, however, when we do nothing. Presuming a proportion between purpose and sacrifice, we acknowledge, "I am not making a sacrifice," and conclude, "so my purpose must not be a great one." Our mind dismisses the deed rapping on our window.

We can draw on this internal process to encourage people's dedication. We hear what they say they believe and *ask them for a sacrifice that fits it.* They may believe global warming is threatening, the world's suffering painful, and the poverty onerous so we look to what they can do and arrange an assignment accordingly. Maybe a volunteer has four evening hours a day to devote, we give him a direction, and he bolts away on it like an Olympic sprinter.

Inviting another's commitment, we offer a connected heart, "Would you like to come and do this with me?" The world's axis will tilt if enough people invite their friends to stand on one side of it with them. When unfamiliar effort stresses people and confronts them with their ignorance or doubts, they depend more on their bonds with each other.

9. Start rapidly

Different numbers of people can influence an issue at different stages. Many may be needed to reform a process like criminal justice, but once in place, its framework can solve problems quickly. A single witness identifies a law-breaker, others carry out their roles, and prescribed guidelines settle the matter. Shifting a handful of Congressional seats may permit rapid change.

But preventing change is easier than causing it and requires fewer numbers, at times just a single person: an executive with a veto, or a committee chairman or House Speaker to sink a bill. Besides the power of a few individuals, the U.S. is unusual in having four institutions that can block change–President, House of Representatives, Senate, and Supreme Court—with the Senate's rules making it even more prone to stasis. Most nations have one or two such institutions, so that in designing four, our nation's founders apparently preferred periodic stalemate to conditions they feared more.

An effect of dividing power among so many entities, however, is economic inequality. Countries with more of them are more unequal, probably because entrenched interests have multiple tools for resisting change, and even short-term gains may require extended effort by a super-majority. When our Supreme Court makes a decision bad for the nation, years may pass before a majority Justice leaves the court, and a brief window for change closes as a President nominates a successor with similar views so that solving a simple problem can take generations. With limited resources available, a movement should understand the numbers needed at different phases of a problem in order to allocate effort. The earlier the action on a given issue, typically the better the results.

Large numbers needed. During the turbulent 1960s when Americans realized that many of them were poor, an organizer named Richard Marks made an observation that still applies. "You can't do things in ones and twosies,'" he said, "when tens and twenties are needed."

We face a certain dimension of effort, was his point. For a big problem, a big concept needs to guide big effort, and conditions define the effort due. With the prospect that in the next 300 years global warming already underway will melt enough polar ice to submerge the world's coasts, we impact nearly half the world's population and much of the natural world, while longer range trends look even worse. Billions affected suggest millions working at it, and for outcomes lasting centuries, generations of effort. The scope of the problems defines the scope of the solutions needed.

If the governing minority were thinking well, it would use its influence to solve common problems and there would be little desire for change or discouragement about government. But when the dominant do not look out for the rest of us, they degrade the system. They use their power to damage the environment, deplete irreplaceable resources, further burden near-broken individuals, ignore the country's crumbling infrastructure, and leave millions scrambling for survival in job opportunity, compensation, education, health, and justice. When the few who manage the conditions appear unwilling to change them despite public protest, others need to take on their role.

To accomplish this, we employ the structure of democracy to restore its function.

Large numbers are necessary because the most direct levers of change are a majority in the House of Representatives, a super-majority in the

Senate, and the Presidency, but with high public interest, numbers can coalesce rapidly.

Organize a crowd. A group could start this way. Imagine that you and your friends sponsor a nationally known speaker and a thousand people show up. Afterward you take the microphone:

"Would everyone please assemble in groups of five to seven. We'll refer to them as Contact groups. Introduce yourselves and name one of you as group Contact. Everyone write out and give to your Contact your name, email, twitter address, and phone number. Then take ten minutes to find out what you have in common."

In fifteen minutes, a thousand people are in 165 groups averaging six people each with their contact data collected.

To scale up, you suggest they all remain where they are so their Contact can find them again, and *ask just the Contacts* to raise their hand, look around for each other, and assemble in groups of five to seven. Those in each group of Contacts introduce themselves to each other, choose one of them as, let us say, their representative or Rep, and make a copy of their own Contact group's information and give it to their Rep. The Contacts then return to their own Contact group and escort it to meet together in their cluster of six Contact groups to make up one 'Organization group' led by a Rep: "Group one will meet in the left rear corner of the hall, group two in the middle rear," etc.

In twenty minutes, 1,000 people in 165 Contact groups have assembled into 28 O-groups, each numbering between 30 and 40 and led temporarily by a Rep who has their names and contact information—the initial conditions for an organizational structure. Each O-group can open a discussion right there, hear participants' interests, and set a place and time to meet next.

Depending on their numbers and the distances people have come, groups can be specified by general location: "Would people from east-city please move to the left side of the auditorium, west-city to the right side, north-city to the stage area, and south-city to the back of the hall?" Sectors of each group can be divided further as desired, but we handle issues about group arrangement in light of our purpose: "Right now we

just want to get a structure going, okay? People can shift around later."
While O-groups can be larger or smaller, the size suggested here would
enable members to get to know each other quickly while beginning
group activity.

If the body welcomes immediate action, another few minutes could
arrange it:

1. The groups whose Contact became a Rep select a different Contact.

2. While the Contact groups are talking, the 28 Reps meet with the
presenter and event organizers for fifteen minutes to agree on a group
action easily planned for a large number such as a march, distributing
information, or a demonstration at a time and place. Even though
organizers could simply announce such an event and let everyone join as
they like, people own a plan better when they help create it and carry it
out with a team.

3. Plan in hand, the Reps return to their Organization group and
present the proposed action. Groups talk out their support for the plan,
resolve details, and assign roles. These steps let people know an action
has developed and they have a place in it. In a few minutes a random
audience becomes an organized force, and a march confirms it.

4. Reps and Contacts have the names and phone numbers of their
members, and before their next meeting connect by phone or face to
face with everyone in their group, a link critical for many to continue.
A few conditions easy to supply cross a threshold for many people's
willingness to participate in a new effort. They need to be comfortable
among others who are like-minded, know some in their O-group, connect
with their Rep, feel their involvement is appreciated, and believe their
values match the group's direction.

5. Apart from O-group gatherings, group members maintain direction
by meeting informally about their common purpose. Two working in the
same building might talk at lunch about approaching a co-worker, three
might discuss a policy relevant to their employment, and four might meet
ongoing over a neighborhood issue. *Steady personal contact sustains
focus.* We do not bind people to a regimen that in turn accomplishes

goals, but rather provide enough framework for them to watch for needs around them and respond.

10. Increase numbers quickly

Gather more people who have understanding and commitment. Remember Diogenes with his candle, searching the faces of Athenians for an honest man? Are we honest enough to bear others' scrutiny? A sincere person seeking a direction needs to believe they can find it from us. George Washington endured Valley Forge with his troops but later traveled to each of the new states to assure people in person of the solidity of the new government. Cesar Chavez knocked on doors. If we expect to affect people, we present ourselves to them directly as a *force* that will not blow away.

This distinction helps define our relation to newcomers. The numbers we need depend on what we ask people to do. The simplest level conveys one idea like "Click here to support House Bill 238." Such information can go coast to coast in a minute because it asks only one response—sign that, call here, show up there. People do not need to change personally in order to comply. Simple responses assume, however, that lawmakers will accept the public's priority and work out the details. Yet the simpler people think, the easier they are manipulated. Leaders can even make war look easy.

Change today depends on complex knowledge. Knowing that we need to change education, transform criminal justice, or go to war is like knowing a river flows south, but each issue signals a massive current of details beneath. To get right the substance of change in the details, some must comprehend them. Many can help spread basic ideas, but at least some need to know how change actually occurs. *A movement depends on people who understand and guide organization, and understand ideas and deliver them, so that our goal is multiplying those particular numbers.*

To accomplish this in less than a century, imagine that a group patiently goes out to meet people week by week with the modest goal of each member bringing in **just one new person per month.** On the face of it, this is not unreasonable. As people take up a new idea, they often share it with a friend anyway. The new person gets a month of one-to-one personal attention in partnering, discussion, and action. Welcoming just one per month means, however, that numbers double monthly. Let's see how this works out.

First month, one person enlists their friend. The two talk and study day by day and engage in activities together, occasionally reaching out to others. Second month, two more join them totaling four. They do activities here and there, and discuss ideas, but they seem to be nowhere. Only four have signed on in two whole months. By the end of the third month, the four become eight as early seeds bear fruit, though numbers still seem minimal for the time spent. But at that pace, *in a year they have 2,048.*

Growing rapidly then, in eighteen months they total 131,042, each enlisting just one new person from a month of outreach, 131,042 in a year and a half from a standing start. By now people get it: *reach others deeply so they develop the same commitment.* Six months later—two years altogether–they have 8,386,688 members and four months after that their members alone could elect the president: 67,093,486. Since adding one new person, per person, per month seems unremarkable, where is the problem?

The critical detail is only that people entering early keep working. In 28 months, the first one starting things off brings in 28 other people. One starting the next month eventually brings in 27, and one in the third month 26. Newcomers change enough in their own first month that they continue to assist others at a modest pace–one new person per month. They learn how to help others develop, and multiplication determines the outcome. Each newcomer enlisting two dozen others in two years solves the national problem.

If two years is too long to wait, instead of a couple friends agreeing, we could start with a thousand hearing a motivating speaker, shorten the cycle to 24 days, and in less than a year have 8 million active. **The indispensable force for change at any speed is enabling new people**

to reach others deeply and the latter doing the same. To personalize this, imagine yourself among eight friends saying to each other, "Hey everyone. If we each just keep welcoming one new person a month, in fourteen months we can be a hundred and thirty thousand. Shall we?"

11. Lead

Understand your leadership qualities. Leaders show the way, explain where the path goes, and why it is important. Two questions mark the scope of your current leadership:

1. Can you ask someone to do something and know they will do it? Answering no means you do everything yourself and have no group momentum. Despite your personal effort, you have no allies to spread your results. You may still be learning, or have inadequately engaged others. If you answer yes, you have a toehold for changing society. You work with others and can invite them to help you.

2. Will their activity continue to expand to others? Answering no means your efforts have plateaued or will do so soon. You do not know how to extend your support, and could use a change in methods. If you answer yes, you need only continue until you turn the nation around.

A personal element matters. Often at the beginning of any enterprise, people are influenced by the qualities of its initiator, which means developing ourselves to be someone others can attach to. In leading we care more and love more, are more unselfish, more willing to expend effort for others. **Leaders give a gift of energy to followers.** If you want to lead, expect to draw on yourself more deeply.

Consider a military analogy, a commander facing a new recruit on his first duty. Does the commander want to "keep him in his place," turn him into a disciplined member of the unit? Perhaps the recruit's contribution is just to be a movable piece easily replaced by someone else, and he only needs instruction on his role.

If the commander's goal instead is, "I want him so strong and alert and confident that if the situation arises, he will earn himself a Congressional Medal of Honor," the commander treats him differently. Facing a new movement member before us, we need to read the future in this person's presence, and recognize that our treatment of him/her today will affect this outcome. A group will accomplish much by its plans and actions, but an element of self-stretching, of pushing oneself to the limit, reveals its *esprit de corps* (spirit of the body), which arises in turn from how leaders infuse meaning, expectation, and support into every contact and group activity.

To be leaders, we develop persevering strength perhaps over many years and once confident of it can invite others to join in. We are more vigilant, more focused on the demands of the situation and helping others succeed, and do not leave to chance things that matter. We gain credibility as others believe we understand and share their experience yet are apart enough from the group's current state to envision what it can become, how to enlarge its potential. ***Four tools at our disposal are personal relationships, our grasp of the group's direction, how we immerse people in ideas, and the tasks we ask them to do.*** We do not obligate or pressure people, but try to recognize what each needs in order to sustain their learning and action.

Different leaders have different emphases. Yours may be either tasks or mutual support. The latter help people feel comfortable together. They converse, make friends, use humor, take interest in others, and usually avoid controversy. They notice what others do, are sensitive to attitudes and viewpoints, show appreciation, and "blot up spilled feelings before anyone can slip on them." They may not think of themselves as leaders, but they meet needs for harmony.

Task leaders get things done. They tend to step back a little from people's attitudes in order to suggest action and enlist cooperation. Because they draw more objections, they need to be willing to face opposition and resolve conflict. Leaders can have both qualities; realize, "This affects people's feelings" and talk it out, then later say, "Let's get to work."

Task leaders may be directive or interactive. The former have a consistent focus, know where they want to go, and readily invite others' effort. This steadies people so they can focus more productively, and is especially welcome when the situation is already organized and a team goes into action, or is chaotic and unformed as at its beginning. Groups in crisis usually welcome someone who takes charge and has clear ideas, while an interactive style works better when some activity is organized and other undefined as in much social action. This leader hears everyone's ideas and seeks agreement.

A characteristic of leaders as we view them here is that *anyone willing to express ideas becomes one.* An organizational leader, in addition, is like the pacemaker for a group's heart, taking in signals from all parts of the body and nudging its rhythms toward optimal functioning. Those presenting ideas well on the media may draw public attention, but the critical activity is to recognize challenges to the strength of the movement and know how to resolve them. As our ship leaves port, we make sure it floats.

12. Conduct campaigns

Apply your best thinking in campaigns. The number who fit around a kitchen table can take an issue public for a few minutes of media notice, post handbills in a hundred locations, or with a half dozen friends hold up signs on the outskirts of an event and are under way. But when our outcome matters to us, we may need to build to it with years of personal discipline, practicing skills, and accumulating knowledge. While initiative drives the day's activity, patience carries through long-term preparation as circumstances slowly unfreeze and change opens. Then in a period of flux action crosses a watershed to achieve goals.

This natural cycle of opportunity opening and closing can generate undue optimism or pessimism. Eventually we realize that no matter what conditions we face, the critical piece is acting now on what we have before us. Action has value even if not perfect. It opens possibilities. As we act, our limitations emerge in sharp relief and we think more clearly. Even a symbolic action like a small visible protest helps maintain continuity. A salesman said once that the goal of every meeting with a customer is another meeting. We move from first contact to final results in phases. Our slow start builds readiness for more action, like a car increasing speed only from its prior speed.

Action has internal effects. When we act on a new idea, it takes on order that helps us pursue it. Getting new people into action early reinforces their vision, stimulates them to learn more, and creates the rough-and-tumble that defines the edges of their reasoning. If a purpose engages a group's interest but not its action, the group becomes a pleasant hangout—a worthy aim but one already well supplied in society. Action is to groups what exercise is to the human body.

Campaigns as development. Campaigns are an arena for people's development, and their development is the basis of future change.

If you can break a task into steps and tell someone each step, you accomplish the task just by directing them. Only a few need the full picture and they assign others their part. But if you want people to recognize by themselves when and how to do the steps without you, you must make them competent with a field of understanding, and elicit their independent will to act on it, implying a depth of development. For sustained effort, people need the competence and resources to restart themselves and others, so we monitor how every campaign affects participants and view every new contact as the beginning of a long-lasting affinity with our goals. Campaigns provide a spectrum of responsibilities that can stimulate judgment and competence.

Kinds of campaigns. Campaigns mobilize activity for a limited time around a specific aim. Besides electing people, they can clean up a city, change economic patterns, preserve historic sites and values, reshape environmental policies, bridge racial differences, and meet needs of particular groups. Sometimes success is in the doing. A group may offer a service, draw attention to wrongdoing, or establish the relevance of a moral principle. A campaign might take on several conditions simultaneously that contribute to one problem. Poverty may be affected by poor education, toxic environments, ill health, unsupportive infrastructure, wage schedules, and hiring practices. Multiple policies can impact a region's physical environment or educational quality.

A vast field of effort is to educate a community about conditions affecting its well-being. Imagine, for example, a public seminar on "The interplay between politics and emotion," using the final section of Part Three above, "Learn from emotions," as a discussion handout. Append the five discussion skills to it (cf. below), divide attendees into groups of five, and turn them loose to reflect on the material as they wish. Other prior sections of the book could be arranged into an intriguing series (cf. Permission, page ii.)

Political campaigns can limit benefit by focusing too briefly on a candidate and office. When their effort appears either to succeed or fail, workers return to their lives, but if they confine themselves to short-term goals, long-term change occurs only by accident. Instead it needs sustained effort such as in ways compiled by former political staffers titled *Indivisible: A Practical Guide to Resisting the Trump Agenda* (71). The guide focuses particularly on Congressmen seeking re-election, and explains practical ways to keep them accountable, tell an opposing story, get responses on the record, and highlight inconsistencies and untruths.

People with no political background and foreign-sounding names get elected by working hard to explain why they are running. A candidate with a thousand people in the streets does better than one with a hundred, but a candidate's own motivation and effort matter. In a municipal election in a small city, a man previously unknown to the public led the entire slate. Asked afterward how he did it, he said he had "knocked on about three thousand doors."

During a storm on a dark November evening, my own doorbell rang. Standing in my porch in dripping rain gear was a former state administrator, already well known, who was running for the legislature. With a smile, he handed me a brochure, said "I'd appreciate your vote," shook my hand, stepped back into the rain, and won his seat handily. Others notice it when candidates put themselves out *especially when it is hardest to do so,* so that those who want it badly enough tend to reach political office even if outspent:

- Have solid, values-based reasons for running.

- Tell everyone about them.

- Push yourself to the limit of your own resources.

- Enlist as many campaign workers as possible.

- Help each become fluent about issues.

- Knock on doors to get the word to voters.

- Organize people to talk to their neighbors and speak up at meetings..

- Register everyone and help them vote in all elections.

- Bring ideas into the mainstream by placards, demonstrations, marches, interviews, and debates.

Political workers already familiar with such activities are the most likely start of a movement. They understand delivering ideas, promoting values, and working as a team. Someone invited them, the effort fit them, others supported and guided them, and they felt they might accomplish something. A movement adds more people, a bigger concept, more attention to individual needs, and a longer time line, but with similar activity. Satisfied that they have secured their own interests, unselfish people step up to defend the birds, the children, and the wild horses.

A university setting. Imagine five friends attending a campus lecture about a social problem. They meet the following week, discuss it for an hour, write a letter to an agency, periodically share what they learn, and have no effect on the issue. Five at another university talk the next day. They

- decide to run with the idea.

- tell everyone they know, invite them to a meeting, and triple their number.

- assign individual responsibilities for writing articles and contacting the media.

- prepare a questionnaire and flier and enlist others to distribute them.

- follow up on each one's personal contacts, enlarging their group.

- invite new people to help so all feel part of the activity.

- bring in speakers to reach the university community.

- circulate a petition concerning the problem locally.

- ask office-holders and candidates to use their influence.

- visit other campuses, promote seminars and talks, and initiate parallel groups.

They devote the central stream of their available energy to generating momentum, and their concentrated efforts reach others.

The Cookie Principle: "If you can bake a dozen cookies, you can bake a thousand dozen." When a replicable action achieves your goal, keep doing it. Don't complicate things. Five activities get steady results. Four are below, and the fifth has its own section following.

1. Street corner information. Go to a busy sidewalk in pairs or with a team. Highlight an issue on placards, or open stands on different corners: "Talk to me about climate change," or "Talk to me about criminal justice," etc. Prepare details explaining how people can follow up. Obtain contact information right there if possible, and offer an event they can attend or a way to connect when they are ready—a card to fill out and mail in, a website where they can register, or a phone number to call. The sidewalk team answers questions, distributes information, and collects people's contact data. On a weekday noon hour, a handful could blanket a city center.

2. Home meetings. Anyone can start an ongoing home meeting by inviting acquaintances and presenting an idea. Acquaintances may be a better pool than friends because there are more of them, and the more you contact, the more you find. Even one is a start. If two of you agree, you can approach others together. Though meetings can be of any size, consider dividing into sub-groups of four or five when involving people in discussion. A large group presentation can impress people, but they usually assimilate it better in small groups.

3. Development. For long-term progress, we:

- keep track of everyone with whom we speak

- sustain our relationship with them

- expand their grasp of the issues

- ask their help approaching others

- support and accompany them when they do so

- engage them in study groups

- help them practice communicating the ideas of the movement

- assign them tasks they can carry out and report back

- take interest in their effort

- assess their success and work out their next direction

- give them responsibility for helping others

We notice people's willingness to change, and supply vision, learning, action, and support to assist them. We think about their needs and remove barriers.

4. Partners. The biggest hindrance to movement activities is probably people's discomfort. Offering information on a street corner or knocking on doors can awaken their fear of rejection. They overcome it best by accompanying others who are already confident. The new person watches their example, imitates it, applies their feedback and suggestions, tries it themselves, and does the same for others starting out. When everyone lacks experience at a group's beginning, doing activities together allays discomfort. If people can commit even a day a month to outreach, we design an activity that helps them be effective and bond with others.

13. Canvassing

Master a personal approach. If a movement is a spear, canvassing is the spear-point. It delivers change one person at a time, altering their thinking by exchanging ideas. If brochures achieve the purpose, then well done, but dropping one off at 200 homes leaves open whether 200 were thrown away. The information on them may even be persuasive, but for impact, a real person may have to deliver it. Multiplication occurs instead when a member reports, "I had solid conversations with eight people today and am following up with them."

Just distributing information can be valid, of course. We may reach a neighborhood days before an election and must make many contacts quickly. But do we think ahead and plan for an army right there, person by person, over weeks and months? We described above how easily numbers are expanded if people are motivated and know how; two aims with everyone we meet–to understand and want to promote the solutions we offer.

Presenting ourselves at someone's door, before we say a word our effort conveys a message: *This matters.* It cuts through suspicion about media slogans and tells a resident, "You matter enough for me to seek you out." The substance of our message stands before them: "We are here for you, to serve your needs and your life. We are your allies."

We remain happy and calm, ready to offer something we believe in. We are not argumentative but helpful, and aim first just to connect through an array of cues such as those noted earlier in our discussion of rapport. People with whom we feel comfortable influence us even with poorer ideas, so we think first how to develop ease with anyone.

Our physical distance (proxemics) is a clue to both our feelings about each other and our likelihood of a fruitful conversation. The farther away we stand, the lower is our felt presence and generally the less our impact on each other. People who feel uneasy or vulnerable instinctively back away. In the U.S. and Europe, the preferred distance for social conversation is three to four feet. This may vary with different ages and populations, but *the closer we can be comfortable, the easier we align our ideas.* Resuming that experience often, our relationship deepens.

Our first words to the person at the door might be, "I'm here about the coming election." We pause a moment, look at them, give them a chance to speak, and listen carefully; not jumping immediately into issues but taking time *to enter their frame of reference.* We match their words, speech patterns and gestures if we can. We notice surroundings, common ground among visible details, and appreciate them: toys in the yard ("How old are your kids?"), car worked on ("You repair cars yourself?"), plants, crafts, etc. We follow out their comments or questions, or ask directly, "What are your concerns?" We might invite their views about issues that matter most to them and respond accurately. About their top issue, we inquire, "How has that affected you?"

They may be open to hearing our ideas. For this, "deep canvassing" has been shown to generate significant change. In a 10-15 minute conversation *in which the other does most of the talking,* we ask a question about a critical issue, hear their experience with it, and draw on their comments to support our position. A key step is getting them to "put themselves in others' shoes" about the issue (72). When they have expressed their views, we ask if we can respond, and fill in gaps in their understanding.

As they welcome hearing more from us, we can bring up topics we have practiced: "In a minute I can explain why our country is having all these problems." With their nod, we sum up our core argument:

> In a study of twenty-six civilizations, a historian found that the main reason they fell apart was their leaders stopped looking out for the whole society and used their power to benefit themselves. When those without power realized the system was not for them, they lost faith in it. Eventually it could not handle its problems and broke up. This has been happening here since the 1970s and has steadily generated an unfair society. Reagan and the ruling elite have instituted policies that over time have gutted the influence of unions, cut taxes for the wealthy, and depressed wages for most workers so that more money has "trickled up" to the richest. Ordinary people are shut out of democracy by anti-union legislation, gerrymandered districts, big money, and voter restrictions. We need leaders who want a democracy that includes everyone.

If they want to know about us, we explain ourselves: "My name is John Jensen, I'm with the movement for change." Adding "I'm not getting paid for doing this" alerts them to inquire about other callers' motives. If their comment is negative, we ask a question about the least negative part of it, and continue doing so. If they express ill will toward particular groups, we invite their own experiences of being treated unfairly.

Their comments may issue from a single main concern. Anger or frustration may signal a larger field. We first try to understand it as they see it, and let them realize we do by describing it accurately. Once they believe we comprehend the problem they face, they are more open to how to solve it. When views come out piecemeal, we try to find a word capturing their tone: "So you have some worries," "Pressure on you," or "Uncertainty about that."

To help focus the conversation, canvassers might bring a simple handout with a few ideas on it, offer it to a resident, and discuss each item. We could also be prepared with a separate fact sheet to back up each of several major themes. To discuss how media may distort information, for instance, one page might summarize Tobin Smith's testimony in Part Two, 7. *The attack on truth.* To discuss challenges facing African-Americans, the material in Part Two 8. *Impact of racism* could be helpful. For job-related concerns, ideas in Part Two 5. *Full employment* and 10. *Who is society for?* could generate conversation. Ongoing research can deepen the impact of canvassing.

If health care concerns them, inquire how they felt about a party trying to pass a bill in Congress, at one point giving a 700 billion dollar tax break to the wealthy while dropping 30 million from health insurance. Even if others thwart those designs temporarily, why would they choose leaders *who want such things?* Ask them, "If you were in a lawsuit, would you hire an attorney who had stated publicly that he wanted the other side to win?" Point out that every Representative of that party was pressured to vote for the bill and almost all caved in, implying risk in electing even potentially good candidates of that party because of its impact on them.

Sum up issues that distinguish between the parties. *Do you want support or cuts for*: science, health, education, consumer protection, net neutrality, bank regulation, environmental protection, reversing climate change, overtime for workers, and a justice system that does not automatically favor the wealthy? And nothing for the average person working to make ends meet or for rural communities, but massive tax breaks for the richest? Take pride in and document what your party has accomplished: "This is what we have done and have tried to do for you in the last half-century."

Impact of curiosity. Curiosity can enhance a conversation. We can carry separate fact pieces with us that relate to people's ethnicity, class, occupation, financial well-being, gender identification, child concerns, religion, or employment, and say to a voter:

"A point about the health care issue relates exactly to your situation. Could I show you?"

"People who have children could be affected directly by something I have here."

"You might be interested in how…could affect your worry about…" or "might relate to the…in your life."

An issue's personal implications interest people more than its broader meaning. About a bill introduced by a legislator in a different state, we can say, "You'd be surprised to hear how a proposal in the Nebraska legislature would affect you if you lived there." Researching bills in other state legislatures could turn up a wealth of curious material: "These are the kind of things people in that party want to do to you" (73).

Offer sympathetic people a way to help at once such as by contacting others, sharing literature, participating in the campaign, or joining the movement. Think what action or learning might fit them: "Do you have friends who might like to know about this? Could we get them together, and go over these ideas with them?" "We need a captain for this block who will get information to the other houses." "Could you do some phoning?" "Could I pick you up for a meeting Wednesday evening?" Your goal is not just for this person to nod in agreement at ideas you express, but to help them lead their own army.

To a resident expressing even minimal interest, we can offer a way to show it by yard signs, bumper stickers, windshield decals, caps, and buttons. Such external signals make their choice of a side real to them because demonstrating their values to other people and hence inviting conversation. Besides displaying targeted messages during election campaigns, yard signs could be used for voter education with messages like these:

- Good of the whole means arranging for everyone to prosper.

- Trickle-down economics is like having three dogs and giving one of them a wiener, expecting him to share it with the other two—Bill Maher.

- An oligarchy means an elite jerks you around and you don't even know it.

- It is hard to get a man to understand something when his salary depends on him not understanding it—Upton Sinclair.

- It is a bad sign if hungry children do not bother us.

- Past civilizations broke down mainly from the selfishness of the powerful.

When people agree to carry out an activity on their own, be sure to return and inquire about their experience. At the start, your interest is the strongest and maybe the only influence on them.

Visit the uninvolved. 45-60% of voters may not vote in a given election, but reaching out to them is an open door. They wait for someone to explain how any response of theirs might matter.

They seldom live in a guard-monitored, combination-protected, gate-mechanized compound. You can walk up to their front door and knock on it, and if you do, they will talk to you. They may feel helpless about politics, and believe they have no say in electoral results, so we want to help them understand the issues and participate.

Their own life may be a struggle. They may work at temporary jobs with low pay and little security, move frequently to look for work, have disabilities or are aging or in ill health, lack any savings to help them ride out problems, and are under-trained for available jobs or over-trained for disappearing jobs. They may have chosen to stay put out of family loyalty but at an economic cost, and may find child-raising harder because they work two jobs to get by and must leave children to themselves. Their daily priority is coping.

Because of the stresses on their lives, they are more easily nudged out of the political process. They may have to travel far to a polling place, wait hours in line to vote, or take off work they can ill afford to miss. With voting designed so they must sacrifice to do it, they give it up, permitting candidates to ignore their needs and views. It helps them if we can reduce stress in any way possible since stressed people are less likely to vote (74).

Approaching them respectfully, establishing rapport, and finding out their interests especially affects the uninvolved. Because their investment in political debates has eroded, *issues are not our natural bridge.* We connect with them instead about themselves with a message like this:

> The dominant minority running society has decided that you don't count, and they don't want you to count. As long as they can keep you out of politics, they can ignore anything you need, want, or believe. They make it harder for you to vote, gerrymander districts, give your children a sub-standard education, and protect you the least from society's downsides. We have to replace those at the top with others who want to take account of everyone. Making your voice heard means learning about the issues and candidates, getting you registered, and then getting you to the polls. Lots of people around here are deciding to do that. Now, where can we start?

14. Act on ideas learned

Link learning with action. Imagine a straight line between this person as they are today at one end, and this person highly effective for social change at the other end: they can speak confidently and persuasively about important issues, are competent with details, act on what they know, and easily connect with others.

What happens between those two ends, in "the black box" in the middle not open to our view?

We might supply people with lots of knowledge—run them through pages of information—and hope to get action afterward, but our observation of educated people does not recommend this. Learning is seldom enough to propel individual change and initiative. The will to share, to be expressive, has approximately zero correlation with the quantity of one's knowledge and maybe even a negative correlation, so that the more we know, the less inclined we are to pass it on. Advanced learning may induce more reserved preoccupation than eagerness to tell others as we become more acutely aware of how narrow a slice of attention people leave open to fresh ideas.

And data of the kind one tells back on a test is not the answer because in so many fields, people with little knowledge may be highly effective, and experienced workers may regard a newcomer's book learning as useless. Having information one does not use also implies knowledge is beside the point, that it does not affect what we do.

Portending the best outcome *is the will to share what one has.* Throughout history, major ideas about religion, society, art, and science have spread rapidly as people eagerly passed on the little they did know. Newness in fact has an impact that soon disappears. Upon first hearing an idea not fully formed, we are freer simply to announce it and leave a complete understanding for later: "Hey listen! I just found out…," or "Come with me. Let's find out what this is about!" Christians will remember Philip telling others about Jesus: "Come and see" (Jn. 1, 43-46).

Sharing what one knows, however limited, is also critical for *stimulating a leader mentality.* People become leaders by proposing even a single idea, and creating change with ideas is the essence of a movement. Cesar Chavez and Delores Huerta changed conditions for hundreds of thousands of farm workers this way and taught the nation about the oppressive conditions they faced. For Chavez, "painting a picture and coloring it in" entailed self-sacrificing effort for many years prior to his early death. For us it means at least being articulate with the picture we present.

Expressing ideas helps newcomers understand the nature of a movement—that ideas become useful as they are passed on. Out of millions of communications between people daily, those shape society that land where someone acts on them. Researchers quietly push the edges of knowledge and others search out best practices and model programs, but leagues beyond other eras of history we are already awash in good ideas (cf. *Recommended reading* below). Our elephantine deficit is failing to act on the ones we have.

We noted above how high quality personal contact initiates a causal sequence that reinforces further high quality personal contact. Learning involves a similar cycle: Gathering information enables us to share it, which increases our competence, which obtains changes in others' thinking, which motivates us to continue learning. The sequence begins in a stimulating way to learn.

15. Become fluent with ideas

When they feel incapable, people do not try to influence society. Unable to act in a way that changes their experience, they find themselves swept along in a system that, while seeming to be free, leads them to closed doors in all directions. When their sense of helplessness morphs into worry and frustration, they are more prone then to stereotypes, prejudices, and resentments, and especially need a sense of efficacy, a grasp of how their knowledge can change their experience. Here we explain how.

Help people practice expressing ideas. We want people fluent with the movement's ideas for two reasons. The basic one is that a movement exists to pass on ideas, which means learning them. By this effort, a group ceases to be complicit in letting mediocre thinking govern society.

But also, *people motivate themselves* by the ideas circulating in their mind. As they master a narrative, it satisfies them to explain it, and they become confident with other ideas. Doing this repeatedly, they realize they can do it with any idea at all, and their pleasure at it encourages them to continue (75). As they see results from expressing an idea, they gain more knowledge, share, see more results, and gain more knowledge. Sharing is a link in a chain. Small efforts develop into bigger ones as expressing their existing knowledge spurs them to learn more. They own a change in themselves, note a benefit and outcome from it, and *realize that personal change matters.*

Most people gain skill explaining ideas only by practice, and are unlikely to assimilate material they only hear. Each one in an audience of a thousand must still mesh the ideas with their own thought stream. To turn a pan of vegetables into a stew, they have to process each one. But upon listening and perhaps even taking notes, how do they make ideas their own?

Small group discussions. The most versatile method is a type of small group interaction. A landmark study about how encounter groups affected participants found that people changed personally and retained their changes when they expressed their ideas in a group, but with a particular condition. *They needed to believe their ideas influenced others* (76).

We can understand how this works. If we announce an idea, and others receive it impassively and turn toward someone else, we have no reason to believe they value our idea or regard it as worth saving. Furthermore a personal discount is implied. The fact that it was we who said it did not matter. When someone with high status states a commonplace idea, people say, "Right on!" while to the same idea from another they shrug their shoulders and think, "Everyone knows that." Others' response raises an idea's significance and enhances the status of the one offering it.

So if a newcomer makes a comment, and someone else takes it up with, "Hey, that's an interesting angle. Could we follow that for a minute?", this lets the person know they are worthy of influencing the group, and the idea itself gains weight. Or someone says, "Let me add to that..." and the original person thinks, "I got something going." Or someone recaps the discussion thread, "Let's see where we've come," and integrates the newcomer's comment into the overall theme, or a participant sums up the newcomer's offering respectfully: "So you're saying that...." Or someone comments, "I hadn't thought of it that way," alerting the group that the newcomer has just led them to "think of it that way." Having their ideas taken seriously is particularly important for young males. Their developmental stage moves them to try to earn others' esteem by expressing their competences, and for myself, I vividly recall how that felt.

To prepare, participants read beforehand the material the planning team selects, and then in the group trade ideas about it. Doing so, they affirm their prior learning and experience, expand their knowledge, improve their ability with words, show respect for each other, and welcome newcomers. Ideas become the content of their personal bonds and guide them toward effective action.

Discussion groups should be small enough for everyone to talk. Five in each seem optimal with four to seven workable. As numbers expand, talking time for each person decreases, while too few in a group lack cross-fertilization of ideas. If a larger group meets regularly for an hour or more, it can divide into discussion-size units for part of its time and retain the same members for a month or so. A few weeks of continuity deepen personal relationships and encourage a common train of thought, but permanent subgroups can fragment a larger body.

People with daytime jobs could schedule sessions after work, in early morning, or mid-day, weighing people's job schedules, transportation, and child needs to find the best compromise. The group's urgency determines its pace. Invited to meet twice a week, participants think, "We have something going!" but tell them, "See you next month," and they relax for three weeks. Session length can vary. A half-hour a week could be effective for participants who 1) think about the ideas between sessions, 2) study new material and prepare to discuss it, and 3) discipline themselves to start on time. This mode may fit especially during periods of intense activity. An hour a week may work better for new people who need to talk out their views about unfamiliar subjects at a relaxed pace.

Particularly when external conditions are changing, we want to regularize what we can in the movement's interior life. Keeping to agreed-on beginning and ending times for discussion groups enhances stability while unpredictability is a stress.

Discussion material draws on three kinds of information—outside, inside, and principles. Outside information concerns solutions to social, political, environmental, and economic problems, and candidates' qualities and policies. It may come from current events, online sources, news media, books, articles, and relevant papers, and explains changes needed in society.

Inside information helps sustain the movement: group development, organization, leadership, communications, problem-solving, planning, supervising, group learning, and mutual support.

Principles affect both. Unconditional love for others and responsibility for the world should infuse a movement's inner life as well as its policies. Values in common are especially important as people collaborate at a distance. A Montana rancher and a New York social worker become a team as they share a field of thought despite different experience. In reforming a state's criminal justice system, a group must recognize long term values and not be distracted by partisan tangents. Grounded in principles, it makes progress despite tradeoffs. This book contains all three kinds of material.

And while people may discount their daily experience as ordinary, it links them to issues confounding the country. Their employment connects to the economy, children's schooling to national education issues, food to inter-continental production and distribution, weather events to climate change, travel to security and global concerns. People who knock on their doors test their personal safety, municipal services reflect environmental policies and needs of demographic groups, taxes connect them to public priorities, and their values to how society treats people. Before they speak a word, participants are embedded in everything important.

Three goals for the discussion are to know the facts, recognize our personal connection to them, and apply them to society. A fourth goal concerns certain direct perceptions.

We aim first just to acquire knowledge. During a discussion, we might summarize a section, point out evidence useful to retain, and understand its meaning like students study for a test. A second goal is personalizing the knowledge. We might share how it has affected our lives ("In my neighborhood…"), explain an idea's significance to us, or how it affects people we know or relates to our values. The third objective is its implication for changing society, how to act on and apply it.

The fourth goal is *articulating what we see*. People may not even recognize conditions that drastically affect them, so we learn how to say, "Look at that! Let me explain what is happening. This is what's going on!" A desire to help people grasp the reality of their experience fueled this book. This focus is particularly important now *because millions grossly misled, confused, and manipulated are even out of touch with the evidence of their own senses.* In such a climate, we will not succeed by accusations but by promoting accurate understanding through respectful, clarifying conversation.

Preparing for the group. Before beginning, participants agree on the general content they want to assimilate, and choose source material containing it. While they might decide to work through the discussion questions listed below, if they prefer their own instead, a simple way to construct them is for the leader *to name any issue relevant to the group's concerns, and ask how participants connect it to their personal lives and values*. Leaders might put their attention on the subject matter well before the meeting time, turn it over in their mind piece by piece, think about its relationship to members' lives, and frame questions that could stimulate discussion.

Starting the group. Seating everyone in a row reduces eye contact while chairs in a circle work better. The leader should insure that all can easily catch the eye of everyone else and might explain why:

"We do this because our basic message is that we value each one's ideas and needs, so we make sure to include them. If we expect to say that to the nation, we begin it right here. We want everyone able to talk, be listened to, and connect with each other easily."

The leader notices how individuals take their places. Newcomers tentative about expressing ideas may move their chair outside the circle, face away from the group, or look at the floor. When they lean forward instead and look at others, they imply, "I'm ready."

When participants already know each other, the leader begins by inviting a short comment from each such as News and Goods–what's new or good in their life. People often arrive immersed in a personal issue, and sharing it in a few words allows others to appreciate their mood. When time is limited, they may do this informally beforehand. The discussion itself can follow several tracks:

–If the group chooses a timely book like this one for their material but participants cannot afford their own, they could purchase one together and proceed through it with questions on key topics. Participants might pass it around reading a half page aloud at a time, and explore its ideas.

–Ending a meeting, the leader could assign each participant a different topic to study and then lead a discussion on it the next meeting.

–The leader might distribute several points for the day, or present a theme or series of questions.

–When each has their own copy, the leader can ask everyone to read the next page quietly and then invite someone to summarize it. The participant explains the gist of the passage, adds his or her thoughts, and others comment as they wish.

–The leader may express their own interest; "What struck me was…," or note an emphasis: "Two things are connected here."

–Everyone together can examine a page or section, note its key aspects, and help each other think through the material and its implication for action.

The discussion should not turn upon the leader's ideas but rather elicit participants' ideas. Leaders' credibility depends not on points they make but on how they involve others. Participants take it where they wish, though the leader may occasionally invite a comment, air a reservation, or instruct when a misunderstanding hinders the discussion.

If the group stalls (or for a change of pace) the leader can use a format called a Consult. In one sentence everyone tells what happened in their own mind after the leader's single-word cue (77). He or she might say "I'm going to announce one word, and I'd like to ask everyone just to notice and then share the first thought that arises in your mind after you hear it. Questions? Okay, here's the word: *Politics!*" Any relevant topic, name, or event can be announced.

From the series of individual responses, the leader recognizes common threads and themes that invite discussion, and can ask a followup question of one participant or invite the group to develop an aspect it wishes to explore. Open-ended questions are preferred, but any question that leads to more comments is a good one:

"Would you like to say more about that?"

"How do you connect that to your life?"

"How would that apply to your work place?"

"Tell us more."

"Your thought?"

"What does that remind you of?"

"You've had an experience with that?"

"You'd like to add to what she said?"

"So what happened then?"

"How do you picture that?"

"I'm wondering…"

"How did your family take that?"

Everyone enters the discussion by invitation or their own initiative. Leaders talk no more than their share, a fifth of the time in a group of five, and avoid implying they have a right answer and others should guess it. When everyone knows more, overviews of the material may be needed less, and the group can proceed to its meaning and implications for action.

Some tend to over-explain their ideas. They assume that others will not understand their first words and they must restate them three or four times, which can reduce others' share of group talking time important for their growth.

When someone has presented an idea and appears to go on to another or repeat the first one, a leader can slowly raise his/her hand signaling they wish to break in, and *sum up the speaker's point thus far:* "So you're saying…." People seldom object to this intervention because it focuses the group on their idea. The leader then turns to others–"Anyone have a comment on that?"–or redirects the topic.

Another remedy that enhances the general quality of the discussion is distributing a few elementary communication skills ahead of time, and making it a group standard that all have an equal share of the group's attention:

- Look at the speaker.

- Use short messages rather than long speeches.

- Ask questions.

- Include everyone.

- Leave a brief silence after people speak (78).

Applying these standards, everyone participates and assimilates ideas together. Looking at others lets them know they have our attention. Brief messages help everyone stay involved and minimize over-talking. Questions draw people out and enlarge the subject. Including everyone enhances belonging. Moments of silence let all weigh the prior comment and choose whether to respond next. The group reads the skills together, and each person plans how to apply them.

The leader can ask for comments afterward on how use of the skills aided the discussion, and suggest everyone practice the set in their daily life. People improve quickly when they check themselves on a new behavior, and may find it transforming to explain their ideas in a safe setting, have others listen respectfully, and build a mutual train of thought.

A stimulating option for ending a discussion is to invite a volunteer to summarize everything said and include each one's contribution, a skill well within middle schoolers' ability. Knowing they may do this, participants pay closer attention, but the practice also validates everyone's offering. Between meetings, all read the material scheduled for the next one in light of the four objectives above. And while we might expect learning to translate at once into action, the two have different tracks. People may already have a personal assignment for the week, so study goes at its own pace to enlarge their perspective.

Give public talks. For practice explaining movement ideas, participants can present talks of increasing length to audiences of increasing size. A handy format follows the acronym SAFW (*Say A Few Words,* the title of a past book about giving talks): State your idea, Accent your idea (rephrase it, tell a little about it), For Example your idea (fill up the time with examples or stories that illustrate it), and Wind up with your idea (re-state how it relates to your audience). The format can work with a two-minute talk or an hour.

Everyone should practice short talks on many issues since capsuling any subject in a couple minutes is a good way to start a conversation. The planning team can maintain a checklist for each member, such as ten "elevator talks" of 1-2 minutes, seven "dinner table talks" of 3-5 minutes, and five "presentation talks" of 12-15 minutes. Short talks develop people's confidence. Select topics by their local audience appeal.

Their own discussion group might be enough practice audience for participants' brief talks, but some should be to larger numbers. The full group might use a portion of its meeting this way, or the talk secretary could announce, "Tuesday night we have eight practice talks scheduled—three elevator talks, three dinner table talks, and two presentations. We would welcome an audience attending."

When members are ready, the movement can offer a Speakers Bureau to the community. Presentations in schools, colleges, rest homes, civic clubs, and via the media circulate movement ideas, but the public might also respond to formal debates on specific topics, with movement members taking both sides and trying to represent opposing opinions in their strongest light. A few well-prepared people can influence a community's mainstream conversation. Talks to responsive audiences might end with dividing attendees into discussion groups, exploring their interests, gathering contact information, registering them for ongoing study groups, and involving them in activity.

16. Allay fear

Address participants' emotional needs. Participants may devalue their own comments and assume they "won't know what to say." Discussion leaders trying to help participants overcome their fear of speaking may themselves worry, "I won't be able to keep things going," or "I don't know all the answers," or "Silence means I'm screwing up," or that they must supply for the group's hesitance by talking themselves.

Upon offering a question that fits them, the leader *is certain* of their ability to answer. Asking, "What strikes you personally about this?" we turn the play over to them, invite their comment, and look calmly from one to another, telling them, "This is about you, about what is going on in your life and the values important to you." We wait expectantly. Our silence and eye contact let them know we are confident they can respond. Silence in fact tends to raise interest and spur even slow starters to enter. Noticing that the leader has passed the ball to them, people eventually begin and build on each other's comments, and we thank them when they are done. While at first they fish around for words, in a few weeks they may express ideas easily.

People tend to rise or descend to our expectation of them. Knowing that each one's years of experience leave them with many ideas, we provide a safe setting for exploring them. They show they are ready to speak by looking at the leader, leaning forward, clearing their throat, nodding, glancing at the present speaker, and then back to the leader. The leader may nod to them, say their name, or "You have a thought"? As participants relax and the group adopts good communications, they respond directly to each other rather than passing comments through the leader. They welcome each other's attempts to talk and realize it is okay for them to flounder a bit.

If they continue to find it hard to express their ideas, the leader may be expecting answers too complicated. Their personal thoughts about the material are enough. If we pose questions beyond their understanding, use unfamiliar terms, or discount their offerings, they may conclude that the group is not for them.

Leading the group does not require specialized training. Many can do it. Even when drawing straws to select a leader, the group defers to him/

her for guidance. The leader stays a few pages ahead, thinks of questions to ask, and models skills that aid the discussion.

17. Study and share

Generate social connections with ideas. This format enables many together to expand their knowledge, develop new relationships, and circulate ideas. Any number can participate, so obtain a room large enough for the expected turnout to be comfortable. Tables are not needed. Chairs should not be fixed in place so everyone can move about freely and arrange seating as they prefer.

People bring one or more books or articles they want to discuss or learn better, drawing from the entire universe of interests. As a common focus they might also have a copy of the same book, such as this one, and if they wish, bring optional material to deposit on a side table for others to browse through. The experience can last two to three hours.

Explain that everyone will change partners several times. First they pair with someone they do not know well and sit together. All read silently for ten minutes in their own material to select points to explain to their partner, and the moderator announces when ten minutes are up. If both partners are ready, they take turns summarizing what they just read or wanted to explain, and discuss it as they wish. After ten minutes at this or when both have had a chance to talk, the moderator suggests that everyone stand, find a new partner, and repeat the same steps, and calls out the same sequence every twenty to thirty minutes.

New pairs set their own pace while dividing talking time equally among reading, listening, and explaining: 1) reading material they brought, 2) explaining to a partner what they read or retained from others' comments, and 3) listening to their partner explain. New partners can tell each other what they already learned, or can read more and then share it. Some may form a small group to pursue a particular theme. The moderator watches for clues to the group's energy to guide the pace of changing partners.

The format opens conversation channels for later follow up, uncovers common interests, generates a group value around absorbing and sharing knowledge, and by establishing a relaxed setting can help smooth out polarized viewpoints. Conveying *what someone else wrote* relieves people's obligation to assert it personally. They are freer simply to present it and then discuss it one detail at a time. A subtle transition occurs from opinions to information, from assertions to sharing, and from the impersonal to the personal.

Because no pre-set slant guides the experience, the design may answer a national need in the lifestyle and economics of small U.S. towns. *Over 16,000 of them have fewer than 10,000 residents.* In each one, many people know many others, their spouses and children, who share common interests and want to help their community. An activist can approach a local organization, arrange a Study and Share experience, promote it via the media and word-of-mouth, and help people develop fresh connections about ideas that matter to them. Uniting around mutual concerns is more important for a town than specific conclusions they reach.

18. Questions for discussion

Challenge people with ideas they can respond to. A single question asked in a discussion group can spark an extended exchange. For those below inviting a yes or no, ask why and follow up people's answer. They can be taken in any order and used both for discussion groups and campaign outreach. While some refer to issues in society, taken together the questions invite participants to align their values gradually to the well-being of others and service to the world. Many points may seem obvious, but by expressing them in their own words, participants grasp them differently. The point is not "knowing the answers" but rather giving intellectual content and interest-energy to their personal readiness for action. Some questions refer to ideas presented further on:

1. What issues concern you most?

2. Which do you feel are most urgent for society?

3. Why do you prioritize them that way?

4. What global trends appear headed worse or better?

5. How have distant events affected you or your family and friends?

6. How do people show care about others who live far away?

7. In your lifetime, how have you changed what you valued?

8. What abilities do you have that could contribute to social change?

9. How could you change in order to be of more help?

10. What has been your experience as a volunteer?

11. Why do people need to work together?

12. What does it mean to work together?

13. Have you ever asked someone to change their opinion?

14. Has anyone ever asked you to do that?

15. What happened?

16. What could have helped a change occur?

17. How do you think small issues are resolved differently than big issues?

18. For something important to you, are you willing to ask others' help?

19. How have you done that in the past?

20. What would you do differently next time you ask someone for help?

21. How do you handle it when someone objects to what you say?

22. How do you work out differences?

23. Do you like to be right?

24. What do you do when others want to be right?

25. How do you feel explaining ideas to others?

26. Are you willing to learn to present them to groups of people?

27. Would you like to choose your leaders yourself or do you trust others to do that?

28. How do people keep their leaders accountable?

29. How do you think group decision-making turns out best?

30. Have you been in groups where people really thought about others' viewpoints? If so, did that help the group function better?

31. Can you ask someone else to do something and know they will do it?

32. What does that say about you as a leader?

33. Do you like to encourage others or direct them?

34. What does integrity mean to you?

35. Is there a link between integrity and improving society?

36. Do you believe you can be the starting point for new conditions?

37. How have you participated in group activity before?

38. What made the activity a success or not?

39. What helped or hindered your own participation?

40. What has been your best experience on a team?

41. What made it good?

42. Did the size of the team matter to you?

43. How did people treat each other, and how was it led?

44. How does it affect you to be welcomed into a group or not?

45. How many people do you know who are really different from you?

46. How do you feel being around them?

47. Do you have feelings that color your attitude toward society?

48. How do others' negative attitudes affect you? How do you handle them?

49. Which would you most want to change?

50. What are you willing to sacrifice for an important reason?

51. Are you ready to dedicate your effort to a high value?

52. If so, what is the value, and what would you do for it?

53. When does working against difficulties discourage you?

54. When do difficulties stimulate or inspire you?

55. What difference has it made in your life to be loved?

56. When have you experienced unconditional love?

57. In what ways do you experience conditional love? What's the difference?

58. Are you willing to take responsibility for conditions that affect many people?

59. What view of government do you want to work toward?

60. Do you think there is something to learn about how to change society?

61. How do you view the level of knowledge you have?

62. Do you know enough now, working with others, to change society?

63. What ideas can you explain comprehensively to others?

64. Can you immerse yourself in something you want to learn?

65. How does your thinking set you up for successful social action?

66. Do you see yourself thinking differently in a year, five years, or twenty years?

67. What ability do you imagine you will have in twenty years?

68. How do you expect to use it?

69. How has your life been affected by others' mediocre thinking?

70. What benefits have you lost due to mediocre thinking?

71. How have your own or others' negative emotions affected your life?

72. How could releasing negativity help you be a better force for change?

73. In what areas of life have you resisted changing your thinking, and why?

74. Do you have strong opinions about inconsequential matters? If so, why?

75. What roles have you adopted that guide your thinking now?

76. What do you understand humility to mean?

77. How have you noticed people's humility affect themselves and others?

78. What have been your experiences opening conversation with strangers?

79. What do you think we could learn from other countries?

80. Do you trust that the group knows more than any single individual?

81. What intangible principles mean most to you?

82. What is the difference between principles and an ideology?

83. What has been your experience arguing with friends?

84. What conditions made it positive?

85. From trends you know of, what do you think life will be like in 50 years?

86. How does that picture affect what you do now?

87. What do you think is the *mythus* of this country now? Of this group?

88. What would help you prepare for the work of getting information to others?

89. What information has the most impact in a political campaign?

90. How is blame used appropriately or misused?

91. Do you think full employment is a better goal than profit for companies?

92. How could that work in practice?

93. Why do you think some people never vote, and others only rarely?

94. What issues of right and wrong strike you personally?

95. Who should have more power in society and who should have less?

96. Does a political party want to take away your rights?

97. How do you best deal with such a political party?

98. What cooperation with churches appears most productive?

99. What implications does religion have for social policy?

100. How has a creative minority helped the U.S. develop?

101. Have you seen the desire for gain affect others' judgment?

102. What evidence shows the impact of selfishness on society?

103. How has a dominant minority caused inequality?

104. How does fairness matter now?

105. What signals tell you society is fair or unfair?

106. How would some people try to make an unfair system look fair?

107. How do you think our system needs to change?

108. What personal experiences convince you of that?

109. Is it worthwhile to try to bring balance and fairness to society?

110. What would balance look like?

111. Do you feel you are included in U.S. society, or do you stand outside it?

112. How have benefit, advantage, and handicap affected your life?

113. What do you think about helping people who are down and out?

114. Does helping them cause a downside for society?

115. How do environmental laws relate to poverty?

116. How do educational conditions relate to poverty?

117. How does the criminal justice system relate to poverty?

118. How do wages and working conditions relate to poverty?

119. Do you think poor people work harder or less hard than rich people? Why?

120. Do you trust market forces to improve society?

121. What has been your experience losing a job?

122. What has been your experience facing discrimination while searching for one?

123. Have you ever worked at a job with high pressure, low pay, and no options?

124. What happens to people who "fall through the cracks" and are truly in want?

125. Is there a pipeline in education, criminal justice, or social services that works against those without influence?

126. What do your values tell you is the right thing to do?

127. What is the ideal role of government to aim for? Why?

128. What social services should government provide?

129. What happens if government does not provide them?

130. Does everyone deserve services and opportunity or are benefits only for winners?

131. Do you recognize a meritocracy in operation? Does it help or hurt?

132. What are the pluses and minuses of capitalism?

133. What is the best way to handle the minuses?

134. How do we deal with economic inequality?

135. What does it take for self-interest to improve society?

136. What changes in elections could enhance democracy?

137. Are there services you would like to supply to your community?

138. What do you think are the most important issues to present?

139. What issues stand out that need new agreements?

140. What breaking points concern you personally the most (cf. below)?

141. What key settings seem to you most accessible for influencing policies?

142. What key ideas do you think deserve most attention now?

143. What leverage structures seem important to improve or develop?

144. What activities or efforts would help you find allies?

145. What campaign would be most important to you now?

146. What do you think would enable it to succeed?

147. Do you think the public agreement is a good idea?

148. What is the alternative if there is no public agreement?

149. What issues do you think you could problem-solve with opponents?

150. What do you think is the most worrisome bandwagon today?

151. How can we get people thinking past their own locality?

152. How have your occupational and social roles limited your thinking?

153. Given what we know now, how can we change the world?

19. The issue of fairness

In *Strangers in their own land: Anger and mourning on the American right*, Arlie Hochschild shares her extended exploration of the conservative values of a rural Louisiana community. Supported by parallel data from a recent Kaiser Family Foundation/Washington Post survey of rural America, a consistent picture emerges:

Though comparable to urban communities on many economic and demographic characteristics and in their use of government services, their residents tend to have a higher proportion of white, Christian, and retired citizens. The measures distinguishing this population most, however, were attitudes about fairness—betrayed by government, losing their culture, and economically disadvantaged. More of them than the general population believed, for instance, that the nation's problems were due to others receiving government benefits who did not deserve them, and that their own patient cooperation with the system was not rewarded; that others—foreigners, non-Christians, and other ethnic groups—were "cutting into line" ahead of them, and they resented this (79).

These beliefs are a call-out to our *mythus,* the good of the whole. We need to be able to explain that the limitations people experience are not due to benefits to the undeserving but from a powerful establishment that has imposed onerous conditions on everyone lacking political power; that their own attitudes have been manipulated, and they need information to flesh out an accurate view.

Several topics apply to this theme, such as blame, fairness, social services, the use of power, and government role. Members can practice these subjects in small group discussion to prepare for canvassing. We gradually open people to different ideas by asking them a question and discussing their answer (cf. 13. *Canvassing* above). They are more likely to change from accumulating small, fresh insights through examining their thought processes with our help.

Blame

1. During the Great Depression of the 1930s, fifteen million people were unemployed and lost everything. Was it their fault?

2. In the financial crisis of 2008, many Americans lost everything and were unemployed for years after. Do you know people who had a hard time then?

3. Are you finding it hard to raise your own economic level?

4. Is it your fault?

5. Do you think it is their own fault, in general, if people do not raise their economic level?

6. How does "fault" apply to people who are really, really poor?

7. Many did well financially in 2008 and afterward. Were they better people, lucky, harder workers, or did the system take care of them?

8. If someone's religion told them they could discriminate against African Americans, should society enforce that discrimination?

9. Would you call that racism rather than religious belief?

10. Doesn't your religion regard each soul as created by God in

exactly the same way?

11. Doesn't that imply equality between us all at the most basic, enduring level?

12. What if someone's religion told them to discriminate against Moslems?

13. Or against gays, lesbians, and the transgender?

14. If we disagree with someone, should we use social leverage to discriminate against them?

Fairness

1. In times of suffering, should everyone face equal burden?

2. On a sinking ship, should first-class passengers get lifeboats before others?

3. Can you rig a system so some always benefit and others lose?

4. If so, how could you tell?

5. Should society give more help now to those it disadvantaged before? If it impoverished a father who left his family poor, should it help his children now?

6. Would it injure society to help poor people with education or health by taxing the rich?

7. Did others aid your health or education? If so, did it make you lazy?

8. Would it make poor people lazy?

9. Should we raise the national minimum wage? Is it right for employees of a wealthy corporation to need welfare?

10. Do you know what a tax on wealth is? Do you think we need it now?

11. Should society subsidize the extra homes and planes of the wealthy?

12. Should high income earners pay into Social Security like others do?

13. Should people too poor to pay court fines be jailed?

14. Do you tend to avoid people of different ethnicity?

15. When would you call that racist?

Social Services

1. Is society damaged or benefited by free school lunches year around?

2. Is anyone injured if society provides free dental and health care for children?

3. Who would be injured and how would the injury occur?

4. How about if it adequately funds early childhood programs?

5. If it educates children free from kindergarten through high school?

6. Through college?

7. If it provides poor K-12 school districts funding to match the rich?

8. If it provides nationwide single-payer health care for all?

9. Do you believe that Social Security and Medicare are good for the country?

10. Do you think we could trust private companies to take them over?

11. Would they tend first to their profits or to citizens' well-being?

Use of power

1. Do you support electing the President by the national popular vote? Why or why not?

2. Do you support a constitutional amendment limiting money in politics?

3. Do you want to make voting easy through voting by mail, extended hours, and automatic registration? If not, why not?

4. Do you oppose gerrymandered Congressional districts?

5. Why do you think some people support gerrymandering?

6. How do they justify this as part of a democratic system?

Government role

1. Is the economic system designed for some people to prosper and not others?

2. Should people whom the government helped to become wealthy pay more taxes to help the poor and middle classes?

3. Have government programs helped to counteract poverty?

4. Should government have that role?

5. Do you support subsidies for corporations and oppose food stamps for the poor?

6. How do you think some make sense of that position?

Ask people to imagine themselves losing their job, having no financial reserves, and trying to feed their family. Do they think their problem would matter to society? Should it? What solution to the problem overall makes sense to them? Fairness does not concern only dollar-for-dollar equivalence, but also public services like education, safety from criminal behavior, equality before the law, and various freedoms.

Help people acknowledge the existence of economic inequality, its importance, how they are affected by it, and how they and society should handle it. Mention a fact and explore its meaning. What does it imply about the economic system? Are the fruits of U.S. productivity distributed fairly? Do people believe the system is equitable and only a minor glitch has produced those outcomes, or were they achieved intentionally by political leverage? How does society account for ten people out of work? Inequality how bad would finally be intolerable? Will it be okay eventually to have a few giga-billionaires who own everything, and everyone else at soup kitchens? Does that go too far?

20. Mass action and personal contact

Focus on the quality of personal contact. Encountering an intriguing idea, we tell our friends about it. Since we average five close friends each, even without technology an idea can spread quickly, leaving the impression that we have achieved change. An idea "goes viral," and we assume everyone thinks alike.

The Women's Suffrage Movement, the Civil Rights Movement, and the Anti-Vietnam War Movement sought straightforward changes: grant the vote, stop the war, and provide blacks the same civil rights as whites. Marches, demonstrations, and personal confrontations jarred government enough for it finally to grant the vote, stop the war, and remove some of the legal burdens on blacks—specific changes like surgical removal of a tumor. Demonstrations usually promote one point at a time, and are not a good vehicle for conveying complicated ideas.

But society's problems now are more like having cancer metastasizing. We cannot excise it like we did the tumor but must address the health of the entire organism. Marches may in effect say, "We have cancer!" but without surgical impact. A million can show up for an occasion, promote a simple message, entertain the public, and make no difference. Shouts, songs, and banners demonstrate that numbers believe an issue is important but without convincing others who wonder, "Why should this matter to me?" A politician threading among margins of support calculates, "How does this threaten my re-election?"

Mass activity may sway those who are truly undecided or who conclude that "Everyone wants this." But the mid-2017 outpouring of objection against repeal of the Affordable Care Act illustrated the problem. Preventing change on an issue may feel like victory *but at best retains the status quo.* The complex changes actually needed on the law involve details, like a medicine traveling through the body to take on a disease in specific cells. The health of the whole body is involved, which means neutralizing injuries to any part of it such as a single voter saturated with false information. In war (an unfortunate parallel), massed attacks such as bombing still need "boots on the ground" to overcome resistance. In social change, the boot is one person offering an idea to another.

We need to master the challenging aspects of change and not rely on repeating the easy ones, so what exactly are the hard ones?

Let us say we are building a boat. We have large and small pieces of wood, and large and small nails. We use the large nails with the large wood, but cannot use them everywhere. We use the small nails with the small wood or we break it in pieces. Some aspects of our effort are delicate, requiring sensitive use of small levers of influence, while other aspects invite collective force. But if we use the small nails well, we fortify the internal structure of the movement so it can sustain strenuous effort, guaranteeing effective use of the large nails.

The basic small nail is high quality personal contact. We change ideas best by talking face to face, for four reasons. One is that we must affect others deeply for them to change their lives to help us. To alter their priorities they need a substantial motive. Facing them, we convey urgency better than on paper, or by technology or impersonal means. We all drive past billboards without them touching us because no person urged us to respond. And if Facebook pages changed us, it was change we sought. We need to know instead how people happen to go in a different direction than they were headed. For this, another person has the most impact (80).

Because of this we make it a group habit *to pass on all the information we can by personal contact* rather than by technology. From a human being we tend to get the essence of the issue at hand, while from mass emailings we accumulate content for our archives. *Our minds, however, grapple with essences, not with archives.* From a trusted individual, knowledge registers more deeply than from impersonal sources.

A second reason is that direct contact affects ourselves. Conveying an idea means we have devoted personal energy to it. We fuse together meaning, value, and urgency in our own mind when we present an idea.

A third reason is that we can fit the message precisely to another's need. A shoe salesman does not sell shoes like tamales, but selects a particular shoe for one foot. So also in a society swamped with mediocre thinking, we reach one person at a time with ideas that align with them and their experience.

A fourth reason is that personal contact skirts the brain's habit of automatically screening out the irrelevant.

Most people do not even notice challenges to their beliefs because their brain avoids them spontaneously. They habitually minimize contrary-leaning media and click off public figures they disagree with. Evidence flits past them like a housefly, dispersed housing insulates them, and their social niche dismisses divergent views.

We all do the screening-out habit with no ill intent just to keep our mental content manageable. We cannot think about everything, so we concentrate on what seems relevant to our lives. *This is a positive feature of our mental equipment,* so while we can own it, we also need to recognize the possible harm from it.

It works this way: Because our senses absorb so much, and everything they absorb has implications, our perceived world is potentially overwhelming. So even before we are consciously aware of it, our mind has to sort what it will actively think about. It bundles up most of what our senses receive, stamps it "Disposable," and leaves behind only a drip for us to examine. It lumps together countless topics it considers unimportant, and employs shortcuts or rules to think efficiently about them. Assigning one meaning to a category like, "The homeless are not my problem," lets us eventually process an array of conditions first quickly, then automatically, and then subconsciously outside our awareness.

So imagine a businessman on a big city sidewalk passing a kiosk that displays headlines like, "Starving child found..." and "Poverty increases...." He has often walked by and dismissed them, but a homeless man steps forward one day and asks him, "Sir, do you have a dollar?"

He has more than a dollar and feels uncomfortable. His rule discarded the *category* homeless, and he often used it in legislative work. But a different rule tells him to weigh among actual people and here is one of them. Instead of dismissing the situation spontaneously, his brain puffs it up for him to examine. His girl friend beside him further modifies his rule and he feels obliged to cope with the situation.

The two tendencies–automatic screening *out* and exaggerating fresh perceptions *in*–point to a movement's problem and its solution: *a guarded mind encountering personal contact*. When a gentler approach is unavailable, we can multiply fresh perceptions *in* by making them novel, specific, and present–the principle behind sit-ins in a Congressman's office. Or on leaving his gated community in a window-shaded vehicle, he passes three people waving signs where he turns into traffic: "Congressman X voted against food stamps," "He receives $1 million in farm subsidies," and *"Hypocrisy?"* We want him to register the moment, and uncomfortably, he imagines his neighbors passing the corner.

If considerateness is so wired into us that we cannot assert blunt truth to someone holding an immoral or destructive stance, we should remember that *offered to us it would be gift*. When we are desperately wrong, others save us from moral disaster by affecting us deeply enough that we examine our actions. So we try to help others make a constructive turn, and jarring them may be the only way. We do not leave them complacent that damaging policies based on false information, moral confusion, or skewed priorities are acceptable. We want them to know that when they depart from positive values, others will "hold their feet to the fire" publicly.

21. Face to face needs

A way to understand the challenge of communicating is to imagine two trapeze performers, one flying in the air and the other catching. The first checks carefully before flying: "Is he ready to catch me?" *We do not let go of our own bar if we don't think the other will be there when we need them.* The one catching must be alert: "Is she coming now? How will I grab hold?" If the one catching does not time their swing to connect in the middle, the one flying falls to the ground.

We are all designed to fly and catch. Anytime we speak, we release a part of ourselves for others to catch, and if they do not do so, we can sustain injury. I have known adults harmed for life by others who crushed their early attempts to express themselves. For us to connect with another, we need to welcome their self-expression so they are encouraged to continue it. *We achieve anything together only after catching smoothly what they send.*

Recognize and meet people's needs early. We each manage a part of the core needs in others, and by recognizing them in the moment we are better able to minimize them as issues. This is important because "needs" mean you cannot avoid them. They hang there and pester you until you deal with them. While anything else happens, people are still stuck in them, awaiting relief, and expect to meet them before or while exchanging ideas. Any or all of three universal needs can be present in a contact with others.

The first related to our purpose is acceptance: "Will they even let me into the room?" Entering an unfamiliar group and looking around, we try to figure out, "Do I have a place here? Am I accepted?" Someone catches our eye and acknowledges us, and we know who to approach first. Until receiving a clue, we hesitated to talk to anyone since there is no point talking to people who do not accept us.

If several notice us, our next need emerges. We want to know who we might be close to, whether anyone actually likes us. We look for a smile, a warm expression, and a tone signaling affection. People already comfortable with each other may be most alert to this quality.

The third prominent need, for control, causes most of the problems. We want to know if our ideas have any influence, if they matter here. We may measure our status by others' deference to our views, whether they take account of us in making decisions (81). Two friends arguing politics assert their need for control, each thinking "I'm not going to let him win!" Insisting on the last word in an argument is an attempt at dominance. It may feel to each that they are being rational, but that they get nowhere indicates they are not. The entire internal process of the movement should meet these three needs.

Ask for what you want. Businessman W. Clement Stone suggested to his organization, "Tell everyone what you want to do, and someone will help you do it."

What if that is true? Imagine the impact a thousand focused, determined people could have on a city of a million. Yet that means only one in a thousand active and spreading a message. Someone explained to them the conditions to be changed and how united effort could do it, and invited them.

Such an effort is more feasible than most realize because people underrate their ability to persuade by about 50%, according to research. Others often say yes unexpectedly, and saying no makes them uncomfortable. The main reasons for not asking are fear of rejection and the often-incorrect assumption that others will do what they please anyway (82). To build a movement, people need to dismiss fear of rejection and ask others' help—and for that need only to believe in their purpose.

People develop their capabilities by the effort leaders ask of them. In school, teachers ask for students' effort, and students learn by the effort they expend. No request = no effort, and no effort = no development. For effort to occur, someone must request it.

The request is essential also because people are constituted to orient themselves to the activity of the moment. They supply the behavior that fits the occasion, but how do they know what it is? Needs around them may appeal to their values and deserve their help, but in practice someone tells them. *Those who arrange the moment say what it calls for,* a principle that applies throughout society as well as in unfolding situations. Leaders can say, "We're helpless to do anything" or declare, "We can't quit now!" Invited to heroic acts in a crisis, ordinary people may step up, but if they hear, "Wait and see," they do that.

Defining meaning is basic to leadership. People can be so distressed that they follow anything with a remote chance of working, making them vulnerable to deception, yet their receptivity is central to a movement. Activists grow by what their group asks them to do. Ask nothing and you get nothing. Ask for heroism, and you may get it, but the reason must warrant the sacrifice.

Social action as sales. We noted above an easy/hard distinction that applies to several issues. We must courageously face the hard so that our tendency to take the easy way does not sabotage us. Enrolling in a college course, we easily attend class, take notes, and participate in discussions, but could fail the course if we fail the final exam, so we give it special effort.

Social action is easy when we hold up signs and walk with our friends, attend meetings, hear speakers, gather in groups, express our opinion, trade ideas, and read articles. We are only out a little time. But viewing social action as sales spotlights the hard part that determines our success. We need confidence and enthusiasm about our product, but these are not enough. **Our sales are in proportion to the time we spend facing qualified customers**—people for whom the product meets their need, they have the money to buy it, and only their decision to purchase remains, which occurs through the sales process.

In social action a qualified customer is an adult able to absorb an idea. The more time we spend offering ideas face to face, the more "sales" we make. No matter how well an idea meets their need, they do not welcome it unless we offer it. Losing candidates often say, "My message didn't reach the voters" as though the planets did not align properly and some cosmic vector intervened. More accurately they would say, "We didn't *get* our message to the voters." We stopped short of the necessary effort. Thousands of organizations plateau because they do not convey their ideas person to person. To a receptive individual who might inspire a thousand others, can you deliver your plan for changing the world? If not, start there. Learn how to change society and explain it to everyone who will listen. Ask for what you want.

Feeling out connection. Even from a social distance we may make small steps of progress:

1. Another's attitude may be a deal-breaker, warning us to expect little positive outcome from time spent with them. They might be defensive about flaws in their reasoning, lack any interest in developing ideas together, resent something we affirm, or dismiss evidence in general. To practice our skills in such situations, however, we can pursue three goals. First, we do not fulfill their stereotypes about us or our group, but continue to give them exceptional listening and respect. Also, we can keep a discussion going even under difficult conditions since it increases our chance of eventually conveying an idea. Third, we may plant seeds we ask them to think about.

2. We absorb each others' ideas only after connecting, which shows up as we 1) have roughly equal talking time, 2) can ask each other questions and get thoughtful answers, 3) weigh each other's views on the same topic, and 4) do not talk past each other.

3. Although we may be anxious to explain many ideas, we listen carefully to people's words, and respond to what they say rather than running a practiced script. Two qualities distinguish successful cold callers. They think about what people say and respond accurately to their concerns.

4. When we get someone's voicemail on a call, we tell our own name so they know we are not a robot, use their name to show we know who they are, and explain in thirty seconds what we would say to them directly. We tell them we will call back with more information if we plan to do so, and educate them that way one idea at a time.

5. We have in mind a next step like collecting contact information, inviting them to a talk, arranging a followup meeting, accompanying them to a workshop, or offering a simple task: "Would you be willing to call these three numbers with this information? I'll check back on what you turn up." *We take each person as far as they can go,* and at the end propose how we can "pick up later where we leave off." If we promise anything, we follow through. A reliable message is more credible.

22. Connect through evidence

You gain wisdom about change by noticing how you were misled in the past. Can you retrace how it happened? Did you give the wrong weight to certain evidence, make a hopeful leap to bridge gaps, believe some people over others, assume more evidence would not help, fail to weigh others' views? Did you indulge in feelings like frustration, irritation, pessimism, or defensiveness? Correcting your manner of going into error may mean focusing deliberately on what makes you uncomfortable, turning slowly but resolutely toward the point you instinctively realize you do not want to think about. Facing it fully, you acknowledge, "Hey, I was mistaken about that."

Evidence as our common arena helps construct civilization by aligning our actions with reality. In Part Three, 7. *Align with evidence,* we discussed its importance and challenges in applying it to our own thinking. All the advances of science, technology, and invention depend on evidence informing us accurately about the world.

But to make it useful, we must convey it. Facts do not assert themselves. For 1500 years everyone thought flies had four legs, but a glance at any fly counts six. The error is astonishing because so easily corrected but it persisted because people relied on Aristotle instead of their own eyes.

"How quaint!" we might think. "People were so *backward* then. We are certainly past such blindness."

Yes indeed. Well past. And soon after the 2016 presidential election, 52% of Republican voters believed that Donald Trump won the popular vote despite steady media monitoring of Hillary Clinton's advancing margin approaching three million. *Tens of millions of people stared concrete evidence in the face and denied it.* How could this jaw-dropping disparity between reality and belief happen?

1. Republican voters wanted to believe Donald Trump won the popular vote.

2. Their experience of victory was incompatible with the idea of losing

the popular vote. Emotional investment in an outcome overwhelmed mere information.

3. They allowed desirability bias to skew their perceptions. If they did not choose biased media in the first place, even from objective sources they steadily chose supportive evidence and dismissed the contradictory.

To talk to someone whose ideas are so confined, we sympathize first that they are entangled in a self-imposed trap, and cannot free themselves of it alone. Such an aberration of rationality usually feels too fused with one's identity to question, but hints of a strong force lying in wait. Occasional jets of smoke and rocks from a normally quiet volcano remind us of the heat churning below the surface. Evidence seldom affects such an emotionally-charged, identity-fused, data-defiant, reason-resistant conviction *and becomes irrelevant.* Any accurate data in their view is consumed by the abstractions used to interpret it, the vagueness of the terminology addressing it, and the emotional purpose regarding it.

Through research that could sharply alter how political goals are pursued, Tali Sharot sums up the difficulty of conveying evidence in her article "Want to change minds? Try this" (83). Acknowledging the distortions created by confirmation and desirability biases, she and fellow researchers examined their implications for changing others' thinking.

Their critical conclusion aligning with our discussion of rapport is that *the brain is more sensitive* to information others supply when people are in agreement. This suggests people try first to find common ground *in order to get their brains working together*–an approach about three times more effective than an evidence-based strategy. If you want to present evidence that vaccine does not cause autism, begin by reminding people first what a good thing it is that MMR vaccine guards children from measles, mumps, and rubella. Asked how we would like our tax dollars spent, when we focus on health, education and security, *we are twice as willing to pay taxes.*

Elsewhere we discuss the value of asking a question about the least negative thing someone says and using communication skills in order to open constructive exchange. Here we have a physiological reason why–our brain works better with mutual, common ground as our starting point.

An ordinary topic anyone can relate to is taking an interest in how another forms their mind, and inviting them specifically to talk about how they reach certainty about issues. We do not contradict or challenge, but rather say, "…so that's how you came to be sure!" Questions get us rolling:

- So tell me how you have come to be certain about things in your life.

- Do some parts of your life depend heavily on facts and others on opinion?

- When you were young, did people around you declare things true whether they were true or not?

- Did one parent tell everyone else what to believe and accept no challenge?

- Think of anyone you knew who did that. Did it help them cope with their life?

- How did you feel when they did that toward you?

- Do you remember adopting that as a strategy yourself?

- If so, how old were you?

- How did it work when you tried it out?

- Did peers who were sure of themselves seem to get the most respect?

- Did you get respect that way?

- Do you know what "group think" means?

- Have you ever been in a group that imposed its views on everyone?

- How did they do that?

- What were the downsides?

- Would you want to know if something you believed were factually wrong?

- Do you like to change at your own pace and not have others correct you?

- Do you remember why Galileo had such a hard time in the 1600s?

- Is there any parallel in events today?

- If 95% of climate researchers say global warming is human-caused, would you agree with them or follow the 5% who disagreed?

- If 95% of doctors told you to take a particular medicine or your disease will kill you, would you do it or follow the 5% who disagreed?

Ask permission to offer details that have impressed you, but judge whether the setting calls for presenting an overview or for a back and forth discussion. Remember the car salesman talking for eight hours at a stretch: *sometimes people are ready to hear a complete picture.* When they are, we need to step up and supply it. If this is instead a back-and-forth time, we notice how much to say at once. Most people can respond to a package of about three sentences, but even then rapport is critical because if their mind is not open, no message of any length gets through.

Having presented a chunk the other is willing to hear, we ask them their views about it and listen carefully with no attempt to dominate them. They are more likely to change their views by our listening. The facts we offer may sink in only over time, so we let this "settling in" process work on them. About a single point they may say, "Well, I agree…" and then divert to ground they prefer to discuss. We continue to listen, ask them questions, and occasionally reaffirm what we agree on.

Evidence and reasoning form a realistic mind and help us approach others. While we may reach agreement actually through emotional connections, evidence enables us to transmit meaning. Accurate terms reduce confusion, such as using "assertion" or "claim" for what some want to believe, and "truth" only with two more conditions: 1) people acting on it would not suffer harm, and 2) objective observers agree what it is.

Objective evidence exchanged even between people who want to be rational may be unconvincing, however, due to their personal channel for absorbing information. One individual might believe ideas only from people they like or authorities they are loyal to. Or they may favor spoken words over written—they like to listen–or they may receive better what they read. Some align with custom and others with people who have economic power over them. Many are contrarian, instinctively arguing any new idea, and others favor the current underdog. We can often guess people's preferred channel.

23. Ordinary communication

Be open to all. The route open to all of us is to bond with others, develop rapport with them in whatever their subjective state, and look for evidence we can agree on. We connect first as people and then by the content of our ideas. Whichever we advance on helps us with the other, but both are important. We prepare by accumulating knowledge in study, and expressing it in small group discussion.

When we are ready, we open a channel with strangers. Researchers in New York, for instance, were curious whether it helped commuters to talk to each other during their morning train ride or if silence and reticence were better. Their finding probably applies to other settings: People enjoyed the commute more if they talked to those around them. Time went by faster, and natural feelings of warmth and support opened. The consistently positive quality of the experience suggested that people needed no special skills. Among all those interviewed, *none reported being snubbed* (84).

Positive communication goes beyond creating good feelings to generate joint purpose. When Italy reorganized its government after World War II, researchers studying the progress of different regions were surprised. It was not factories, natural resources, social structure, nor even education that mattered but whether people talked to each other in small groups; in choral societies there while here might be in bowling alleys, hair salons, churches, barber shops, sports and entertainment events, waiting rooms, lectures, and buses. We express our natural interest in each other and discuss our common experience. Conversation about mutual concerns generates positive outcomes and laces society together. Their connections shape people's beliefs and values, help them understand the events around them, and generate action. Local culture drives economic growth (85).

While this view may seem commonplace, it suggests a starting point for a municipality changing course: *Are we talking to each other?* Doing so may aid regions where big companies or technology have moved employment elsewhere. A community's conversation may help resurrect its economy (cf. 17. *Study and share*).

A safe beginning is usually to catch the eye of someone near us and comment on a feature of the immediate setting. The other can choose whether to pick it up and converse with us. Location may suggest a topic: In an airport, the extent of security procedures. At a football or basketball game, player safety and regarding college athletes as employees. With a company team at a bowling alley, job security and CEO pay. On public transportation, spending for mass transit or airport expansion. We think about the other's possible interests. How has climate change touched them, how would business handle a higher minimum wage, how would it affect the local economy, how are people they know recovering from the recent recession? We ask a question that invites alternate viewpoints: "How do you read the current Congress?" Sometimes a straight-out "permission to speak" fits the situation: "Hey, could I ask you a question?" If they answer, "Sure, go ahead," it means they see us eligible for contact. If they feel reserved today, they let us know and we pull back.

When the other answers, we can restate their content if it is long or unclear: "So you're concerned people will go overboard and…." Putting our words to their ideas, we understand them better, let them know we want to, make it easy for them to continue, and show respect.

If their answer has a negative tone, we either continue to listen carefully and summarize what they say or, as we discussed earlier, ask a question about the least negative part of it. If they object to "the governor's anti-business attitude," we think of a positive inference on the same topic: "You must have had experience managing a business." If they present an ideology or a complaint, we find a constructive aspect. About even racial bias we could respond, "So you've had good experiences working with people of your own background, you like to be around people who are similar to you." We want to show we understand them and are not frightened off by differences.

"What do you think?" they may ask. If they do not, when they pause we might offer to talk. After we listen for a time, most will welcome our thoughts. We might sum up the narrative outlined in Part Two: "I've been learning about what makes civilizations fall apart, and I'm worried about ours."

If we disagree with them on evidence, we can propose a resolution: "I believe your information isn't right. If we look it up and it turns out wrong, would you change your position?" If they won't, we offer a rationale for using evidence in place of imposing views on each other. If they have listened to us, we can ask them to sum up what we have explained: "I'm not sure if I've been clear. Could you tell me what you got from what I said?"

We model a way to listen. If they adopt it, it helps them change. By even putting words to an idea different from their own, they stretch their thinking.

24. Healing by respect

Focus on what you can respect in others. We want others to treat our limitations kindly and appreciate the pressures we face, and we weigh intuitively whether they are critical of us. We absorb their eye contact, tone of voice, body language, and words.

We can also expect them to guess about us: how do they think we judge them? If we appear unsafe they lock their door to us, perhaps opening its three-inch port and asking, "Who are you and what do you want?" Recognizing a familiar face, they open the whole door. To do that despite disagreeing on ideas, we need a harmonizing focus. How differently, for instance, would we relate to an opponent we know is a great parent?

Many traits in others deserve our respect, and keeping them in our mind's eye *changes us internally,* displacing oppositional force we might otherwise project. The two of us may be embedded in different policies, religions, or life experience. Difference is just a human condition, but we control opposition. For constructive change, we do not project a force that alienates others. They may regard us as opponents if they wish, but from our side we can establish a harmonizing tone by focusing on what we appreciate about them, qualities like:

Hard-working

Loyal

Devout

Passionate

Calm

Disciplined with details

Firm

Easy-going

Consistent

Versatile

Good memory

Engaging

Ability to conceptualize

Can "nail a point" quickly

Generous

Open to diverse perspectives

Sense of humor

Loyal to constituents' interests

We may know of particular achievements of theirs that warrant our respect, or an aspect of their *intent* even though we disagree over how they carry it out:

A critical person may want to correct mistakes.

A suspicious person seeks to avoid being lied to.

A competitive person puts out energy to win.

A resentful person resists being burdened by others' needs.

A selfish person may guard against being hurt.

One dismissing evidence may hold out for a few prime values.

One aloof from strangers may be loyal to those he knows.

In my counseling work, I have seen this principle operate: "If you can find *one thing* you can respect about someone, you can change *their* behavior." Our respect is a force that helps connect another to their positive qualities, an influence often clearer in reverse. When we focus on the negatives in another, the best we may hope for is to limit the damage they cause (e.g. we put people in jail), yet our focus on their negative qualities *can multiply the qualities instead.* We make matters worse by failing to recognize cause and effect.

A geopolitical instance: Saddam Hussein, the dictator of Iraq whom we removed with trillions of dollars and thousands of lives, *tolerated religious diversity and advancing women's rights.* Christian churches had been accepted in his country for two thousand years—a condition worthy of western nations' respect particularly because his country's dominant belief was Islam. But after his overthrow, sectarian feelings intensified, women's rights were reversed, and over a half million fled the country with their churches in rubble behind them and the entire region mired in sectarian war.

Was a lesson missed–that we are to cooperate with even a limited good in others? There was something to build on had we wished to try; if we had had less cupidity for oil, more respect for people, and more determination to be constructive. As the U.S. prepared for war against him, Hussein put out frantic signals via diplomatic back-channels that he wanted to negotiate, but our leaders ignored them because they wanted war.

Slight changes can have significant outcomes. Imagine an aggressive, powerful individual who at times can be gratuitously destructive, but a passing influence moves him not to be gratuitously destructive. Though he is still aggressive and powerful, society may benefit greatly by his slight movement toward less evil. One tilted against us may enable a positive outcome by aligning with us on a single point.

Facing someone we believe is wrong, without realizing it we easily encourage conflict. We picture the situation as us against them, our feelings correct and theirs not, but our feelings have nothing to do with whether our idea is better or likely to be accepted, and instead are a tone we place on the exchange.

A way to think about this is that to accomplish anything at all, we use either our proactive or receptive capacity. Sometimes we assert our own ability or ideas to accomplish a goal, and sometimes we receive and cooperate with others' initiatives. So about the person before us we ask, "How are they employing their natural power? Is it proactive or receptive?" Understanding which it is, we note, "Okay, I can respect that."

Appreciating another's humanity changes the energy issuing from us and helps us alight on qualities we can encourage. Someone preoccupied with conspiracies, for instance, may oppose manipulation and want important information accessible to all:

"So, if I understand," we say, "you are really concerned that some people can take advantage of others and leave them worse off... You have a protective sense for society and don't want to see it damaged... You want an honest society where people are not deceived and misled...." Such a response aligns with the emotion behind their basic aim. Before commenting on their approach to a problem, we first appreciate and respect even one of their qualities.

They will show that they accept our view by their smile and eye contact, enabling us to talk instead of argue. With this tone established, we find out if they can hear a suggestion about how they can achieve what they want while balancing other values.

Ask permission. On presenting a challenge or change *to anyone any time about anything,* it is respectful to ask permission:

"Is this a good time?"

"Could I make a suggestion about that?"

"I have a thought about that. Could I throw it in here?"

"I have a slightly different perspective on that...."

"May I stop by tomorrow with some information?"

Such comments manifest respect for the other's boundaries. We are constituted to be able to shut out what we don't like, and when we broadcast ideas at people who have closed their door to us, we invite them to double-lock and nail it for good measure. We have wasted the time of both of us by trying to bull our way into their thinking when they have told us they do not welcome it.

But once they say "Sure. What is it?", a mental toggle switch is thrown that changes the direction of the next transmission. We agree on which of us is talking and which listening. We cease talking past each other, and actually consider each other's message.

25. Resolve conflict

Differences are to be expected everywhere because of diverging interests and life experience, but they need not develop into conflict, which directs negative feelings toward another. In a divided family, volume can rise suddenly in making a point, a retort is equally intense, and in a few seconds people are shouting. A voice pleads, "You don't need to shout," and another answers, *"I'm not shouting!"*

Shouting signals a drive for dominance. If our idea is actually better and the other would have to concede it, their wish for dominance tells them intuitively to shout to express more power. They may be unable to concede a point when sensing that doing so would weaken them.

Concern for dominance confines what people admit into awareness and carries its own rules of logic. As we noted above, *it is more important to human nature not to be dominated than to be logical,* so that normally reasonable people may startle themselves upon noticing their words are heated. Any of us can feel this way though we manage the feeling differently.

A path of agreement, again, is to focus on the other's intent. We look for a positive desire in their words so we can remove dominance as an issue and talk as equals:

"So it's important to you that the nation appears strong around the world."

"You really want fairness in the courts."

"So you really want to shake things up."

"You really want the best person to win."

"You want people to be sensible."

"So you object to unfairness in how people are treated."

"You have great confidence in this person's ideas."

We do not bend what they say into a meaning we can argue but want to be so accurate in stating their intent that they immediately say, "Yes, that's what I want." This changes the context: *We are discussing what you say you want.* For people reading from the same script, dominance is neutral. We let them make their point the way they want and try to understand where they wish to go with it.

A problem-solving perspective. Solving conflict in our group, we first ask, "Does the issue affect our purpose?" It deserves a strong opinion only when it affects the group's progress, which makes it the group's business. Otherwise, parties can have their differences. Either can say, "Okay, let's do it your way" without impact on the group. In such cases, suggest to individuals that *they dismiss intense assertions about inconsequential matters.*

Two initial choices can help. 1) We take personal ownership, asking "What am I doing to contribute to this?" Aware of a negative feeling in ourselves we examine it to find its source, deal effectively with the reason for it, bring our reaction into balance, and avoid upsetting others. 2) We release *others'* negativity. Deciding not to react as they do, we more easily manage our own mood and do not allow their state to affect ours. When we do not take responsibility this way, the issue falls to the group to sort out.

To solve a problem, the hardest step for a group may be defining it, because its nub may not be obvious. It may arise from people's beliefs about the meaning of life and man's place in the universe not settled by material evidence, can express suppressed emotions or hidden distresses, may occur on the edge of awareness, or may signal someone's need for recognition, or tension with another system. We need to understand the problem we are going to solve. Seemingly insignificant pieces we ignore get back at us when a situation is multiply caused. Tie up seven legs of an octopus and the last one clings to a rock.

We figure out the question that needs answering. "Are two people clashing continually?" differs from "Are they pursuing divergent purposes?" or "Is the structure set up for conflict?" Perhaps the group is too stretched, or a step is too confusing. Responsibility may be murky or communications lame. A clue to misframing is the problem lingering after we answer our question.

When we think we understand the problem, we try to identify the activity that can solve it. We may need to listen to everyone's views and fill in our understanding. Hearing two people may be enough–problems often evaporate with feelings aired. We may need to gather information, accept irreconcilable differences, or clarify responsibility.

When parties agree we state the problem accurately, we list alternate remedies, weigh each, choose the best, and agree on a follow-up plan. When people's values are simply opposed, however, even perfect communication may only define each one's stand, and they are left to cooperate on goals they do agree on.

Managing differences.

1. Opponents may become friends through respect for each other's qualities. Competitors often do this because knowing few others who talk their language. A description of friendship, in fact, involves sustaining connection across differences. We learn from people who approach an issue in a way we do not.

2. A group should welcome a free play of ideas until a common direction is determined and then unite around the plan. Ineffective groups do the opposite. They standardize thinking around a leader's ideas up front but when a poorly made plan struggles, individuals must adapt later to make it work. A group does better by listening carefully to everyone before acting.

3. A new person saying, "We could see this differently" might have a clue that rescues a big effort, but may not be able to influence the

group to implement it. If others with more status ignore such ideas, the group loses the wisdom inherent in the 360-degree vision of everyone's experience.

4. People may not notice how their manner of disagreeing can affect others. We all constantly assess our acceptance, closeness, and control as we noted above. Common expressions of them are: "Do I have a place here? Am I accepted?" "How close are we? Do people like me?" "How much influence do I have? Does my opinion matter?" From others' comments they may conclude incorrectly that they don't belong, others don't like them, and their views don't count. Others reassure them by listening to them, agreeing on a point, respecting part of their statement, asking permission to offer a different view, and incorporating their comment into a larger context.

5. A putdown or criticism from someone esteemed by the group strikes harder than from an outsider. People who feel they have low status depend more on supportive communication from those who have high status.

Defuse negatives.

1. The group incorporates practice in communication skills into all its activities, and finds ways to improve them. Leaders model the skills they want others to employ.

2. They draw aside any who cause stress, listen to them at length, and carry out problem-solving steps with them. Someone's strong feeling about an issue does not make them wrong but does leave it to others to resolve the conflict.

3. The planning team can explain a touchy point to all group members and invite their suggestions for resolving it or arrange for anonymous written feedback. Sometimes people with key information do not come forward, fearing blowback on themselves. Anyone needing considerate treatment can be incorporated into a team already functioning well: "Let's put him with Roger's group. They'll help him."

4. When an individual resists feedback, others' boundaries matter more. *A single negative person can destroy an organization if others let them.* We are constituted to absorb the feelings and attitudes of those

nearby, and preserve our positive state only by deliberately choosing not to adopt the negativity. Exercising this discipline enables us to remain positive alongside unhappy people, constructive but firm around the uncooperative.

We perfect ourselves through what is under our control rather than by correcting others' deficiencies, but must establish deliberate boundaries. We direct our own actions regardless how others act, cannot blame others for feelings we indulge, but always answer to our own values. A group can maintain its purpose despite negative elements within it and a society improves itself despite intractable flaws. Limitations are constant and simply mark the point at which, for now, resistant conditions stalemate our capacity to pursue our purpose. We can address them with a positive or negative attitude.

5. An issue's impact on group effectiveness is a criterion for problem-solving: The group 1) re-affirms its purpose, 2) identifies the activity that achieves it, 3) *notes how conflict hinders this activity,* and 4) explains the changes needed from everyone to resume movement toward its purpose.

To make frankness acceptable, people must believe in what they do, care about each other, trust each other to respond moderately, and be honest—"You're doing this and it has this effect"—confident that the other welcomes the feedback. Participants' love for each other strengthens them, but truth promotes their goal, *microscopic honesty about anything affecting the group's well-being.* "Soft punches make strong organizations."

Harmonize conflicting views. Social issues usually contain a mix of values, goals, worries, and pressures so that a way through may not be apparent. Imagine weighing two policies, to help a minority catch up (like affirmative action) or to urge self-responsibility. Each view is appropriate sometimes. We get past a disaster "with a little help from our friends," but afterward "row our own boat" and either may be plausible just now. One candidate may want a limited, practical step on a problem while another wants to pursue an ideal, but no presumptive standard guides which to adopt.

Confronting a conflict of ideas, our mind remains uncomfortable with it and the discrepancy stimulates us to be more creative. To encourage this creativity, we resist resolving the issue prematurely and instead leave an opening in which a synthesis or the better of the options can appear. We help ourselves at this by putting into words the view least familiar to us–"Let me try to sum up your side, okay?" Till a resolution is clear, we accept the discomfort of holding the issue open.

Some people call up possibilities more easily. Imagine a man who at different times in his life was a Republican businessman, a religious Democrat, and a skeptical Independent, and remembers each experience clearly. He can adopt each frame of reference, recognize overlapping features, and foresee how a given issue might play out with each view. While few people may have all three experiences, we can easily find three individuals, each with one of them. Good communication enables them to draw the best from their collective knowledge.

26. Learn deeply

Learn how to make a movement effective. Learning is the launch pad of a movement, gathering mute information into an active force. The critical change is moving it from the side-eddies of people's attention into their central focus. This can be hard because they are drawn in so many directions. Social action may take on one issue, and then after a surge of effort, people quit and return to their daily lives. Their activity was an add-on, and add-ons easily become drop-offs. The intent we want instead is, "This need deserves my steady effort for years to come," which implies continually feeding our mind with learning.

Our learning has to connect with our goals, however. The main reason people do not learn is that they see no way to apply it. Curiosity may suffice for a time, but learning needs an outlet. We move ourselves when we want to be more effective at what we do, and immerse ourselves then in the knowledge that aids us.

Personal learning. Besides learning via group discussion to expand our fluency with ideas as we explained above, we also need to build our personal base of knowledge.

All of us do roughly the same thing when we really want to learn. *We sink our mind into a subject and keep it there.* Our consistency at it reflects our dedication to our purpose. We might ponder ideas, write them down, speak about them, and speculate how to apply them. We could read the same book three times and think about it through our day; read a section of it, recall its gist, tell it to someone, refer to it often, discuss it, and decide how to implement it. We may write notes on good points, index special ideas, save them so we can retrieve them easily, make marginal comments, carry the book with us, connect the content to what we notice in our personal experience, tell someone about every idea that attracts us, and add daily to what we can say about it. A medieval comment on argumentation was, "Beware the man of one book," meaning originally that someone who actually masters one book will crush you in an argument on the topic.

Three activities sum up this picture. We 1) gather some ideas, 2) hold onto them, working them into our thoughts, and 3) express them to others. We know we do this well when we can explain an idea a week or more after we last thought about it. Retaining it fully even this long shows that our mind has a grip on it, that we are making it our own. The proportion of time spent on each of the three activities, however, affects our results.

You may have read a book and noticed its themes floating spontaneously through your mind. But a week later a friend says, "Tell me about that book you were reading," and you can barely connect one sentence to another. It did not affect your thinking enough for you to share it. You relied too much on the first of the three activities above and do better by adding the second—trying to hold on to specific ideas or pausing to integrate them with what else you know.

Learning efficiency jumps sharply, however, with the third step. A study many years ago documented that the most efficient way to learn was *to spend forty to eighty percent of learning time in the effort to recall.* This means as much or more time in output—calling up the information from our mind through remembering, explaining, and discussing–compared to the time for input by reading, collecting, copying what we want to learn, and listening. We actively express the store we already have instead of passively absorbing more, and may need twice the amount of time expressing it as gathering it (86). We engrave a picture deeper into our own mind by trying to paint it in another's mind, which is the universally accepted teachers' axiom: *To learn a subject, teach it.*

Who we imagine we are also influences the competence we develop. To be a person who can make changes in society, we read about those who do that. To make a profit, we read about people who make a profit. If we want to do what Mother Teresa did, we read about Mother Teresa. To go to war, save animals, or make scientific advances, we fill our mind with images that sustain what we want to do.

We suggest here that besides how to earn a living and raise a family, we learn how to save civilization. Forces operating today make it vulnerable. Compare the effort to space flight. Miss a factor in a launch, and expensive hardware sails into the void. Might turning around a nation of hundreds of millions or a world of billions depend on people's best ideas? Without effective policies, our hard-won civilization could drift cold and lifeless into deep space, never to be heard from again. Our collective thinking has not yet determined how to tame edges of chaos, violence, and social fracture that appear.

Spurred by such needs, we turn to knowledge. We are most proud of the features of our culture that issue from it. Society's very structure has come from those who mastered universes of information and made it easy for the rest of us to ride along, taking its perks for granted. But we can predict the future by this: *we will construct only what we understand and agree on.* Our future depends on our knowledge. Ivan Pavlov expressed the attitude that earned him a Nobel Prize: "A scientist must accustom himself to the gradual accumulation of knowledge," a standard at the heart of great achievements, while mainstream attention today is preoccupied with zing and flash.

Building on truth. A culture labeling itself "post-truth" that dismisses facts, rocks the basis of democracy. The best thinking of the majority should prevail because, as we noted, the most people together have the most accurate grasp of reality, and hence are better able to make good choices averaged out over time. Though it can be misled, collective thinking depends on absorbing reality that is never out of date and never errs. Only representations of it can be mistaken.

We value truth because it represents reality, and act on reality only through our formulations of it, our symbols for it in numbers and words. The critical quality is that the two must match. When a symbol accords with the symbolized, we call that a truth. When the symbol distorts or diverges from the symbolized, it might be an assertion, an interpretation, a generalization, a claim, an opinion, a view, an assumption, or an accusation. It also might be a lie, a distortion, a manipulation, and so on. These terms each have their own useful context, but we serve society by respecting truth where it is due. Otherwise, *we inevitably install error into our thinking and decisions.* The impact of erroneous thinking on his community spurred an activist I know to pursue for many years a solitary personal agenda–as he put it– "to make war on misinformation."

Some assert as already true what they want to create, and when they do it persuasively, others pay attention. We seem conditioned to believe people who exhibit conviction, a tendency that probably aided early survival as the older and presumably wiser set a tribe's direction. Others believed their judgment by and large to be best, but today's complex society needs the refined, individualized realism drawn from all. The experience of the elite is too narrow to supply reliably for everyone else's.

The easy part of establishing truth is collecting evidence. The hard part is restraining ourselves from distorting it so it supports what we believe or want. We may fail to notice that our desire for a particular outcome warps our interpretation of evidence unless we consciously resist it.

Helpful disciplines are to avoid premature conclusions, seek evidence that could negate our theories, and sustain a hypothetical spirit, respect for probable error, and an attitude of gentleness toward elusive data. We might search out how we can conduct a randomized controlled trial on the issue at hand. With sensory-confirmed, accurate details we continually refine our maps of reality. When our observations contradict our expectations, we sustain the difference long enough to inquire why, maintaining the objective mode of thought that science and the modern world depend on. If we do not, we find ourselves battered one way and another by emotion-driven assumptions.

Optimal communicating enhances mutual trust and leads us to better conclusions. In addition to employing the skills explained above, people should communicate as equals instead of from rank, remain provisional instead of asserting certainty, use reasoning rather than authority, aim for problem-solving consensus instead of control, be spontaneous rather than strategic, be empathic rather than emotionally neutral, and describe evidence and seek information rather than evaluating and blaming (87).

Incorporate the abstract. While we absorb the real conditions of the world, we also stretch to the less tangible–to principles, beliefs, and dreams–because evidence does not stand alone. *Our abstractions guide our use of it,* emphasizing aspects that have meaning for us. Our values guide our experience and direct us to the people and resources we need. We form within us the reality we wish to implement, live in it, and love what we create in order to establish the field that gives evidence its due place.

A businessman I knew who gave away a million dollars said that ninety-five percent of his work was inward. Reflecting on his life and business made his decisions continually on target for a good reason: *Many implications of our decisions are not yet framed in words,* though we may vaguely sense them as impressions, hunches, or a gap in information. While consciously we may think we have all the data we need, our deeper mind may nudge us to wait for an essential piece. It is only by slowing down our thinking, and calmly sinking our mind into the field of these elusive impressions that the factors that improve our decisions arise eventually into our awareness.

The critical knowledge is not in a database but in our minds, the personal store of knowledge enabling us to act wisely. Our deeds cannot exceed our understanding, so that to tackle a complex goal we accept personal change. Jack Welch, former CEO of General Electric, pointed out the shift in focus: "Before you are a leader, success is all about growing yourself. When you become a leader, success is all about growing others." Within a movement, we ourselves become different as we learn how to change society, and then pass along our knowledge. Mind forms a model of what it wishes to bring into outer experience.

Reasonable. People wanting a better society recognize a need, talk it over, and settle on a response, but with a universe of information to draw on, our challenge is in sorting. How can an ocean of knowledge elicit good judgment from itself and translate it into social form? We can assess our strategies for how they answer that question.

A few years ago, after interviewing a spokesman for the LGBTQ community, a TV commentator referred to him as "dangerous." Someone asked later why he might be dangerous.

"Because he sounded so reasonable," was the answer.

People want reasonable. They want credible ideas from others who do not deceive or distort. We need to think rational, sound sensible, and because we solve problems also be buoyant; happy about solutions we can offer, and open to others' helpful knowledge. We listen to both allies and opponents for what we can learn, and refer to our sense of the good to guide us.

27. Turning points for action

Monitor where effort affords the most gain. Conditions that can arise with nearly any issue may signal where our effort matters most, and help us assign resources.

Breaking point. A breaking point is a turn for the worse portending further damage. Runoff of herbicides and pesticides may cause an outbreak of toxic algae. Industrial chemicals may kill a fish run down river. Air pollution boosts respiratory diseases, and gases depleting ozone increase skin cancer in polar latitudes.

In education, a bright student could become a physician. But squirrely in kindergarten, distracted in first grade, and his single mother not a savvy advocate, he gets an incompetent teacher the district cannot remove. This is his breaking point, his unseen turn for the worse where he accesses the low end of the system's resources. His teacher expects little of him, and he eventually leaves school an underachiever.

Breaking points channel the poor into a problem-beset life. A worn-looking man on a street corner holds a sign, "Will work for food." We may accept separate worlds for survivors and non-survivors; assume that he is alcoholic, lazy, or unbalanced, but breaking points may have preceded his vigil. A few dollars less per month and he lives in an abandoned car instead of a heated room. With child care and transportation, people get to work on time or they stay in the penniless subculture. They resolve a health problem early so their employment and parenting continue and their children avoid serial foster homes or kin-care. An increment of counseling preserves a couple's marriage and keeps their children from jail. Small events set up or avert a troubled life (88).

With thousands similarly affected in a city, we look for patterned solutions such as an effective educational system, accessible and affordable health care, and getting to work. Public transportation has changed economic life, yet some cities remain unfriendly to those without cars as land use planning moves homes far from jobs. People closest to breaking points understand them best, so we need to listen to what they tell us.

Key setting. Societies make decisions and allocate resources in defined settings. For the student above, the state education appropriation and teacher retention policies generated a breaking point. Control of early key settings insures influence later, which explains why many change efforts fizzle. Initial conditions limit later options. A key setting nationwide is a state legislature appointing its Congressional redistricting commission.

When I participated once on a task force for needs of youth, a legislator's staff member suggested I volunteer as secretary to write up the first draft because, he told me, the first form of an issue influences it from then on. Beginnings portend endings.

To implement a solution, we shepherd it through the jumps where opponents or circumstances might derail it. Key settings for an electoral victory might be friends meeting about a candidacy for one of them, detailing a campaign message, gathering allies and funding, the campaign, and finally the election. The first people active for a candidate influence later policies. Legislation passes through a dozen key settings, and opposition at any of them may block an outcome.

We need to master early events because the later we arrive, the fewer means remain but we also monitor the late ones. Good laws can be sabotaged by unsympathetic administrators. "Don't worry," says the committee chairman to the lobbyist for the special interest defeated by legislative vote. "We'll take care of you in the regulations." Because good ideas remain vulnerable until they become a stable part of the legal system, supporters need to follow their entire implementation.

Key idea. A key idea moves a problem toward a solution, even one as simple as, "Let's work together on this" or "You have a point." Grasping the idea key for the moment lies at the heart of social action.

Technology has made it easier to transmit ideas *in globo*. We can send massive information nearly instantly nearly anywhere so that millions can get the same news at once. But harder than mass distribution is placing just one where it is useful, fitting one idea to one receiver. Who exactly needs to know this, for what purpose, in what context, at what moment, and with what result? An idea may become key by reaching one individual.

After years as a state legislator, my father became legendary in applying influence as a lobbyist. When a senator would hold up something his organization supported, he never tried persuasion himself. With a team, he would think, "Who can get to him?" The result, passed perhaps through several hands, would be a personal friend accosting the legislator on the sidewalk to scold him about the issue. We may want to spread a general point like, "The issue is fair use of resources," or insert specific data: "On page two line twelve, change the million to two million."

Democracy is a key idea. The role of government is a key idea. No one would earn anything, ever, without a stable society, a body of laws, a criminal justice system, and people able to purchase goods and services. Productivity occurs within a framework built for it. No company produces in a vacuum, but borrows opportunities from an infrastructure operated with trust. So from a million dollars earned somewhere in the country, society's question is how to distribute it through profits, taxes, education, safety, security, and compensation for individual effort.

Though our attention is easily captured by issues requiring vast input, even one person mastering a problem can be key. During my time on a municipal assembly, agenda items typically passed through many stages of input and debate between staff, assembly, and the public. On one occasion a knotty problem came up, and a single man stepped forward for public participation. *He then answered every question that staff and assembly posed to him,* and when he was done, the assembly concluded the issue unanimously. When answers are out there, someone needs to collect and present them.

An ongoing local need is to identify those in local and state government whose decisions directly affect important values, and assign one or more members to stay familiar enough with developments to be able to give feedback: "It would work better if we did this." Issues may concern police, education, social workers, jails, traffic, services for the poor and homeless, the needs of children, public protests, and so on. We need a sufficient grasp of the decisions affecting such issues to be able to go public persuasively at an appropriate moment.

Leverage structure. We want policies that obtain a continuous benefit with the least effort, a big advantage from a small motion. Energy transformed smoothly solves a problem efficiently—a type of thinking basic to civilization.

The mechanical advances of civilization are leverage structures, but human actions contribute, like traffic rules to reduce accidents. Center lines and medians minimize head-on collisions. Lights, wider shoulders and longer sight distances increase response times. Mechanical elements can interplay with human, such as pilots' hours of rest and a no-fault system for reporting incidents. Technology attempts to streamline the complexity of health care into simple steps.

Where we place our lever can solve or perpetuate a problem. We might assume that homelessness arises from unemployment, substance abuse, mental illness, illiteracy, crime, or maladaptive attitudes, or that it arises mainly from not having shelter. We may improve people's employability by solving a score of problems, but may also address shelter directly through zoning, rent levels, tax breaks for landlords, pension levels, addiction treatment, policing of facilities, referral agencies, and safety nets. With stable shelter, people do better with their lives. Many facing eviction need help to work through this personal disaster.

We pattern for efficient outcomes in many ways: retirement accounts and insurance for financial continuity, plumbing for water and waste disposal, electricity for light and heat, telephones for communicating, factories for mass production, taxation for achieving collective purposes, and representation for drawing on citizens' dispersed wisdom. Our universal reliance on these systems reminds us constantly of the need to make them work.

Efficiency is less important than effectiveness, however. In a few minutes ten thousand people can sign a petition emailed to Congress but have more impact contacting their Representative personally. Despite the omnipresence of efficient methods, the way that takes more time and effort is usually more thorough, as in a craft shop's advertisement: "We work cheap, fast, and good—pick any two." If we work cheap and fast, it won't be good, and fast and good won't be cheap. There are inherent tradeoffs between the resources we expend, the results we get, and the speed with which they happen. Our facile use of the wonders of technology can make us think that everything should be easy, so that we may fail even to notice when sustained hard work is indispensable.

While leverage structures in society invite constant weighing between short and long term benefit and upsides versus downsides, they challenge us also to balance human values against efficiency. People attending to their own lives for a decade awaken one day to discover part of their life controlled by an efficient monopoly. A few who own the machines or manage care or design systems may become powerful and wealthy while a majority barely survives. Maximizing efficiency, the powerful few quietly impact the three-quarters of the population living paycheck to paycheck, an oligarchic government offers opportunities to those who profit from them, and inequality steadily worsens.

Articulation between actions. System is necessary where one action repeatedly impacts another, "articulates" as between bones of the arm. We want activity passing smoothly between parts, automatic adjustment by transfer of information or energy. Problems show up at meeting points like a 3/8 inch nut facing a 1/2 inch bolt. A country's trade policies may depress another's economy, an industry pollutes water and air, suburbs invade wildlife habitat, and refugees cross deserts seeking safety. Articulation is all around us.

When the same solution works for a recurring problem, a pipeline can move incoming problem-data directly into outgoing solution-data. A rubber tube across a road attaches to a traffic counter, supplying an objective basis for upgrading. Increased traffic leads to installing turn lanes and overpasses. Otherwise, planners must constantly re-gather familiar information and re-argue outcomes. Since each student needs a desk, a school orders more automatically, but when money fluctuates, students may sit on the floor. Teacher-student ratio may be affected by salary levels, changes in the local tax base, voters' willingness to be taxed, and the cost of facilities.

Slippage can occur where automatic adjustment is due. Environmental protection sees many partial links between common problems and standard solutions. While disintegrating roads and oil pipelines need replacing, some criteria are set strictly while others lack agreed-on values. Novel conditions slow progress to people's rate of re-education. Instead of change occurring through agreement on principles, every new person may challenge the prior consensus, but when the current situation resembles the previous, planning is easier: "Points one through nineteen are the same, but twenty has changed," so we turn to point twenty and move faster. As hard as it may be to obtain, automatic adjustment marks a solution likely to work long-term.

Will to change. People vary in their will to change. In early 1968 I was living in the Lower East Side of Manhattan, then the poorest and most violent part of New York City. The Poor People's Campaign was marching in Washington in a few days, and I was helping solicit contributions for it, inviting pedestrians to drop coins into our cans. Most responded politely. Near the more prosperous edge of the district, I approached a young man wearing a three-piece suit.

"For the poor?" he said derisively. "There are no poor!"

"No poor?" I said. I was startled. "There are people sleeping on the sidewalks."

"Those people are *sick!*" he retorted as he turned away.

This is denial of observable reality, which always surprises us. Seventy-five years after the gas chambers, some still deny Nazis' liquidation of Jews, or believe Wall Street engineered the financial crisis of 2008, or that global warming is a hoax, or that no one is poor.

The technique of asking a question about the least negative part of their comment noted earlier could apply even to those with seemingly paranoid views. Many in fact have a positive intent: "You don't want to be misled, do you? You're skeptical others will tell the truth, aren't you?"

We build on their agreement: "What condition do you think has brought down civilizations through all history?" We affirm what we can in their answer and offer Toynbee's research: "Societies went downhill for the reason ours does now. People in power manipulate the system to gain for themselves instead of providing for the whole. That's the core fact."

The will to change gains strength through personal contact, so that by avoiding people we insulate ourselves from their needs. We may convert the homeless, jobless, sick, mentally ill, and on welfare into a different species freeing us of any response. As we edge closer to them socially, their thinking impacts us more, so that knowing even a single person may open a train of thought: "Well, I know one guy who...." As our interest in others rises, we may decide to support experiments to find out what helps, and eventually involve ourselves with meeting their needs.

The influence that moves this change best is letting others' viewpoints touch us, usually by personal contact.

To help others, we first find out, *"Will you let me listen to you?"* When the other grants even this much by speaking to us, we can elicit their ideas in a gradient from impersonal to personal. We

invite their comment on impersonal, neutral topics like weather and traffic

express our view about casual subjects and be heard

refer to events in history

explore relative values reflected in those events

open present day issues

explore relative values reflected in present issues

understand the effects on society of different values

agree on ranking values

agree on practical steps that apply our ranking of values.

These six turning points together–breaking point, key setting, key idea, leverage structure, articulation, and will to change—help focus action. *Seeking agreement on effective ideas, we invest long-term effort in key settings to forestall urgent breaking points and create systemic leverage structures that work by automatic adjustment.*

28. A spectrum of goals

Engage with varied goals. A movement gains strength by effort outside election campaigns. "The good of the whole" is not defined only by cyclical politics. Local and regional issues deserve attention year around, and are a natural bridge for people into meeting systemic needs. Many turned off to politics but committed to their community welcome local involvement.

Community enhancement. Every state and community need deserves thought such as flowers along a street, concrete-and-asphalt infrastructure, caring for people one by one, and policies that affect community well-being. Needs are unlimited, and people may take interest in a particular kind. A group can periodically invite anyone to present "a commercial" about a local project that might warrant the group's support, and together work out priorities.

Volunteers' service tasks hold a society together. A movement can address needs such as shelter and food for the homeless and hungry, or help for the ill, young, or aging. They might aid those released from incarceration to find successful roles in society, or promote particular economic policies. Services for youth might be in tutoring, coaching, volunteering for organizations and facilities; helping young people reclaim streams and wetlands, and remove invasive species. Upon securing human life, we improve the biosphere.

Service tasks can aid the movement. Volunteers arrive early and arrange rooms, prepare food and clean up, maintain facilities and grounds, account for supplies, respond to communications, and make phone calls. Services can be unobtrusive like research, or involve presenting ideas. Some people prefer non-public roles, and those with moral or religious boundaries about politics may welcome community service. The movement might invite a member to start an independent non-profit to meet a specific local need, and be a back-up support for it.

We discuss common purposes with other groups, and inquire how churches may wish to collaborate to help the community. We contact organizations about their programs for local, regional, and global needs, and where interests may be aligned; inventory the Internet and follow up on contacts; seek out partisans for opposing views, and determine what we can learn from them and might accomplish together; sponsor workshops that draw in people of all opinions; aim for agreement about trends and conditions that affect life on earth at neighborhood, local, regional, national, and global levels; and design and carry out ways to solve problems of any dimension anywhere.

Political and social change. A movement can inform the public by study groups, lecture series, TV programs, marches, demonstrations, petitions, voter initiatives, forums, talk shows, rallies, interviews, and research papers; sort out views on local and regional needs and link campaigns with groups elsewhere. One group's target may be a redistricting commission, and another's a Congressional primary, state house race, or municipal office (89).

The most labor-intensive but effective route to influencing public opinion is old-fashioned presence face to face, door to door, street to street (cf. 13. *Canvassing*). Getting relevant information out in person can utilize all the energy available, and especially fits a movement because self-giving increases impact. Appealing presence lends substance to values.

Organizations may assume they can promote general positions via mass media, but the less personal today's message, the easier it is dislodged by tomorrow's and lumped with social noise readily dismissed. Each movement member instead might view themselves as leading their own army. They can arrange to connect with and support everyone to whom they pass on information, and enable them to do the same for others, and they to others.

Our goal is not just to transmit information, however. The more efficiently we do that, the more impersonal our means tend to be. Rather, *we do so in a manner that fuels action on it.* Imagine Marines sitting through classroom instruction on the layout of Middle Eastern towns compared to the same ones as a unit learning about a specific town the night before a raid. The motivation to learn changes. For a nationwide boycott, or for demonstrations in the capital cities of all fifty states on the same day, we want to convey the plan in a motivating manner—people communicating with other people about it.

Selecting objectives. A few criteria can help a group sort among objectives:

1. *Whose problem is this?* Who suffers from it? We affirm connection with them.

2. *What are our sympathies?* They motivate us but can lead us to ignore other needs. We want to balance our personal tendency with sympathy for all.

3. *How desperate is this need?* The worse the situation, the more attention it warrants. Someone should do something.

4. *How much can they help themselves?* If they can handle their

situation, we defer to them, but misguided assumptions can generate disaster such as turning out the mentally ill to live on the streets. Children in poverty cannot improve their school nor the incarcerated the justice system. Those unable to remedy their needs due to age, infirmity, ignorance, or lack of influence especially depend on outside help or political decisions.

5. *Is someone else picking up the load?* Society already plans for many needs but may execute poorly. We might help insure that the designated agency has the resources it needs.

6. *How much can outside help solve the problem?* We back off if we might make matters worse, do not know the action to take, or lack the ability. The Theory of Minimum Change guides us, applying the smallest step that remedies a problem.

7. *Does this outweigh all other needs we could address?* We monitor a score of problems for the one we can best respond to.

Generating urgency. A team concept affects motivation. Imagine a hundred people, each believing they work alone, who by chance on the same Saturday decide to approach someone else about a movement idea. When seventy-five find their person unreceptive they assume they failed, give up, and turn to other interests the next weekend. But a *we* exists that did succeed. Meeting later as a team, the hundred discover that twenty-five received a positive response. They realize, "If we just do that four times, we reach a hundred new people! We can double our number in four afternoons!" A *we* is the actor. Random aggregations lack the strength of group purpose.

Urgency fuses time pressure with a felt sense of an issue's importance, resulting in an impulse for action now. Thresholds can contribute: effort is important today because conditions will be worse tomorrow. Melting Greenland ice is objectively urgent, but the challenge is for it to matter, for people to believe they must respond at once. Leaders generate this by offering reasons and a plan of action, weaving personal tasks into a tide of shared energy.

Multiple cues close in time convey urgency best. Recall when an issue absorbed your attention. Perhaps 1) details concerned you and a response from you was fitting. Bad things were about to happen. 2) People you respected drew you in and asked you to take action. 3) Activity awakened feelings for your fellow workers. 4) Your own small steps made you feel responsible and involved. 5) You adopted group attitudes, exchanging ideas with others who felt the same. 6) Leaders removed blocks so you could act quickly, sent fresh data to you at once: "I got this to you as soon as I could," implying "so you could respond right away," or "I wanted to make sure you had what you needed." 7) You pounced on new data and passed it on, kept ideas moving. Every place information stops makes a purpose less important. If you act as though time does not matter, others will believe you.

29. Agreements, principles, and processes

Progress typically depends on agreement when we talk to a public entity, official, opponent, or ally though it carries no assurance of wisdom. Masses with a common conviction are often wrong. Characterizing a healthy society, however, is what we might call "the public agreement," *a belief that benefits be shared.* It ultimately includes everyone, and we reason to it from how human nature prospers. A child's right to food means others are responsible to provide it. Another benefits from a service my taxes support but I don't use—an airport, a highway, an education. I affirm his self-benefit as I assume he does mine, like a national potlatch where each one's gift benefits all.

Determined to pay only for our own gain, we violate the public agreement, taking from it but not giving to it. Parents sending their children to private schools may reduce their support for public education, live in a security-guarded compound and minimize police services, travel by helicopters and commuter planes and vote down mass transit, have health insurance for their family and send others to crowded emergency rooms or let them languish. The party ends and the agreement fractures when power expects only to take and the pot is empty before everyone is fed. Those finding nothing left for them may want to sabotage outcomes for all.

Principle, process, and particulars. "We agree in principle," we may say about an issue, "but still have details to work out," and for that need a process.

The principle of civility, for instance, implies processes like meeting physical needs, family survival, personal safety, freedom, rule of law, talking thoughtfully about issues, and trading products of our culture. Democracy as principle implies processes like the right to advertise views, vote, organize, and persuade. With equity as principle, a court system as process solves thousands of particular cases. Self-determination as principle united the early colonists and they objected to the particulars of taxation. When England refused to resolve this through the process of representation, they revolted.

Principles may compete, and we can choose which to emphasize. On the excuse of security after 9-11, the government instituted secret military tribunals potentially affecting twenty million citizens. Suspending civil rights could threaten Americans' freedom under law, so we must decide if we want safety at that cost, or accept that freedom implies risks.

Driven too far a principle like financial gain works against us. Larger profits for us imply less for the other when interests collide, but as self-interest moderates, we want both of us to prosper. Ethical/moral/spiritual principles are not limited this way. We can want as much truth and goodness for others as for ourselves, but are ethically challenged with personal benefit at stake.

Separated from its principle, a process is readily subverted. Oligarchs attack the processes of democracy because they do not believe in its principle, and people permit this because they pay little attention to their system's integrity. Principles administered only by formal bodies are vulnerable. A majority must guard them or the dominant minority gradually dismantles them. Explaining movement goals, we begin with principles such as the good of the whole, inclusion, unconditional love, and responsibility. We clarify a social policy by defining the principle at stake, the processes that apply it, and the particulars affected by it.

30. Key electoral changes

Electoral change is our main goal. We want to help good people into office by means of a body of activists numerous and focused enough to win every significant election. Here are targets for it:

1. "Democracy or not?" is the meta-issue that should color every debate, interview, and demonstration. Voters need to understand the destructiveness of gerrymandering. It is not just a political strategy, and movement members and candidates should not let it be framed so superficially. It affects national survival. We cannot let an anti-democratic minority normalize an unfair system. The same applies to voter restriction. Because these so clearly attack the nature of democracy, the argument against them needs to be pictured, exampled, probed, and analogized in every possible way. Candidates supporting those practices should be confronted with their intent: ***You WANT to oppress others!***

Because the issue depends on appreciating principles of fairness, rights, and democracy, many people do not get it. They are unfamiliar with grasping abstractions, and teaching them to think that way could take hours of conversation if it is even possible. A political cartoonist might help: Picture a candidate with his foot on the throat of a voter struggling on the ground within sight of a polling place and holding a sample ballot. The caption reads, "Don't complain! I'm not stopping you from voting!"

2. The pivotal change is to wrest control of the system from those who now manipulate it by a three-stage strategy: 1) State legislatures appoint a commission that, every ten years, designs Congressional districts. 2) Congressional districts distorted to favor one party result in an anti-democratic minority dominating Congress. 3) An anti-democratic Congress rewards its supporters to perpetuate an unfair system. The first lever for change then is selecting state legislators.

3. The leading national objective is electing the President by popular vote. A compact of states holding a majority of electoral votes is a worthy objective *but a needlessly high bar to start with.* Federal law already authorizes state legislatures to allot their electoral votes as they

wish, so that individual states can now assign them to the candidate with the most votes nationwide. Even Delaware or Montana with three electoral votes each would stimulate voters everywhere because not just those states' voters would be affected. Knowing even a few electoral votes could swing an election, people in every polling place would know their ballot added to the total that determined at least some electoral votes. A shift could occur gradually as a few states showed how easily it could be done. It is undemocratic for a few in swing states to determine how the nation is governed.

4. Add a "None of the above" option to each race on every ballot. A majority marking it would dismiss all on that slate. Present occupants of those offices would remain temporarily but be ineligible to run in an election, say, two months later when a new slate would appear (nominated, for example, by random selection from the list of registered voters). This would allow voters to remove candidates seen as a body to be co-opted by special interests.

5. Let voters select first, second, and third choices for a seat. Any receiving a majority of first choices would be elected. If none did so, the second choices of the lowest vote-getter (dropped off the list) would be reassigned to the remaining candidates with a third round if needed. With their first choices voters could encourage candidates unlikely to obtain a majority, knowing their second or third choice would advance an acceptable compromise candidate.

6. Open state primaries to all voters regardless of party. A democracy has no business disenfranchising growing numbers of independent voters. A party wanting to unite around its own candidate could have a closed election ahead of the open primary that admitted all voters.

7. Cease using party affiliation to advance winners of open primaries to a general election. The two top vote-getters in a primary, regardless of party, would move up as California now permits. This would stimulate voting across party lines and broaden candidates' appeal since crossovers would often make a difference.

8. Direct state redistricting commissions to make Congressional districts compact and stable while minimizing gerrymandering. Remove

restrictions on registration or register all citizens automatically. Expand the times and means of voting, and move election days to weekends.

9. Select state governors at the quadrennial elections for President so more voters could choose them.

10. Set a two-year goal to elect 450 members to the House of Representatives who agree to restore democracy, reverse economic inequality, sustain the good of the whole, remedy global warming, and solve national and international problems by constructive cooperation.

11. Energetic canvassing of voters *who support opposition candidates* can help rein in the latter's more extreme policies. Provided with upsetting information, citizens usually politically passive are more likely to call their Representative's office and ask, "What about this?" Even if not removed from their seat, Representatives are more likely to restrain their excesses.

12. Candidates need to be likeable, principled, hard-working, articulate, and interested in elected office. They tend to emerge from groups that already believe change is urgent, and are more likely to undertake a grueling effort on knowing they have others' respect and support. Those seeking national roles often start in local or state offices or on boards and commissions that give them a hands-on education.

13. Estimate candidates' knowledge and values by naming a topic and letting them talk about its specifics. The following address allocating the benefits of American productivity, help for those struggling, taking care of the physical world, and enhancing democracy. Each contains a general subject and a facet of it that concerns us:

Discharge of pollutants into air and water, temperature of the earth, quality of food, education of children, safety of the community, freedom of religious expression, freedom from religious persecution, privacy of personal lives, health of inhabitants, fairness of opportunities, protection from criminal activity, correction of delinquent children, rehabilitation of adult offenders, support for the mentally ill and disabled, security for the aging, decency of foreign policy, reach of military power, justice of courts, survival of family farms, productivity of soil, health of oceans, purity of water, safety of products, sustainability of energy sources, recycling of non-renewable resources, security of ports and travel, investment in infrastructure, efficiency of transport, easing of hostility, survival of fish, birds, and animals.

From their comments, we can judge: 1) Is their mind filled with political pablum, vague generalities? 2) Are they familiar with details that can actually aid problem-solving? 3) Do they exhibit a thoughtful range of priorities? 4) Can they state an unpopular truth that challenges their audience, and say the same to both supporters and the undecided?

14. The proposals above help sustain democracy. People may legitimately disagree when comparing candidates but should not about founding principles. If Principle A inherently implies A-1 and A-2, we can reach out to someone who agrees with A but not yet A-1 and A-2. We present the obvious link until they get it, a task due now in twenty-two states where restrictive registration and voting requirements (A-1 and A-2) contradict the meaning of democracy (Principle A).

Some who wish to do the right thing may welcome the following explanation, while others who regard it as limiting their advantage will need it thrust before them by personal contact, town halls, mass media, challenges, sit-ins, picketing, and debates. We contrast their self-interest with the idea of democracy:

"These changes apply America's belief in majority rule, that we are more secure when a majority chooses our country's direction instead of a few powerful people. Do you disagree with that? Do you think a few should run things, be able to grant favor to whomever they wish? That's called an oligarchy, where a minority controls government. Or do you believe democracy is such a bad idea that you would rather have a king or an aristocracy with an upper class in power? Or people with lots of money choosing candidates, a plutocracy? Do you think democracy is obsolete, that we can't trust everyone together to think for the whole? Certainly they can't when no one listens to what they say. Making it harder for them to register and vote silences their voice, right? When you studied American government in school, did teachers tell you democracy was better than other forms of government? Did you believe it was a good idea then, and if so, are people carrying it out now? If you shut out the majority so a minority runs everything, are you proud of that? Don't you want a government that still works for you when you lose an argument?"

Open-minded people will acknowledge an unhappy fact: those who want to gerrymander and suppress opponents' votes would rather impose an oligarchy than participate as equals in a democracy. *They would kill off our form of government before relinquishing power,* and need to face their choice. Power is more important to them than sustaining a democracy, a downhill intent for their nation.

15. A path is open with the 45-60 percent of eligible voters who do not vote in a given election. Each of them needs a human being to show up before them, connect with them, help them think through their values and options, and get them to the polls. This is only a quantity of effort. Whoever cares enough to put out the effort wins.

At this writing in mid-2017, the Republican Party controls all branches of government but conflicts among its factions hinder its ability to govern while the Democratic Party wonders why Republican difficulties do not translate into support for itself. Each might provide a clear answer to the question, "How do we intend to serve the American people?" If the two cannot cooperate on one answer, they could instead answer for their own side and get it to voters. If they do not, the other will be glad to define them by their most vulnerable features.

31. Communicate with opponents

Collaborate with opponents when possible. Some avoid talking to opponents to weaken the latter's position, may believe talking does no good, or may fear their influence. We raise fences out of worry over what might come across the fence.

But for constructive social change, people who disagree usually need to talk. By refusing, we stress others and ourselves, impairing the judgment of both of us and reducing the pool of usable information. Much of what we want to talk about concerns the essence of democracy, so we remind people of this. Under a dictatorship, you keep your views to yourself and act as authorities demand. In an oligarchy, you may vent your views but it makes no difference. People in power do what they want, but you can think you are part of the process if you like. Even in a democracy, leaders ignoring or retaliating against criticism can depress participation.

A democracy presumes that people as a whole have the best ideas but must exchange them enough that the better ones stand out, implying a certain quality of communication. A chorus of voices may be only a mob able to sing in one note. People instead need to examine ideas piece by piece in order to recognize and promote the best ones.

If we do not deliberately engage others' thinking this way, it tends to stay the same. The Occupy Wall Street effort, for instance, publicized the potentially electrifying difference between the fortunes of the top 1% and the bottom 99%, but did not accomplish broad change. Even a far-reaching rationale has little effect unless it wins over the uninformed and oppositional and steers them toward corrective action. Technology does not remedy this need. Facebook, Twitter, YouTube, and the Internet have connected millions, but offering no message of change, they have not ignited a movement. *If we have nothing to say, it does not matter how many we can say it to* (90). When mass distribution of information misses the mark, we return to nature, we appeal person to person. African Americans in the Civil Rights Movement, working people in the Labor Movement, and women obtaining the vote put themselves out personally.

Though we go first to the undecided and uninformed, progress may be possible with adversaries. We contact them, inquire how we can address concerns together, open to their goals and aspirations, and affirm common experience. If we can shake hands on even a partial solution with them, we can appeal to the undecided together to complete the picture. We focus our limited resources on the tools for change, valuing ideas that prepare us for action, constantly on guard against our ignorance.

Conditions aiding change.

1. In a group that standardizes thinking, the daily impact of peer opinions absorbs people's attention and makes it harder for them even

to hear a new idea. The presence of a group also causes them to ignore details. They think, "Someone else will check that out," so that they more easily accept false assumptions. Apart from the group, however, the same people are more likely to respond with, "Sure. Let's go to the sources." Recognizing a need for physical distance in order to change, they may move to a new neighborhood or the opposite coast, or change jobs. About a political opponent, we could ask, "How can I get him alone so we could talk this out?"

2. Solitude can help. In relaxed surroundings people may more easily return to their stable values, rediscover their right and true. Solitude allows us time to reflect and develop better ideas. Fishing or hiking with an opponent for an afternoon might serve the need. On returning from an extended vacation, an opponent may react less to hot buttons and be open to thoughtful exchange.

3. A movable edge of thought such as a suppressed doubt can matter. We listen for hints about any our opponent may carry, and enter their mind on one side of a conversation already going on in their head. Group views can be driven by assertive members who override others' opinions, leaving some unable to think through their deeper concerns and hence receptive to a personal conversation. Removing pressure on people allows doubt to come into awareness.

4. Listen to their thinking. To do this well we stop trying to get our point across and instead absorb what comes to us. Most of us, most of the time, think our own point is key, but insisting on ours drives others to assert theirs. To help them change one comma of it, we aim first to understand them. We follow their thought processes, draw out their views for five to fifty minutes, and weigh what they say.

To assimilate an idea that conflicts with our own, we do not just hear it but engage it with our thought processes, *and cannot do this while immersed in our own views.* By explaining the other's idea cogently back to them, we discipline ourselves to welcome it at a deeper level. We can say to our opponent, "I'm not sure if we're hearing what each other wants. Could I summarize what I hear you want, and then you do the same for me?" We then capture accurately the purpose they may not even have expressed in words and their feeling about it, and continue correcting our version until they can say, "You understand me perfectly." Then we ask them to do the same for our ideas.

5. When we make up our mind about someone who resists information and evidence and treat them like a category, they have no reason to open to us. We can instead take a genuine interest in them personally. A rule-of-thumb measure of our interest in someone is how much we know about them, so we can inquire about their life.

I learned about this from a classmate who seemed talented with people, who was friends with everyone. Walking with him one day, I asked about it.

"Charlie, you seem to get along with everyone," I said. "How do you do that?"

"It's easy," he said with a smile. "Just ask people a lot of questions about themselves."

Later I watched how that worked. A single question was merely being polite: "How are you doing?" "Great." A second question suggested a little more receptivity, but three or more questions appeared to cross a threshold. People might think we wanted their life story, and by answering they let us know they regard us as eligible to relate to them. To the extent that they are ready to listen to us, our sharing comparably helps to sustain a sense of balance.

6. When the other vents negative feelings, a simple tack noted already was used by a young man whose family asked him to visit his great aunt in a nursing home. No one wanted to be around this lady because she was so negative, pouring out an endless stream of complaints. It was suggested to the man that he ask her a question about the least negative thing she said, and continue doing so with each of her comments.

The result was that the two had a pleasant conversation for a couple hours, but the nursing home staff reported later that the lady remained in a good mood for three or four days afterward. Many apparently negative people do not want to be, and offered an alternative will take it.

My parents faced a similar problem when a distant relative reputed to be stern, cold, and uncommunicative was passing through town and it was socially correct that they invite him to dinner. They discussed how they were going to handle this, and my father finally suggested, "Let's just draw him out."

Afterward they exclaimed what an interesting person he was with many unique experiences, and how much they enjoyed the evening. They "drew him out."

7. We can arrange to get to know people personally. Common experience is a social language. Thrown into one arena, we realize we can develop ideas even while uncomfortable, come to know others as individuals, and appreciate their values. Addressing local issues we mingle with people we know and make progress from pick-and-shovel effort over bits of common purpose.

While my father was in Alaska politics, my parents would invite legislators to our home, both opponents and allies, with the understanding that they leave political issues alone. Over dinners of fish, moose, caribou, and deer my father had taken himself, guests discussed hunting, travel, weather, resources, family, and other non-political topics. The result was that in his legislative work, my father never had to talk to strangers. As a child one evening, I had his worst political enemy take an interest in a clay figure I was working on and was startled to discover that to me he was a nice person.

The same could happen in Washington. The President could invite all Congressmen and their families to an annual picnic on the White House lawn, houses of Congress could seat their members alphabetically, parties could play more baseball, and members, finally, could choose to collaborate. Doing so, however, offers both a benefit and a drawback: *personal relationships make shared decision-making more likely.* A party that believes it has all the power it needs to obtain all it wants has little motive to share anything. When it realizes that collaboration results in better decisions, personal bonds are a first step.

8. Expect interest rather than conflict. Many avoid expressing their beliefs because they dread conflict, yet a movement presses this boundary by trying to place ideas where they were not before. We reduce our hesitance by viewing our activity as sharing something positive:

"Here's an interesting idea." Or we provide a service or offer a benefit. Diverse views need not be contentious. By remaining happy and interested, we are more likely to elicit the same in others.

9. Ask others' permission to offer an idea. By respecting their right to refuse ideas, we avoid needless invasion. If we discover information they can use, we provide it *and stop there.* Testifying before legislative committees on several occasions, I realized that my comments bore no fruit because I did not align myself with the committee's concern. Our words seem irrelevant if we do not respond to others' needs, which we discover by asking. We should communicate in so satisfying a way that, even if we disagree, they welcome resuming it. We convey every idea so as not to close off the next one.

10. Distinguish degrees of certainty. Remembering how badly we want to make our point at times, we can sympathize when others do that. They may be unwilling to hear any dissent and expect us to agree or give up. Although careful listening may not change their view, it often lightens their emotional charge and clarifies pieces we can deal with.

It can help to *put words to their degree of certainty several times in a row.* Unconscious priorities may block good reasoning, so bringing them into awareness tends to move people toward reasonableness: "Wow! That sounds like it sums up for you the entire issue, that there is nothing more to be said," and then, "It sounds like you mean that for everybody in all situations, that there's no other way to look at that!" and then, "Something in your life must have convinced you deeply of that." Once they know we recognize an idea's importance to them, they are often more willing to consider details: "Are you more certain about X or about Y?" "Is your personal experience related more to X, Y, or Z?"

11. Distinguish what is essential to us and what we can concede. We may be able to ask them for something indifferent to them that might help us significantly, or offer them something indifferent to us that they might value. We discover these helpful tradeoffs only by extended, thoughtful communication. While we could regard this as compromise, we do not expect both sides to concede equally from an arbitrary starting point. A comic's riff illustrates:

"Can I burn down your house?"

"No."

"Can I burn just the second floor?"

"No."

"Could we talk about this?"

"No."

"You're not compromising!"

Sometimes we must stand, fight, and nail opponents' errors, yet doing this with hostility can perpetuate problems. We want to make compromise possible by noting common ground, "Well, I agree with you that…" before addressing differences.

12. Understand that being right may not resolve a conflict. Believing our analysis is already correct can halt collaboration. Often we can frame a problem in more than one way. "The problem is loss of wildlife habitat" and "The problem is loss of jobs" may both apply, but different formulations block progress. We can define a problem we would both like to solve: "How can we preserve habitat and jobs at the same time?"

We note conditions under which we can conceive of others being right. Expressing even a possibility stretches comprehension. An environmentalist might say to a polluter, "Your discharge would matter less to me if organisms were less sensitive to toxins," and the polluter answers, "Your regulations would be easier to bear if the benefit from them matched their cost." A common direction could be learning how toxins might do less harm while improving cost/benefit. We try to affirm even potential validity in their view: "If this were true, it would strengthen your position," or "When this happens, your view applies," or "I see that your stand is based on…."

To assimilate their thought processes better, we can switch sides and try to present theirs convincingly, though they may be unable to do the same. Once committed to their own conclusion, defensive people may feel they surrender by putting words to another's perspective.

13. We can assume that both we and our opponents thread a path through an issue tangled up in our own head. The one we see may occupy only an incidental corner of the one they see. Sometimes we have the

knowledge or resources to help them but only if they "let us in." If they do, *we try to help them solve the problem they experience*, and begin by appreciating it: "Tell me what you are facing, the pressures you are under. What options do you have?" We let them explain what is unfamiliar to us.

14. Look for incremental change. When problems appear intractable, we focus on small gains around the edges like, "Could we agree on a fair competition of ideas?" In polarities such as labor and management, left and right, white and black, we need not expect permanent struggle. Instead of asking, "Which of us is right?," we go to smaller questions like, "Could others be partly right?" and "What is the next step for us?" Huge changes may be needed but only small ones in reach. Perhaps an earthquake-damaged wooden building should be torn down and a better one built, but we could also jack it up, square it, patch it, and return it to use for less cost and delay.

Trying to address an entire complex problem at once, we are more likely to run aground on another's emotional stance about it. Better to identify a single part where the other's reasoning is murky and say, "Could we just carve off this one piece to look at?" We accomplish many purposes better a step at a time.

15. See others as a source of information. Sometimes theirs broadens our own. We site a bridge with a base in both river banks, a peace treaty accounts for both sides' needs. Asking our opponents, "How are you receiving me?" and "What are you wanting to send?" we remedy our ignorance of each other. The more complex the issue, the more information we need from others. When sending an aide to meet with a Congressman, President Lyndon Johnson would urge him/her to extend the conversation, talk longer than needed, since useful details often emerged after business ended.

16. Search for common values. Some refuse to collaborate because they distrust others. They think they cannot rely on their opponent's agreements so they resign themselves to power-based competition. But we can legitimately say, "We seem to be stuck over here, but maybe we can make progress over there." NRA members meeting mothers on

welfare can find similar values. The former have children and the latter want a secure society. We do not embarrass or humiliate an opponent if another way exists to avoid an evil, but hold open the possibility that even this person could be an ally.

17. Reverse what we want to hear. Sometimes opposition is incomprehensible and our visceral reaction is to avoid even listening, insuring that we do not learn what others have for us. When we hear something we do not like, our tendency is to dismiss it, but such ideas may offer progress. Though we may not find common ground, we may at least learn where the other is vulnerable or incomplete; may conclude that they are liars and cheats and we must struggle against them, but we understand the task facing us by advancing into their idea and assimilating it fully.

18. Ask to be corrected. Accepting correction presumes the other may know something we do not, so it takes humility to say, "Correct me if I'm wrong here, but…" or "Do I have this straight?" or "Is it accurate from your knowledge to say…?" We view others' experience as a resource even if we disagree with them, and weigh their feedback.

19. Invite a change of perspective. To help even narcissists stuck in their own view to be more open to ours, we can ask them to put themselves in our place or imagine how they would feel in another's predicament. This single shift has been found to help even self-absorbed people feel empathy. Whenever we want to move someone frozen in an idea, we can ask them to imagine reversing positions and put into words how they might see the issue differently.

20. Make belief and behavior consistent. A movement asks society to align its actions with its stated values. Contradiction between the two feels uncomfortable, but few of us monitor this in ourselves because our mind skates over the difference, skipping from one pole to another without noticing their incompatibility. Grasping the inconsistency *can require someone waving it before us*: "You say you're not racist, but that was a racist remark." "You say your religion instructs you not to condemn others, but now you do that." "You say you dislike income inequality, but object to policies that could remedy it." To someone we

dislike, our comments might sound attacking, but to a person we care about, whose thinking matters to us, the same ideas can convey concern: "I'm worried for you." Our attitude determines what the other hears in our words.

21. Plan a problem-solving workshop. Discomfort with opponents can halt constructive effort, so to obtain solutions, people often must work through it. *A Community Unity Workshop* could help a town polarized between competing religious bodies or police and black citizens. Invite equal numbers from each side so neither feels sandbagged, and spend an afternoon this way:

Distribute the five communication skills listed earlier, explain them, and ask participants to agree to practice them.

Pair people first with someone from the other side whom they do not know well to search for agreement on values and suggestions for the community.

As pairs agree on what they can, they join a different pair and share with each other the agreements their pair reached.

The new group of four compiles their agreements, adds more, and incorporates more people into them.

The groups continue in this way for the time available—reaching agreement on more topics and combining groups. The larger groups become, the more important is their use of the communication skills. Those remaining in pairs or small groups may help by examining an issue of their choice. At the end, a speaker from each concluding group reports to the whole assembly on the agreements obtained. This format works *by focusing steadily on the positive,* and can be combined with other presentations and activities.

22. Advocate for our opponents' interests. Before challenging what our opponents do wrong, we commit to their prosperity and well-being. We want to enlist their goodwill and help them toward constructive goals by solving the part they cannot while they solve the part we cannot. Good of the whole, for instance, implies populist interests committed to commercial prosperity. It makes no sense for people who depend on a paycheck to wish ill for their company or for the social structures that

make it viable. In the other direction, Henry Ford applied a principle of economics almost revolutionary for his time by raising his employees' wages without being forced to do so because, he said, they needed to earn enough to buy the cars they were making. More money circulating benefited everyone. A manufacturing company years ago established a policy of never having to fire anyone, and with layers of contingency plans and strategies—"What do we do *if...*"—rode out many ups and downs.

23. Use our time efficiently. While engaging with opponents may yield returns, it can also waste time. When others' ego needs, rigidity, or economic or political intransigence stand in the way, even superb communication may accomplish so little that our time is better spent otherwise. We need not give up on people, but should weigh the benefit likely from effort toward all our goals.

32. Arguing with extremists

Learn how to communicate under difficult circumstances. Toward someone determined to convince us of something untrue, we tend either to avoid them or assert our own view more forcefully. Instead we can recast the situation: "Great! Wonderful! I have a chance to practice some skills I rarely use!" The other only has to be willing to talk to us, which means that *he codes us as acceptable to speak to.* We proceed:

"Right now you want me to have the correct viewpoint and you believe that that is (we sum up their idea briefly). Hmm. I also want to have the correct viewpoint and I'm glad to have information that can straighten out my ideas if they are wrong, okay?"

So far, this response mutes the issue of personal dominance. We state that we submit to "the correct viewpoint" and we welcome the other "winning" if the information indicates. We then turn a crucial corner by insisting on being corrected by the evidence, which has the benefit of focusing us together on evidence.

"If you want to correct my ideas, and I *want* to be corrected, there should not be a problem, right?" Here you pose a basic standard of rationality by asserting that you regard it more important to have valid ideas than to win an argument. You continue:

"To correct an idea, people go to the evidence about it. For this issue, could you and I start with an Internet search? Is that okay? Let's go do that."

Doing so with a single insignificant issue offers the other a way to win but also involves them in using a problem-solving method. The approach works even better if, the first time you do it, **you lose on the issue you look up.** You say happily, "Hey, you were right! Great! I'm glad we got that point cleared up." Then you scour up other issues enabling you to lose gracefully. Winning an argument through simple research alerts the other to more ways they could use that strategy, and sets up a meeting ground for other issues.

When opponents' minds are fixed but a need requires that you work together, *you especially need to be flexible.* For two people in the dark to shake hands, the one who can see better has to find the other's hand. We want to be versatile enough to connect with their thinking. This need not mean concessions but rather doing what moves the discussion. Focusing on a quality we can respect like "Your candidate represents a key value for you," invites the other to open up more. We alter our words to bridge differences, want to understand how they put everything together, and do this sincerely because we all live under a mystery. No scientist, prophet, or philosopher has adequately explained how human beings can be free to think as they do. Our brain does not explain its own consciousness. If we are curious about how others form theirs, they typically welcome our interest.

We can invite them to explain their purpose: If this is what you want, we can talk further about how to get it, and perhaps collaborate on a means. A conversation might pass through stages:

1. "What is your purpose? What do you want to accomplish?"

Your own aim is for them to express ideas you can support. They may not have regarded their thinking as having a purpose, but you can point out that every action has a result. What did their thought process produce, and was that what they wanted? Their initial answer may be incomplete, so you guess where the parts they do express might be headed and state them as best you can: "So you're worried that people believe they can add to the national debt endlessly and will never have to pay it back. Your purpose then is the stability of the financial system." You try to frame accurately what they tell you about the outcome they want.

2. "So then for you, electing Tom seems to be the best step for bringing down the national debt."

Note the period at the end of the sentence. It expresses our guess about their purpose as a statement rather than as a question. *When we instead ask a question, we draw the other onto our ground.* We focus them on meeting *our* need, filling in a detail we think we need to know, but in doing so we take over the direction of the exchange, and may quickly find ourselves following our own ideas while their answers steadily become shorter.

Framing our response instead as a statement stays on their ground—we are trying simply to follow the track of their idea. It is more freeing for them because they can politely convert it into a question they can answer, change the subject, or select a part to develop. By whatever they say, they continue to own their train of thought.

If people believe we genuinely want to understand their views, they are usually glad to correct our response and will expand on their idea. We continue summarizing what we hear until they have clarified their purpose and the actions that accomplish it. The critical element for them, however, is often the feeling they attach to it, so we include that in our summary of their idea.

3. "You feel the long-term danger to the nation is really, really important. It stands out in your mind and you worry about it."

People may not feel understood until they believe we sense the intensity and quality of their feeling, so we try to put accurate words to our guess about it. Once they believe we grasp both their meaning and feeling, they are more receptive to our interest in them and after a time more likely to open to our ideas. We may be tempted to deliver our own idea at the first opening, but often do better by continuing to focus on their purpose and its emotional resonance for them.

4. "How do you see the danger actually coming about? What would happen?"

People want to be emotionally clear on an issue and often sense they are not quite there. If we want to help them toward it, they may be willing to think about it with us. We inquire where their connection to the issue originated, the points on which it alights, conditions associated with it, how their thinking developed through time, and concerns that have similar emotional potency for them. Multiple circumstances may carry emotional loadings that converge in one issue.

5. We help them take steps toward even the capacity to work together. As a conversation unfolds, we may note a small opening when we can propose action or solutions, but doing so too early can exceed the envelope of comfort already established. Our assertive move may stimulate their defensiveness, leading them to screen our comment for threat.

The problem is that people tend to open to challenging views by small increments. Beginning with ignoring us completely, after a time they may regard polite daily greetings as okay but not conversation. Later a superficial exchange is okay, but with only a few sentences. Then deeper conversation may be okay but not mutual purpose, and mutual purpose coming later may still not include changing their ideas. In the slowly expanding envelope of safety we share, we proceed by a string of yeses so that a small point of acceptance leads to another and another. Our next comment is never too big a jump past their previous degree of openness.

6. "If you woke up one morning and things were the way you wanted, what would they be like? What would you observe? What would make you happy?" We ask them to turn vague concepts into practical images, to picture the tangible experience of being at their goal.

What do you see happening in society as you want it to be?

What activities are present and what are absent?

How close to that ideal are we now?

What stands in the way of achieving it?

What could you and I do to help make those changes?

7. People alter their views more easily when we acknowledge their freedom to choose whatever view they want, as we discussed above. We can extend this influence by pointing out the logical consequences of their viewpoint, and that we respect their obligation to accept them *even if other values conflict*:

"Since you really believe torture can be necessary for military purposes, I can understand how you could want police to use it to bring down a drug ring or solve a murder, for instance."

"So then, because you support the death penalty for bad crimes and it seems to work in your view, I can see how you might want to apply it to other crimes then. I understand."

"You believe people are entirely responsible for their own lives and the government should stay out. I see your consistency then in wanting to eliminate job retraining, unemployment compensation, food stamps, and government help for medical facilities. I understand."

The point is not that these are good ideas or even that the other believes them, *but that they are consistent with what else they believe.* By putting words to the implications of their beliefs, we invite them to expand their perspective.

Return to basics. If people call themselves "loyal Americans,"we can draw on that belief by returning to ideas loyal Americans typically subscribe to. We might ask them, "So how does your view fit with the introduction to the Declaration of Independence?"

> We hold these truths to be self-evident, that all men are created equal, that they are endowed by their Creator with certain unalienable Rights, that among these are Life, Liberty, and the pursuit of Happiness. That to secure these rights, Governments are instituted among Men, deriving their just powers from the consent of the governed.

We can memorize the passage, relate a few lines to a voter, and explore their implications (91):

- "Self-evident" truths are obvious to everyone. Are they obvious to you?

- Do you believe all men are created equal? Why would they say that?

- Do you believe all men have inalienable rights? Does that include women?

- Do you think "inalienable" means that other people can't take them away?

- Do you believe the nation should secure, safeguard, and protect people's rights?

- What do you think those rights are?

- Do you believe in the idea of government?

- What do you think its role is?

- Where does its power come from?

- Does everyone have a place in your view of government or just a few?

By opening a picture they subscribe to in general but that challenges their current attitude, we elicit cognitive dissonance. We hold up to their mind the inconsistency between two beliefs, and continue to remind them of the discrepancy until they align their attitude with founding documents.

Analogies can clarify a principle. To a southerner insisting on his heritage, you could point out, "If you had an uncle who robbed banks and killed people and then was shot himself, would you celebrate his achievements as family heritage? A heritage should connect us with positive values and principles of the past, right? So what exactly are the positive principles and values that the Confederacy passed on to you? Could you name a few that inspire you? Which ones seem constructive?"

We can inquire how their stand fits with their ancestors immigrating to America: "Your forebears crossed a bridge into this country and now you want to pull up the bridge?" Concluding a conversation, we say as we walk away, "Next time I see you, I'll ask you how you put those two things together," leaving their mind with a challenge to resolve.

Seek rapport. We are more influenced by people we like even though we disagree with them. Liking keeps communication open for future exchanges and is enhanced as people match each other. We tend to seek out friends with experiences like ours, so that with the same occupation, interests, religion, age level, demographic background, etc. we feel more comfortable together.

Around people apparently unlike us, however, we establish a connection by entering their frame of reference however we can. We noted above being fascinated at how they construct their mind—a point of matching. We acknowledge their feelings and thoughts accurately—a point of matching. We use the same kinds of words they do, and adopt the same manner of expression they do—more matching. Like facing someone who speaks a foreign language, we connect poorly if theirs is Spanish and ours English but switching to Spanish, we connect easily.

Subtle cues taken together are an intuitive language. People unconsciously notice sentences long vs. short, speech slow vs. fast, words short vs. long, pitch high vs. low, position standing vs. sitting, and so on. As two wish to relate better, they spontaneously adopt others' cues. Watching a couple at a restaurant, we might notice, "Those two are in love." Their body position, nods, facial expressions, head tilt, responsiveness to each other's ideas, and beginning and ending each other's thoughts are all ways their bodily matching displays their connection (92).

Adapting ourselves to another may seem an extra effort, but *the more versatile one in an exchange prevails,* like a boxer able to land a punch or a gymnast who can stick a landing. As we vary our response according to the other's needs, we are better able to suggest an idea that connects us.

Freedom to change. A focus that aids change is people's realization that they are free to select their beliefs, as we noted above. It is a self-imposed box for them to believe they have no choices and must follow one direction. Questions can re-engage them with their options:

- Do you believe you could change if you wanted to?

- Do you feel you have to appear completely certain about everything you say all the time?

- When you became an adult, did you give up some childhood ideas?

- Did that feel like a betrayal, like letting yourself down?

- Or did you see it as improving your thinking?

- Do you let yourself down if you think an idea you learned last year doesn't work this year?

- Or does the change just improve your thinking?

- Are you married or in a relationship?

- In your personal life, do you sometimes find value in someone else's ideas?

- Do you have give and take between you?

- What helps the give and take start off?

- Does one of you propose talking about common concerns?

- And then the other person agrees to try?

- And you listen to each other's views for awhile?

- And one or both of you modify your idea?

Coping with argument. Though we approach our contacts with others as exchanges or discussions, we may need to master the conditions of argument.

First, we arrive optimistic, interested, and happy so that a smile comes naturally to us. Smiles are disarming, suggesting good will toward the other, hope we could become allies, and assurance that we will not cause the other unnecessary stress. We supply humor if we can.

Second, we believe that the other ultimately wants good ideas and may not realize how their views could hinder their judgment. We expect the best thinking eventually to prevail. Information often plays on people's minds unobtrusively, opening them gradually to new perspectives.

Third, we try to comprehend the other's context. Though it may not fit our own, in some framework it must make sense to them, so we try to find it: "Okay! I believe I understand. If I were in your position, I would be thinking…."

Fourth, we can practice recognizing errors in argumentation. We encounter them sooner or later, and correcting them can have more impact than information we supply. Consider, for instance, the nuances of meaning in President Trump's statement, *"This is a witch hunt!"*

A "witch hunt" originally meant tracking down supposed witches in medieval Europe, and killing them by burning, drowning, or torturing, and means now an intent to pin great evil on someone falsely. The objective data are that two Republican-controlled houses of Congress and the Special Counsel are conducting independent investigations that could involve President Trump, but since they have made no accusations, the data do not support the claim. In ordinary politics, media and the public criticize or support a President based on approving or disapproving his actions, so it would be a wild exaggeration to refer to that as a witch hunt. Criticism goes with the territory.

The President's intent, however, helps explain the phrase. He wishes to establish *that because he is innocent of wrongdoing* (presuming the conclusion), *others must have an evil intent.* Any accused may gather exonerating evidence, but by using "witch hunt" the President appears to try instead to de-legitimize accusations that could arise: "If others attack me, I can paint it as a truly evil thing." Supporting this strategy is that in many corners of our culture, one does better by making assertions than by presenting evidence.

A group project could devise or draw from current news an example of each error below to help voters recognize attempts to manipulate them:

1. Over-generalizing one case to all cases

2. False comparison

3. Selecting only supportive facts

4. Either-or oversimplifications

5. Bandwagon—everyone agrees

6. Incorrectly linking cause and effect

7. Logical jump

8. Assuming the conclusion

9. Diverting to unrelated issues

10. Missing intent to find the truth

11. Confirmation bias–believing what supports prior views

12. Desirability bias—believing what we want to happen

13. Incorrect context

14. Insisting an assertion be taken as fact until disproven

15. Inappropriate analogy

16. Personal claim–"I am entitled to my opinion."

17. Attacking the person to invalidate their idea

18. Asserting that prior errors invalidate current evidence

19. Unverifiable assertions

20. Wishful thinking

21. Emotional attachment to a viewpoint

Such errors are often introduced subtly into a conversation, and we may sense only that another's words do not quite fit. One voter listening to a news report on criticisms of President Trump muttered, "I just hear they're still disappointed Hillary Clinton didn't win," a comment that could fall under errors 6, 17, and 18 above. A reply could have been, "You're saying that when a candidate loses an election, their supporters cannot report news accurately afterward? If they have personal feelings, their reporting must be false? So therefore, when you personally feel strongly about anything, I should never believe you?" We examine the rationality of their thought word by word.

33. Obtain the skills you need

Commit to long-term personal development. Jump ahead 30 years, look around, and notice that not all problems in society are solved.

How do you picture yourself? The question is significant because people are more likely to care now for their future self if their image of it is clear to them.

How healthy will you be, how happy?

What will you look like?

Will you be a couch potato or still be working on the issues?

Will you be developing your capabilities?

Will you be more competent?

What will you be able to accomplish?

A large goal implies large development. From today onward, you inescapably form yourself around your highest value, so you might notice what it is. How do your actions reveal who you are? To change society, you will need to understand basic ideas, assimilate them into your personal thinking, communicate them to others, have good judgment about organizational effort, and sustain others' motivation. No single choice enables you to know those things. Presuming that we want large scale change from others, we focus on ourselves. Wishing others to be open to change, we do it first.

A tension exists, however, between two impulses. One is our drive to define ourselves and nail down elements of our life, and the other is the fact that we are continually pressed to change. Instead of insisting we are already correct and complete, a more realistic view is that we are "righting"–in error yet adjusting to truth. We assume we have a healthy mind able to absorb reality but that this is a process rather than an achievement. We constantly re-balance like a sailor on a rolling deck. Self-righting is easier done together, challenging each other but dreaming as one, recognizing an emerging possibility and giving it life by sharing it.

Don't let yourself down. In practically everything humans do, part is easy and part is hard. Because we like easy, we tend to do more of it, put off the hard and do it haphazardly. In maturing we finally face that we must do the hard part thoroughly, and that if we do not, we will not accomplish what we want. The hard part demands more intense thinking and action but we choose it because it will work.

A disciplined focus affects every sector of life. People do their work excellently and results follow. A day's work for Albert Einstein was sitting in a chair and thinking. Others applaud, draw on the achievement, and it finds its place in our culture. Mastering the hard parts, we move our lives and world ahead. Letting ourselves down means a standard matters to us but we avoid it because it is difficult.

If we have no idea how we might let ourselves down, we probably are not living up to our potential. We solve only the problems we face–for instance, are our eating habits and exercise what they should be? We are concerned here, however, with traits affecting society like responsible effort instead of passivity, respect for others rather than biases, and communicating instead of remaining aloof. We benefit others as we work on ourselves.

Patiently improve judgment. Today's evidence may not adequately define a future we can only partially foresee, which invites us to employ judgment to assess implications of the evidence. How well we do that today determines our success later. *We restrain premature finality* while searching for the best course. Viewing how often people's plans went awry, Kurt Lewin, a pioneer in social psychology, proposed that *if you think you understand something, try to change it.* Think you understand society? Try to change it. Your results will reveal your comprehension. A judge threads among degrees of confidence and prioritizes values. Familiar phrases express this attitude:

"You'll have my verdict in two weeks."

"Let me think about it for a couple days."

"I don't know anything about that."

"Where could I find out?"

"I have only scraps of information now."

"We're collecting evidence."

"I wonder."

To solve problems of any kind, a helpful attitude is first to *arrange any tools, conditions, or ideas that are easy (i.e. that you can do)*. When nothing else remains under your control, *shift your focus to perceiving the remaining task patiently and thoroughly until the next easy step becomes clear.*

Recognize the gap. Perhaps the hardest aspect of wisdom to develop is the shift from knowing something to recognizing what is missing. Our tendency is to leverage what we know beyond its usefulness. We apply our education confidently to our job, nailing details we were taught were important, but may then apply it where it does not belong, and overlook gaps.

Let us say we learn numbers perfectly from 1 to 100. Later discussing a problem that uses numbers in the 50s, as the other explains their idea we slowly realize that they *learned the number sequence 51, 52, 54, 55.* In order to recognize the missing 53, we need to have learned the sequence correctly ourselves but also must watch for the integrity and accuracy of whole sets of information. This concern has countless applications in social affairs:

A great deal of blame but no compassion.

Plenty of assertion but little evidence.

Much communication but little reflection.

Sharply defined differences but little similarity.

We love our sameness but fail to distinguish difference.

We reflect continually alone but do not share it.

We compile evidence and leave it voiceless.

We open our heart to everyone but skip accountability.

The critical understanding is that if multiple causes impact a situation *and we ignore one of them, we guarantee problems later.* Once I worked for a man running a large organization whose standard answer to literally everything you asked him was, "Lemme think about it," even to points seemingly simple and obvious. Then a day or two later he would find me and give his answer. In time I came to respect this, because it meant he slowed down his spontaneous reactions enough to survey the impact the decision would have as it rippled through the organization.

As we noted above, these implications almost by nature cannot be obvious at first. They arise from the fact that *reality is intrinsically broader* than our conception of it, and we spontaneously try to make our concept more efficient by pruning away details that appear unnecessary. We have to allow our minds the reflective time to allow reality to stretch and update our conception.

Be vigilant. Being rational means that the quality of our mind matters more to us than the point we want to make. We need to watch how our need to be right (to have influence, to get our point across) can injure our thinking. Because we do not instinctively form an accurate model of the world, we must analyze our thinking before it damages us, and notice how we bend what we receive. We try to gather others' messages accurately and learn what they have to teach us, release resistive emotion, and examine our deficits curiously.

We do not easily manage this alone because we act within long-standing limitations. Like fitted with a prosthesis after losing a leg, we learn to move within its range of motion. A group effort to change usually succeeds better. Insight is available from asking those who know us, "How am I to work with?" They may suggest how we might connect better to others, that we hold things up, go off on tangents, exaggerate non-essentials, are judgmental and rigid, or do not follow through. All of us have limitations and by facing them we improve our group effort.

David Briggs cites developing research about how humility enhances personal relationships. Humble people are more realistic about their strengths and limitations. They are more open to others' ideas, talents, and needs; are less selfish, more understanding, and able to see the world though others' eyes. They have more self-esteem yet take correction better. They are more forgiving because they understand people's weaknesses, and retaliate less for wrongs done to them. More willing to be trustworthy, they elicit trust from others and are self-sacrificing in a good way (93).

We can understand humility also by answering the question "What is life about?" Answering, "It's about *me!*" we lack the trait. A humble viewpoint looks instead at every being as its own center, having its own life and destiny. As we appreciate and love each one, we realize that there is no center. Instead there is a *whole* and we inhabit a corner of it. Due proportion about our place in the universe is an objective basis for humility.

Form subjective reality. Each of us is governed by a personal subjective reality, what we commit to sustaining in existence *in our mind,* like what a *mythus* is for a society. We each carry an interior, invisible plan to guide our lives, a foundation enabling us to express our values through our actions.

This foundation helps displace the power of our "little self" that takes its direction from outer conditions; that feels threatened by unpleasant circumstances, lets itself be pulled down so that frustration and hurt erupt spontaneously, and depends on others' validation to feel okay. The world may supply it with moments of relief and flashes of happiness when a plan works out, but it may soon revert to being mildly overwhelmed. In difficult circumstances, our little self retreats before pressures and defends its views, fears, and opinions.

Because the little self relies on temporary conditions rather than enduring values, it is a weak foundation for initiating change. It has minimal interest in learning, preferring to ride out assumptions it claimed before. Presenting an idea to others, our little self refuses to let go of it because we own it, while others release our idea because they do not own it; both reasons unreasonable. We should turn loose poor ideas and keep better ones regardless of their source. We improve the little self by patiently weighing the quality of our thoughts, feelings, and actions and adopting the better ones. Others, of course, may rely on their own little self, so that to change their activity, we are faced with modifying their subjective reality. How we expect to do that guides what we need to learn.

34. A continuum of change

Make decisions that change you. Imagine that a carpenter slapped you together with random-fitting pieces of wood, and the result was not pretty. But he gave you a rasp and a plane and flexible arms, and said, "Take off the rough edges, smooth out the curves, and you'll look fine." Undertaking that as a multi-year effort, we steadily alter a little here, a little there, and form the character from which we operate day to day—our interior strength, principles, and values.

We train ourselves also for tasks we face. The more complex they are and the fewer skills we have for them, the more training we need. Think of the effort to become a trial lawyer, a surgeon, or a quarterback. All of us face an even bigger task that till now we may have ceded to others–managing the world. Measuring our personal skills against that standard, we fall short and need more learning, assertive action, better reasoning, higher quality communication, superb problem-solving, wiser planning, and so on.

Below are a couple dozen choices about helpful skills. Though arranged in a rough sequence from basic to the more refined, many can be undertaken at once. They refer to qualities of character, activities toward the world, and ways of enhancing the movement. Any bypassed could signal a need left unaddressed.

They have in common that *they all depend on decisions sustained by intention and will,* and distinguish a values-based life from the little self. The latter just reacts somehow to whatever comes up while the former pursues substantial change. With the first point of the series, for example– thinking through what we believe–we can decide to give it time and attention or dismiss it with "Oh, whatever!" and continue reacting to circumstances. Here first is the series, and then a paragraph about each. We decide:

1. To think through what we believe and what we do about it.

2. To accept long-term change in our thinking.

3. To make changing society important to us personally.

4. To adopt the good of the whole as an organizing principle.

5. To expect that everyone has something to teach us.

6. To continue to learn about everything.

7. To work together with others.

8. To do reliably what we agree to do.

9. To be willing to take time for others and for group action.

10. To become skilled at listening, and listen to others in depth.

11. To improve our ability to communicate truth.

12. To invite others to join us in action for change.

13. To encourage personal connections and effective action in the group.

14. To help develop the group's ideas.

15. To face the limitations of our thinking and welcome correction.

16. To confront the limitations of others' thinking and actions.

17. To talk out issues with those who disagree when possible.

18. To discipline ourselves to do what contributes to group effectiveness.

19. To ask for action that increases others' skill and expresses the group's values.

20. To plan together for group activity.

21. To promote constructive principles for changing society.

22. To move toward balance and harmony.

23. To accept total responsibility for others and the world.

24. To adopt unconditional love for others and the world.

25. To spread truth.

26. To correct group think, short-term self-interest, and moral confusion.

27. To meet others' needs.

1. To think through what we believe and what we do about it.

We can think on the surface–answer when spoken to, take account of others, and meet needs for food, shelter, and survival. But weighing the future, we look past circumstances to form images of where we will go, what we will do, and the challenges we will face. We gradually distinguish what is important to us and think more broadly about our impact on others—family, friends, and community. We consider how we might apply our values–perhaps to join a group or church, take part in community activities, or express our views. By our choices, we conform our lives to the values we say are important, an activity ours alone. No one else controls the focus of our mind nor the intentions we pursue. Family and society may urge roles and ideas upon us, but we keep or discard them. We choose our beliefs and actions.

2. To accept long-term change in our thinking.

Once we begin clarifying our beliefs, we discover that this effort has no end. We realize we will continue to change for better or worse till we pass away, and decide to apply steady conscious attention to our learning and development. We acknowledge that we can let the impact of personal experiences change us in ways we do not choose, or can manage that journey deliberately according to our values.

3. To make changing society important to us personally.

To adopt such an expansive goal, we clear an interior space clogged now with other concerns and shift the scope of our thinking. We enlarge a particular focus, give it emotional meaning, and declare it a worthy purpose. We may be asked to master evolving issues, and set aside personal needs in order to respond to those of others. We grow in generosity and in understanding people, and become a first cause, an origin of activity that will mean a better society. We demonstrate this as we engage in activities we never did before, and declare it our business to change the world.

4. To adopt the good of the whole as an organizing principle.

It is easy to think "common good" in the abstract, but we are challenged by details that demand a refined sense of balance. We need to counteract our tendency to use others' actions as excuses to go out of balance ourselves or let them anger us. Good of the whole implies fairness in accounting for all values at stake in a given issue. Other balances self, elsewhere balances here, thought balances feeling, invisible balances visible, old balances young, rest balances action, and one person balances another. We look for the greatest good for the greatest number, and accept the discipline of thinking of the whole when we attempt to settle a part.

5. To expect that everyone has something to teach us.

This decision relieves the most common hindrance to discussion, that we have already made up our mind. But if others know *anything* we don't know, we might learn it from them. Because so many ideas are necessary for society to work, we cannot presume that our own should dominate. Rather we seek comprehensive understanding, and others, with their years of unique experience, can add to it. Every job, educational program, encounter with a stranger, or family experience may have a clue that expands our knowledge. Our interactions alert us to the weaknesses in our attitude and our incorrect assumptions about the world.

6. To continue to learn about everything.

We humans are helpless unless we learn, and we master our world not through instinct but by ideas we form consciously. If we fail at this, we accept dominance by others who may damage us. Ignorant people are easier to manipulate. While we need volumes of passive learning that help us understand our world, the goal for a movement is acquiring active knowledge about changing the world that we can explain to others at any length under any circumstances. We master whatever we can use for enhancing our life and changing society.

7. To work together with others.

We counteract our tendency to isolate ourselves. Loneliness has worse survival factors than obesity many times over. We may control our results by working alone and demonstrating our personal competence, but the impact of our work shows up as we affect others. Social change means millions deciding to treat other millions differently. We start by doing ourselves what we eventually want society to do—work together for the good of all— so we find others who have the same purpose. We do less well if our starting point is to defeat others or push them away. The extent of our collaboration is the extent of our eventual success, so we seek out or form a team whose goals we share.

8. To do reliably what we agree to do.

Strong people ally with each other in a movement, and reveal their strength through their habit of carrying out their agreements even if they are tiring or hard. If we agree to conduct a discussion class, we do it. If we agree to canvassing, we do it. Because this trait affects every effort for a movement and all gains for society, we make clear agreements with others and, where needed, provide them the means to carry out their part. We make reasonable requests, explain why they are important and appropriate, obtain others' commitment, and follow up with them afterward with recognition and appreciation.

9. To be willing to take time for others and for group action.

Since the world depends on us, we are alert to what we can actually do. We may give ordinary time and courtesy to others, receptiveness to their ideas, and active involvement in plans developed together. Recognizing others' needs, we respond to them unselfishly instead of continually pursuing our own preferences and habits. This simple practice demands continual self-discipline, and guiding our actions steadily by our higher values. Daily we are glad to spend minutes or hours in consideration and service toward others.

10. To become skilled at listening, and listen to others in depth.

Listening is not merely silence while others speak, but rather active thought about their ideas. Such attention is a gift to them because most develop their thinking by speaking it. Expressing themselves to a good listener, they feel freer to follow their thoughts into corners they would not explore otherwise. Many have never in their life been asked, "What do you believe?" because no one has regarded their answer as significant. By exploring how they form their mind, we imply to them, "Your thinking matters." Our careful listening conveys respect and improves steadily as we master our own thoughts and feelings, and try to understand those of others.

11. To improve our ability to communicate truth.

We learn to communicate truth by doing so, first in a safe setting such as a discussion group; then with friends and family, and eventually in groups of diverse composition and in meetings with larger numbers. We learn to separate truth from opinion and distortion, and observe how its use leads to constructive outcomes. We uphold the truth about everything and pass it on, particularly what affects the well-being of others. Leaders especially need to grasp the facts, meaning, and motivations about a course of action and make them clear to all. Their ability to explain what is worth doing can bring about turning points in history. For truth to govern us, we declare it, and challenge lies and distortions.

12. To invite others to join us in action for change.

Our development moves along a path of increasing personal responsibility and understanding, but we limit our outcomes when we isolate ourselves. We affirm our commitment and values most clearly when we involve others in deliberate effort. We explain to others what we believe, and invite them to join us in acting on it. Doing this marks the depth of our belief and is the key influence of a movement. Believing something important we ask others' help in achieving it and do not allow fear or inertia to hinder us. We have more effect on others than we may realize because people tend to accept invitations. Their connection with us assures them of a positive experience.

13. To encourage personal relationships and effective action in the group.

People tend not to develop and change their thinking by themselves, but are influenced by the group's welcome and inclusion, and their participation in its activity. As we offer people a bond, they are more likely to find a satisfactory role. For an effective movement, we observe their needs, plan ways to meet them, and together engage in learning and action that encourage everyone. We learn about others by our study of human nature and careful listening, and help them deepen their involvement in pursuing the group's objectives.

14. To help develop the group's ideas.

Since our thinking as a group directs our actions and accomplishments, it is important we do our best to increase our combined fund of knowledge. As part of a group, we share in its collective intelligence. We do not need to understand or master everything, but only contribute what we can about what we know. With the group, we help to choose a goal, develop an action plan, and carry it out. As we project toward the next step, we continually expand the group's knowledge, particularly where our own experience and effort can make a difference.

15. To face the limitations of our thinking and welcome correction.

We apply to ourselves our understanding of human limitation. We all are limited due to our mind's inherent tendency to focus on one thing at a time and extinguish unused knowledge. Because of this, we can all expect lapses in our memory, reasoning we miss, applications we overlook, and assumptions that do not work out. In a group, some retain knowledge others do not, so that feedback and mutual questioning are indispensable for common effort. We avoid becoming defensive and turf-protecting as we welcome others' offerings, particularly where we have gaps.

16. To confront the limitations of others' thinking and actions.

We apply to others what we apply to ourselves—acknowledging limitations and errors. As hard as the prior decision may be, this one is harder because we wish not to discourage others or cause conflict. Because confrontation may hurt their feelings, we use the possibility as an excuse to accept their errors. Yet once people know others care about them, they are more likely to value truth offered to them and appreciate a "heads-up." The depth of our bonds is the depth of the truth we can share. We express our insights because we know our accomplishment together will not exceed the quality of our thinking. We can overlook others' personal idiosyncrasies, but for actions that affect the group's effectiveness, we speak truth and realism kindly.

17. To talk out issues with those who disagree when possible.

We want to resolve quickly any differences that impact group activity. Small things may stand in our way. We may be embarrassed at an oversight or mistake we make, sense another to be touchy, or face explicit contradiction. A movement's message to society, however, is that people can work out differences if they are willing, a standard we share with newcomers. We think carefully how to achieve the best outcome with this person, and do not avoid discussions from fear of negative feelings. Both the movement and society can expect contrasting ideas when many try to agree on plans. One person's caution can alert others to values or ideas to consider more deeply.

18. To discipline ourselves to do what contributes to group effectiveness.

Discipline is first internal as we direct our thoughts and feelings, but manifests quickly in our behavior. We direct our energy along a path that advances our skills and takes us toward a goal, but this often depends on bonds with others who agree that our effort together is worth it. An effective team matters to its members enough for them to expend the best that is in them for its success. Teams drive themselves to their limit by reinforcing this value in each other. Our common action becomes important to us as we believe in each other and work together for a reason we value. Because our movement can affect the future of the human race, it deserves our determination to become an effective team.

19. To ask for action that increases others' skill and expresses the group's values.

We encourage ourselves when we are competent at tasks that matter to us. This occurs spontaneously in a movement as people apply their existing ability and their group invites them to a further step. As leaders in an active group, we aid people's development by recognizing what they can do, understanding the conditions that could further it, and arranging an appropriate challenge. We express a need to them, ask for their help, offer them a responsibility, and discuss with them their picture of their progress and accomplishment.

20. To plan together for group activity.

We take responsibility for group activity, know that people's needs can be met well or poorly, and that we can make a movement more or less effective. We aim at developing the group's potential and putting it to work on issues it faces. We understand others' readiness for action and willingness to do more, and apply a tool kit of methods and perspectives;

show our determination for results by cooperating with a planning team that absorbs members' thinking, aligns with their values, draws the best ideas from all, and designs group actions.

21. To promote constructive principles for changing society.

As our sense of responsibility for society expands, we reach out to others more assertively. A single person can approach a city councilman, supervisor, or school board and say, "That policy is wrong, and I can explain why." We think in terms of how good ideas can affect society everywhere. Sometimes we implement our analysis by ourselves, sometimes with a handful of friends demonstrate or visit an official, and sometimes achieve outcomes with the body of movement members. We understand how responsible people change society by conveying positive values and ideas.

22. To move toward balance and harmony.

In action, we fuse together two essential elements. On the one hand we master plans and methods, and on the other, account for intangible principles, emotional balance, and thoughtful priorities to refine our sense of direction. Our capacity to engage in varied activities stimulates us to think carefully about the standards that govern us. Recognizing how the quality of thinking determines the outcomes of social policies, we weigh all conditions for what brings balance and harmony to the situation. Balance may move us to act alone or with others, may invest us less in personal gain and more in serving others' needs.

23. To accept total responsibility for others and the world.

We make real a stance of total responsibility for the world first by our readiness for whatever task life presents us, and then by the practical steps we undertake. Late in our series, this decision implies that by now we manage an array of competences and values with which to carry out our intent. As we own our abilities and limitations, we become fearless in our actions, and are habitually willing to expend our energy for values that matter to us. While we cannot do everything, we remain open to what the world asks of us, and look for the closest match between our capacities and the needs they could meet.

24. To adopt unconditional love for others and the world.

The basic meaning of love is to will good for another. Adopting this as our perpetual condition of heart, we express it to friends and family, but do not limit it to those of our circle, or who please us or agree with us. Extending to everyone a desire for their well-being is a premise of democracy—that all have a place and a right to the conditions enabling them to pursue happiness. This decision calls us to examine the less obvious effects of our actions so that we do not participate unwittingly in oppressing people and burdening their lives. To express unconditional love a society arranges less for winners and losers and more to keep everyone participating.

25. To spread truth.

Spreading truth begins with appreciating the real and good everywhere. Truth describes and conveys it, and since truth lies at the heart of good judgment about our world and affects the health of society, we notice when it is distorted or undermined, and do not allow error to continue unchecked. When correcting falsehood is critical, we seek out ways of doing it that can succeed. Declaring a truth, we may invite opposition and criticism upon ourselves, so our decision implies a willingness to sacrifice. While we may aspire "to speak truth to power," speaking truth to anyone who avoids it can require courage, understanding, and self-discipline.

26. To correct group think, short-term self-interest, and moral confusion.

With this decision we confront the most difficult problems of society such as communicating with those immersed in a self-reinforcing mistake, or who manipulate others for gain, or damage society long-term, or devise policies with negative moral impacts. While we may appear to want to dominate others and may arouse their defensiveness and opposition, it is at this boundary of differences that great values rise and fall, and important changes are possible if we are determined to engage others.

27. To meet others' needs.

This decision incorporates all of the prior and opens us to unlimited activity. Meeting others' needs is the basic role of a constructive leader and distinguishes him/her from a destructive one. A need entering our awareness invites our help. To prepare ourselves to respond, we draw on every experience, resource, and tool available. Often we work with others to help them meet their own need to forestall dependence on us, and may engage group resources to meet the needs of many together. We determine that meeting others' needs is for us a lifetime purpose. As our competence and wisdom develop, we learn how to meet needs of greater scope.

References

1. *Hope in the Dark: Untold Histories, Wild Possibilities* (Third Edition), Rebecca Solnit, Haymarket Books: Chicago, 2016, page 136.

2. "Trump's Appeal: What Psychology Tells Us," *Scientific American Mind*, March 2017. "Behind his unforeseen success in the 2016 election was a masterful use of group psychology principles."

3. The 1966 booklet of organizing methods was republished later as *Dedication and Leadership*, Douglas Hyde, Notre Dame University Press: South Bend, 1992.

4. In a lecture titled "War Made Easy," Norman Solomon (*Alternative Radio*, December 4, 2005) traces the historical record of how governments enlist the media when they want to go to war. Practically identical words and thinking are used to appeal to the public from decade to decade. Solomon cited the words of Hermann Goering, which in their more complete form are available at *http://enominepatris.com/politics/goering.htm*. Quotation used by permission.

5. "Why We Did It," *MSNBC Documentary*, narrated by Rachel Maddow, March 6, 2014.

6. *Motivation and Personality*, Abraham Maslow, Harper Brothers: New York, 1954. His work offers many insights into how people's life experience influences their motivations.

7. *Republic of Plato*, edited by Alan Bloom, Basic Books: New York, 1968, page 198.

8. "Scientists nearly double sea level rise projections for 2100 because of Antarctica," Brady Dennis and Chris Mooney, *Washington Post* (online), March 30, 2016. Authors note new research: "The melting of ice on Antarctica alone could cause seas to rise more than 15 meters (49 feet) by 2500." Because of the technical nature and complexity of projections about global warming, nearly any specific assertion can be argued. One forecaster declares effects negligible and another disastrous. We focus

better on the obvious, universally-accepted, measurable trends and their implications: atmospheric pollution is increasing, the world is heating, ice is melting, oceans are rising, coastal areas are vulnerable, and do we want those outcomes? Substantial data agree that the climate has already passed a tipping point portending destructive effects for centuries to come.

9. At a time when I was in despair, I was walking down a steep sidewalk in Seattle. A woman walking up the sidewalk whom I had never met suddenly glanced up and smiled a warm and personal smile as she went past me. Though it happened decades ago, the impact of her smile still affects me, and I am grateful to her whoever she was. For many people, the only significant information they know is that they are loved.

10. "America has never been so ripe for tyranny," Andrew Sullivan, *Huffingtonpost.com*, May 1, 2016. A thoughtful exploration of the problem democracies face in navigating between freedom, reason, stability, emotion, frustration, and tyranny. The danger lies in how easily general frustration leads to abusive government practices.

11. *https://www.niddk.nih.gov/health-information/health-statistics/ Pages/overweight-obesity-statistics.aspx.* Our point is not about individual body types but rather that something systemic has gone wrong that shows up in the overall statistics.

12. *Whatever happened to justice?* (Revised edition), Richard J. Maybury, Bluestocking Press: Placerville, CA 2004. Maybury explains two factors at the heart of western legal thought: Do all you agree to do, and do not encroach on other persons or their property. The history of mankind and the social sciences as a body inform us in detail about what does and does not aid human development.

13. *The Sixth Extinction: An Unnatural History*, Elizabeth Kolbert, Henry Holt: New York, 2014. Documents the ongoing impact of human activity on the disappearance of living things large and small.

14. *A Study of History*, Arnold Toynbee (abridgment by D.C. Somervell), Dell Publishing: New York, 2 volumes, 1965. For a parallel reflection on our own period, see Paul Krugman, "How Republics End," *New York Times*, December 19, 2016. He recounts the actions of the powerful that

hollowed out Rome till it fell, and similar conditions doing the same to us now. He does not find any force in the current social scene strong enough to prevent the same outcome.

15. *Collapse: How Societies Choose to Fail or Succeed*, Jared Diamond, Viking: New York, 2005, pages 421 and following.

16. "Economic Inequality: It's far worse than you think," Nicholas Fitz, *Scientific American Mind* (online), March 31, 2015. The article deserves careful study because the actual data differ sharply from public assumptions and confirm a basic theme of this book.

17. "The US is not a democracy but an oligarchy, study finds," JC Sevcik, *upi.com*, April 16, 2015. See Princeton website for full study. Also, "Jimmy Carter: U.S. Is an 'Oligarchy With Unlimited Political Bribery'," Daniel Kreps, *Rollingstone.com*, July 31, 2015. The 39th president said the Citizens United ruling "violates the essence of what made America a great country in its political system."

18. *www.goodjudgmentproject.com.*

19. Many influential people, notably House Speaker Paul Ryan, are devotees of Ayn Rand who promotes an imperious, cavalier attitude toward society. A sample: "Capitalism and altruism are incompatible; they are philosophical opposites; they cannot co-exist in the same man or in the same society." "Any white person who brings the element of civilization has the right to take over this continent." "The question isn't who is going to let me: it's who is going to stop me."

20. *USA Today*, October 12, 2016. Later legal action obtained clawback of some of Stumpf's compensation, but further revelations indicated even wider problems with the bank's accounts.

21. "Restoring Civic Virtue in America," Jeffrey Sachs, *Boston Globe* (online), December 4, 2016. Sachs's other two points are our country's secretive security state, and mass media replacing political parties as a means of participation. He urges ways to address all four, but is most concerned about the separate worlds inhabited by lawmakers and the general public, and suggests ways to let citizens use the Internet to influence laws directly.

22. "Oxfam says wealth of richest 1% equal to other 99%," *BBC.com*,

Jan. 18, 2016. The richest 1% now equal the wealth of the rest of the world combined, according to Oxfam. It has calculated also that the wealthiest 62 people in the world own as much as the poorest half of the entire global population. Different measures supply different proportions, but the general picture is consistent.

23. "Lies, damn lies, and fake news," Jon Perr, *Dailykos.com*, July 30, 2017. A compelling summary of decades of out-and-out lying emanating from Republicans and their media for political and economic gain. It cannot be an accident that large proportions of Trump supporters believe many patently false assertions: that the country is worse off now than eight years ago, fewer people have health insurance, world climate is not changing from human activity, Saddam Hussein probably or definitely had weapons of mass destruction, Obama is actually Kenyan, Russia did not hack Democrats' email to influence the election, millions of illegal votes were cast, and Clinton's campaign emails contain code words for pedophilia, human trafficking, and satanic ritual abuse. Such distorted thinking could only occur from willful intent to deceive by some and others' willingness to align their thinking with their emotional biases.

24. "Fear and unbalanced: Confessions of a 14-year Fox News hitman: How Roger Ailes & Fox News got rich scamming America's LaZBoy cowboys and selling out America's soul," Tobin Smith, *Medium.com*, May 26, 2017. Smith recounts vivid incidents illustrating his theme.

25. *On Tyranny: Twenty lessons from the twentieth century*, Timothy Snyder, Penguin Random House: New York, 2017. Yale history professor outlines twenty ways to defend truth under current circumstances.

26. "How the racists of the south have ruled this nation from the very beginning," Susan Grigsby, *DailyKos.com*, November 16, 2016.

27. "Even more black people were lynched in the U.S. than previously thought, study finds," Mark Berman, *Washington Post*, February 10, 2015. Summarizes the progress of studies of lynching, and how updated numbers were determined.

28. "Math is racist: How data is driving inequality: Wealth: America's other racial divide," Aimee Rawlins, *CNN Money Online*, September 6,

2016.

29. "ASU president paints bleak picture of Arizona's economy, future," Paul Maryniak, *Awatukee Foothill News*, December 29, 2016. In a talk, ASU president Michael Crow outlined worrisome trends affecting Arizona, and noted this 10 year prediction passed on to him by the second highest executive in Google X company.

30. "March of the Machines: What history tells us about the future of artificial intelligence—and how society should respond," *The Economist*, June 25, 2016. Research is ongoing on the issue. "Is guaranteed income for all the answer to joblessness and poverty?: Experts disagree, but a number of experiments could offer insight," David Noonan, *Scientific American* (online), July 18, 2017.

31. "Poll: Americans Have Little Faith in Government," Charles Babington and Jennifer Agiesta, *Associated Press*, January 2, 2014.

32. A long history behind such thinking in the U.S. began with what educators thought schools should produce. In "The Structure of Success in America," Nicholas Lemann (*Atlantic Monthly*, August 1995) summarizes a trail of events. See also his book, *The Big Test*, Farrar, Straus and Giroux: New York 1999. Two American ideas compete. One is a natural aristocracy or meritocracy which generations of American elites have ascribed to themselves and which the SAT test has increasingly determined. The other is the idea of universal individual opportunity, stronger in America than anywhere else. Lemann notes that these concepts were separate for a long time but "what seems to have happened is the funneling of opportunity toward a smaller and smaller group."

33. *The Power Elite*, C. Wright Mills, Oxford University Press: New York, 1956.

34. *www.eisenhower.archives.gov/farewell.htm*

35. "The Fog of War: Eleven Lessons from the Life of Robert S. McNamara," *Sony Pictures* (documentary) by Errol Morris, 2003.

36. "Reduced self-referential neural response during intergroup competition predicts competitor harm," M. Cikara, A.C. Jenkins, N. Dufour, R. Saxe, *Sciencedirect.com*, June 21, 2014.

37. *War is a Racket,* Smedley Butler. Written in the 1930s, this book is available on the Internet at *http://lexrex.com/enlightened/articles/warisracket.htm.*

38. *A House Divided: Six Belief Systems Struggling for America's Soul,* Mark Gerzon, G.P. Putnam's Sons: New York, 1996.

39. "Why we overestimate our competence," Tori DeAngelis, *www.apa.org/monitor/feb03/overestimate.aspx* (February 2003, Vol . 34, No. 2. Print version page 60) is a good summary of the issue, and notes contributions by Dunning and Kruger. With just one data bit, one has only the choice of asserting it or not. But as more data bits accumulate, one realizes that multiple aspects may be relevant, so that gathering more data seems sensible. Unfortunately the tendency to exaggerate our knowledge can apply to those claiming expertise: "You don't know as much as you think: false expertise," Jessica Schmerier, *Scientific American Mind* (online), January 1, 2016. Self-proclaimed experts often honestly overestimate their knowledge and others cede ground to them. This may seem logical because we have to judge from secondary indicators of people's ability, and don't know the reality of it. One signal is their apparent confidence in what they know. Also, "You do not think alone: A new book argues that thought and knowledge are community efforts," Gareth Cook, *Scientific American* (online), June 21, 2017. Cites book *The Knowledge Illusion* by Sloman and Fernbach, that our thinking is vastly more dependent on others around us than we realize.

40. *Catch-22,* Joseph Heller, Simon and Schuster: New York, 1961.

41. In a letter to activists December 2, 2005, Robert McChesney, the director of Free Press that is devoted to freedom in the media, noted seven current attacks on the media: infiltrating public broadcasting, manufacturing fake news, bribing journalists, lying, eliminating dissent in the mainstream media by punishing reporters, gutting the Freedom of Information Act, and consolidating media control. These manipulative activities appear to have intensified during and after the 2016 election. In 2017, media reported that far-right Sinclair broadcasting's acquisition of media outlets across the country has established a propaganda structure that will affect public opinion far into the future.

42. There is a case to be made that because punishment makes people feel worse, it motivates them to change. People may scream at a family member to affect them enough that they will do the right thing. But because this strategy is often counterproductive, many need to learn how treating others positively but firmly is more likely to obtain the behavior changes they want.

43. "A Case Study of Innovation," Elting E. Morison, *Engineering and Science Magazine*, California Institute of Technology: Pasadena, CA, April 1950, in *The Planning of Change*, edited by Warren Bennis, Kenneth Benne, and Robert Chin, Holt, Rinehart and Winston: New York, 1961, page 602.

44. "8 behaviors that really are contagious, psych studies find," *psyblog.com*, April 8, 2016. Some ordinary behaviors transmit easily to others such as happiness, anxiety, rudeness, laughter, risk-taking, yawning, smiling, and shivering. Why not use for a positive reason what we are designed to be good at? Also, "Step by Step, Your Brain Mimics His Moves," Ker Than, *Psychology Today*, July/August 2005, page 26. Also, "Optimization Versus Effortful Processing in Children: Cognitive Triage: Criticisms, Reanalyses, and New Data," C. J. Brainerd, et al., *Journal of Experimental Child Psychology*, V55, N3, p353-73, June 1993.

45. "The Political Brain: A recent brain-imaging study shows that our political predilections are a product of unconscious confirmation bias," Michael Shermer, *Scientific American* (online) July 1, 2006. It appears extremely difficult for people to be directly aware of how they distort what they receive. This study describes the process as de-activating the brain's reasoning function while a series of emotional processes advance. A more recent study explains the problem in more detail: "The irrationality within us: Why we are not as rational as we think, and why this matters," Elly Vintiadis, *Scientific American* (online), December 12, 2016. Physiological changes happen in us that mark negative or positive emotions signaling to us which options to prefer and which not–i.e. "gut feelings." Emotion and intuition actually guide most decisions. Article examines what should be called "rational" by courts and others. Also,

"Why facts don't unify us," Tali Sharot and Cass Sunstein, *New York Times* (online), Sept 4, 2016. Because people welcome information that supports what they already believe, a single body of both positive and negative information will gradually divide a unified group because each side cherry-picks evidence. This is not rational but is a subtle influence working over time. In "In Lieu of Manners," Jeffrey Rosen (*New York Times Magazine*, February 4, 2001) points out how confirmation bias has led to litigation as a substitute for manners and respect for others. Upon taking sides in a contentious situation, we tend to become more committed to our views and interpret evidence as more supportive of them. Litigating these disputes leads to greater polarization.

46. "Why good thoughts block better ones," Merim Bilalic and Peter McLeod, *Scientific American*, March 2014. Explains the *Einstellung* effect, the brain's strong tendency to stick with the familiar solution that comes to mind first. Its most potent impact is diverting us unconsciously from information that could change our thinking. Consciously we feel open to whatever ideas reach us, but exclude entire categories unconsciously to protect choices we assume are already correct.

47. "Bill Maher's excellent and sobering commentary on the wealth gap," *Dailykos.com*, BruinKidFollow, May 11, 2013. An engaging and well-reasoned summary of the problem.

48. "Some 95% of 2009-2012 Income Gains Went to Wealthiest 1%," Emmanuel Saez, *Wall Street Journal* (online), Sept 10, 2013, and "Incomes of super-rich outgaining middle class," Josh Boak (AP), *Arizona Daily Star*, July 2, 2016. Attitudes behind these numbers are a significant force: "Someone finally polled the 1% and it's not pretty," Auriandra, *Dailykos.com*, May 29, 2014. Multiple polls sharply contrast the views of the general public against those making approximately $1 million annually. The 1% want less environmental protection, health care, and social security by 8, 19, and 33% than the number of those in the 1% who want more of them. The public instead have dramatically different priorities: 29, 44, and 46% more of the public want more of these things than those who want less of them. A score of other measures distinguish similarly between the two. When society lacked such specific

data, cries of unfairness were universally dismissed as envy or class warfare. This defense has been routed by the objective facts of inequality and better familiarity with causative attitudes.

49. "Who gets food stamps? White people, mostly," Arthur Delaney, *HuffingtonPost.com*, February 28, 2015.

50. "Most Americans don't have enough to cover a $500 emergency," Gail MarksJarvis, *Chicago Tribune*, January 7, 2016. Cites national survey.

51. For a thoughtful summary of poverty in the U.S. and its causes, see "9 Questions about Poverty, Answered," Peter Van Buren, *Mother Jones* (online), June 6, 2014.

52. *Made to stick: why some ideas survive and others die*, Chip and Dan Heath, Random House: New York, 2007. Chip was a teacher of Jonah Berger, author of *Contagion: Why Things Catch On* (Simon and Schuster: New York, 2013) which offers many insights on how appeal is transmitted that could aid a campaign. For timely, sticky ideas we might keep our ears open to the nation's comedians.

53. *Collapse: How Societies Choose to Fail or Succeed*, Jared Diamond, Viking: New York, 2005.

54. This list is adapted from a shorter one in *Effective Classroom Turnaround: Practice Makes Permanent*, John Jensen, Rowman and Littlefield, Lanham, MD, 2012.

55. "Actors Gang: How Tim Robbins has cut reoffending rates," Kate Bissell, *BBC News*, Los Angeles, March 14, 2016. Robbins developed a format in which inmates take roles of characters in a play to practice working through anger and other emotions. The method has cut reoffending rates of participants at least in half. The original meaning of "penitentiary" was a place where people learn penitence, remorse for wrong they do; and upon turning around their thinking, learning how to apply themselves constructively. We enlist the voice of goodness in their conscience that they may have discounted. The national shift in terminology from penitentiary to correctional facility probably implies that society gave up trying to affect inmates' inner state and relied instead on modifying their behavior, yet the two are inextricably

entangled. *Locked In: The True Causes of Mass Incarceration and How to Achieve Real Reform*, John Pfaff, Basic Books: New York, 2017, identifies as a core factor that prosecutors send far too many people to jail who could benefit from other forms of guidance or intervention. Further investigation also is warranted about the connection between aggressive behavior and male testosterone levels, which when voluntarily regulated can significantly decrease unwanted impulses.

56. This definition suggested by Hunter Thompson invites us to address courageously the issue of control, and bring it into balance with values it impacts. Because control of others has been such a terrifying force in church history, churches today bear a special responsibility to bring balance to the issue. It is a contradiction to spiritual values.

57. "The Christian Paradox: How a Faithful Nation Gets Jesus Wrong," Bill McKibben, *Harper's Magazine*, August 2005. McKibben details discrepancies between U.S. beliefs and practices on the one hand and Christian teachings on the other. Americans possess a "Ben Franklinized" Christianity–"God helps those who help themselves"–replacing Christ's emphasis on service to the poor and love for our neighbor in need. U.S. policies have shaped Christianity instead of vice versa. We are the last among rich nations to feed the hungry, we are more violent and retributive, sustain a wider gap between poor and rich, indulge in regressive and repressive legislative policies, jail more people, lack self discipline, act on impulse, are poor stewards of both our personal and collective financial household, divorce more, and leave more children uncared for. Christian thinking is preoccupied with issues peripheral to what Jesus talked about: pursuing the self-satisfied life, inveighing against gays and abortion, and a preoccupation with the apocalyptic. Tax cuts for the rich, the war in Iraq, and the death penalty for offenders have been presented as Christian duties. McKibben believes a genuine hunger exists for a true spiritual mission that Christians do not hear in Sunday sermons. We might approach church organizations with an offer to discuss social issues in light of Biblical references: Genesis 4,9 (brother's keeper), Amos (entire book concerns repression by the rich), Luke 14,12-14 (make your feast for the

poor instead of wealthy friends), Luke 16,19-31 (conversation with a rich man in hell), Matthew 5-7 (peacemaking, forgiveness, love of enemies, hypocrisy of judgment), Matthew 25,31-46 (serve dire human needs), John 8,7 (don't condemn others).

58. While strolling in downtown Amsterdam, my wife and I came upon a small museum of torture. I do not want to burden anyone's imagination with what we saw, but humans have found ingenious ways to inflict pain and horror leading to a slow, excruciating death. That people eagerly designed and used these implements *because of their religious beliefs* should spur a daily examination of conscience by every churchgoer to remind themselves to restrain their desire to exert power over others. The moment they notice their way of promoting their religion causes distress or pain to another, they must realize that they have "gone over to the dark side." If they believe it important to correct others' errors, they should recall Jesus' emphatic teaching that we should not judge each other and that he would eventually do all the judging himself.

59. A personal note. The circuitous route of my own life followed this shift. I found it easy as a Catholic priest to fulfill the duties assigned to me, but recognizing the larger field of needs that lay outside my priestly work led me eventually to a leave of absence and then to much learning and change. The unexpectedness of subsequent turns hints that those embarking on an uncertain path by relying on Divine Providence may be led where they could not have envisioned.

60. "Liar, Liar: How the brain adapts to telling tall tales," Simon Makin, *Scientific American Mind and Brain* (online), Oct 26, 2016.

61. "How winning leads to cheating," Jordana Capelewicz, *Scientific American* (online), February 2, 2016, and "Why being in a group causes some to forget their morals," *psyblog.com*, June 21, 2014. Researchers have found that when people win what they perceive as a competition, they presume that they have more power, and are more prone to cheating even in fields unrelated to the competition. When people compete against objective standards or values, or simply make a gain not compared to that of others, this effect disappears. People are more likely to "turn corrupt," in other words, when their success is in reference to

others. Dacher Keltner, psychologist at U of Cal, summarizes: "…dozens of studies have found that the simple feeling of power makes people feel above the scrutiny of others and act in impulsive, self-gratifying and unethical ways…and can indeed lead to various abuses like lying and stealing."

62. Sinclair's famous quote appeared first in his book, *I, Candidate for Governor: And How I Got Licked,* about the 1934 California governor's race. On the same point, "Study: Rich Republicans are the worst climate deniers," Chris Mooney, *Mother Jones* (online), July 10, 2014. Among low income Republicans, 17% match the proportions of Independents and Democrats in the belief that climate change is not very or not at all dangerous, but 51.2% of rich Republicans answer that way. The wealthy's myopic view of their world has a long history, but their tendency offers a lever for helping them acknowledge their irrationality: "If this is true, it threatens your finances so your mind doesn't want to face it. Are you able to understand that?"

63. "Social Status and subjective well being," Cameron Anderson, Michael W. Kraus, Adam D. Galinsky, Dacher Keltner, *Psychological Science*, July 2012, Vol, 23, #7 764-771.

64. *Encounter Groups: First Facts,* Morton A. Lieberman, Irvin D. Yalom, and Matthew D. Miles, Basic Books: New York, 1973. Careful research explained the qualities of small group experience and leader styles that contributed most to people's personal growth. Warmth enabled changes to occur.

65. The single most powerful motive easily available at all school levels is that students love to be able to perform and be applauded for anything they can do competently. *Effective Classroom Turnaround* (cf. Recommended Reading) explains how to apply this principle for maximum interest and retention of learning. Classrooms that employ psychological and pedagogical principles correctly typically turn around in a few weeks.

66. During the meetings of the G-20 in Hamburg, Germany, on July 7, 2017, thousands of protestors turned out to object to international trade policies that fed global inequality and other problems. Some protests

turned violent, and a common viewpoint reported among them was, "Peaceful protest is not enough," which underscores our central point. To change systems, we must move their levers, and street protests of any dimension are typically too far removed from them. And when peaceful means fail to remedy frustrations, the instinct of many is to increase violence, with bloody revolution as the ultimate change agent.

67. Malcolm Gladwell reports numerous data converging on 150 as the brain's practical limit for the number of people we can know personally (cf. *The Tipping Point: How little things can make a big difference*, Little, Brown and Company: Boston, 2002).

68. "The most surprising attribute of great leaders," *psyblog.com*, August 1, 2014. The article cites several research studies identifying humility as the factor that turned leaders from good to great, particularly for helping others develop leadership qualities. But also, "The irritating reason overconfident people get all the breaks" (*psyblog.com*, August 28, 2014) probes how overconfident people gain for themselves by deceiving others, and others allow them to do so.

69. *Effective Classroom Turnaround: Practice Makes Permanent*, John Jensen, Rowman and Littlefield: Lanham MD, 2012.

70.   *http://www.nlpco.com/2013/04/subtle-skills-for-building-rapport-with-nlp/#axzz4T9n2g3w9*. Excellent brief summary of easily-learned techniques for generating rapport by matching another's qualities.

71. "Indivisible: A Practical Guide to Resisting Trump's Agenda" is available to read at:

https://docs.google.com/document/d/ 1DzOz3Y6D8g_MNXHNMJYAz1b41_cn535aU5UsN7Lj8X8/preview#.

For a download of the guide go to *www.indivisibleguide.com*. "Former Congressional staffers reveal best practices for making Congress listen." Many suggestions explain how a few people can achieve significant impact.

72. "How to shift anti-transgender attitudes," Bob Roehr, *Scientific American* (online), April 7, 2016. "A new study shows that door-to-door 'deep canvassing' conversations can change real voters' attitudes to be more tolerant." A rigorous research project found that significant change

occurred when canvassers spent 10-15 minutes eliciting voters' views, exploring their experiences of being discriminated against, and then applying these to transgender persons' experiences. Better results are likely on many issues when canvassers take more time with each voter, mainly listen, and pursue the theme, "How have you experienced a similar issue yourself?" The principle of taking an alternate perspective has many applications. To a young person engaged in risky group behavior: "Tell me how you would feel if one of your friends got seriously hurt." We can gladly offer anyone 10 minutes of careful attention and then say, "Well, I need to be going."

73. "The emotion that does motivate behavior," *psyblog.com*, June 22, 2017. Explains how to utilize the powerful influence of curiosity to engage people about issues that affect them.

74. "Want to suppress the vote? Stress people out," Chris Mooney, *Mother Jones (online), June 23, 2014.* People who are prone to stress are more likely to skip voting when voting is stressful. But on a positive note about voting: "How science can help get out the vote. Research offers several proven strategies for boosting turnout on Election Day," Supriya Syal, Dan Ariely, *Scientific American* (online), Sept 1, 2016. People are more likely to vote if they make specific plans for the time of day, where they will go, how to get there, etc. Also, they like to think "Everyone else is doing it," rather than that few are doing it and thus their vote should matter more. They like to think they are among a crowd that will succeed together. Finally, how they connect voting to their identity matters most, generating almost 11% increase in voter participation. We ask, "How important it is to you to be a voter?" or "How important is it to you to vote?"

75. We can readily enlist the motivational force of competence. According to Jacob Bronowski, "The primary civilizing force is that man loves to do what he does well, and having done it well, he loves to do it even better." *Ascent of Man*, Little Brown and Company: Boston, 1975, page 116. Being able to express ideas others will listen to and accept is a universally significant capability.

76. *Encounter Groups: First Facts,* Morton A. Lieberman, Irvin D.

Yalom, and Matthew D. Miles, Basic Books: New York, 1973. Participants grew and sustained their changes best when their ideas influenced others. The study also demonstrated the ineffectiveness of a dominating leadership style.

77. This method (emphasis on the first syllable) is helpful with all age groups. For a fuller explanation, see reference 69.

78. This set came together when I tried to understand the factors driving an exceptional evening with friends. The first point, looking at others while they speak in a group, lets them know we are thinking about what they say, so we do this steadily. When we talk to an individual, however, our intent guides our eye contact. Addressing someone we wish to influence like a misbehaving child, firm eye contact lets them know we expect them to comply with our wishes: "Now look at me and tell me what you are going to do." Determined sales people usually maintain direct eye contact. Smiling while nodding affirmatively as we ourselves speak conveys to the other that we like them, and adds to our influence. When our aim instead is to persuade with thoughtful information, we may wish to leave the other free to agree or not. Another sensing that we want to dominate them may view eye contact as a threat instead of an offer, so as we speak we glance at them occasionally to let them know we want to communicate as equals.

79. *Strangers in their own land: Anger and mourning in the American Right*, The New Press: New York, 2016. Also, the Kaiser Family Foundation/Washington Post Survey of Rural America, *www.kff.org*, June 17, 2017. These two sources together supply critical perspective for activists working in rural communities to understand voters' needs, wants, and feelings.

80. "In-Person requests are more effective than electronic ones: People respond better to face to face requests than to e-mails," Matthew Hutson, *Scientific American Mind* (online), May 1, 2017. In-person requests appear more effective by giving greater urgency to the request and more respect to the other person. Personal contact improves results by many multiples over the impersonal.

81. These three dimensions are the basis of the Fundamental

Interpersonal Relations Orientation (FIRO) developed by Will Schutz in 1958 that have been applied ever since for personal change, and in testing instruments available from different vendors. Since people vary in how they welcome others expressing these dimensions toward them and they toward others, watching for the operation and effect of the factors can help resolve organizational difficulties.

82. "A fact about social influence that very few people know," *psyblog.com*, April 14, 2016.

83. "Want to change minds? Try this," Tali Sharot, *CNN online*, September 14, 2017.

84. "Study: Talking to other commuters is not a drag after all," *Good News Network*, May 7, 2014.

85. "Bowling Alone: A Harvard Professor Examines America's Dwindling Sense of Community," Robert D. Putnam with Scott Heller, *The Chronicles of Higher Education*, March 1, 1996, Volume 42, Number 5, P 10(2).

86. These estimates for the proportion of recall time compared to input time came from an obscure study over a half-century ago, but have seemed valid in practice ever since. The teacher axiom "To learn a subject, teach it," expresses the same idea–multiple occasions of output compared to input. Applying the general principle, I developed a method for achieving perfect memory of key information suitable for any student age and material. See reference 69.

87. "Defensive Communication," Jack R. Gibb, *Journal of Communication*, 1961, 11, 141-148. Gibb explains the importance of these aspects of communication for creating trust.

88. *Evicted: Poverty and Profit in the American City*, Matthew Desmond, Crown Publishing: New York, 2016. I've known many people who had successful adult lives despite a difficult childhood. Families faced with job loss, parental death, eviction, and other setbacks can still love and support each other, and make their way together. Often the sacrifices of a generation of parents are rewarded only later in the success of their children. A single mother at the poorest end of the economic spectrum raised President Obama. But that some do make it despite challenges is

often misapplied by politicians who generalize from individual successes to the theoretical possibility that anyone can succeed. The demographic data point out instead that the more burdens people carry and the fewer their "assets," the more likely they will have a troubled life. There are just so many Harvard scholarships to go around. People deserve at least that policies do not inflict damage on them that can be easily recognized and avoided. How hard is it to intervene concerning lead pipes, poor education, toxic environments, job discrimination, and illness?

89. "198 Methods of Non-Violent Action," Gene Sharp, *http://www.aeinstein.org/nonviolentaction/198-methods-of-nonviolentaction*. Lists innovative ways an activist group can reach the public and affect political decisions, and references more extensive work by Sharp.

90. "The short life of viral social movements: social media charity campaigns spread like wildfire but burn out fast," Sander van der Linden, *Scientific American* (online), February 15, 2017. "Viral social campaigns can effectively capture the attention and support of mass audiences, but in order to make viral altruism stick, more gradual and deeper engagement with a social cause is required over a sustained period of time." The article's concluding idea could not state better the need for a movement.

91. For movement members to distinguish themselves within their social group, two characteristics to be known for are: 1) "Those people are exceptional listeners," and 2) "They can explain the Preamble to the Constitution and the introduction to the Declaration of Independence."

92. In developing Neuro-Linguistic Programming, Richard Bandler and John Grinder crystallized significant insights about many aspects of human behavior, with rapport an important one. Many have built on their work in the last forty years, notably Anthony Robbins in *Unlimited Power*, a misleading title for an excellent and now inexpensive book about how people change. Helpful explanations of rapport are available also from an Internet search of "Building rapport." See reference 70.

93. "Here's what science says is the secret ingredient to making your love spark," David Briggs, *Washington Post* (online), February 12, 2016.

Recommended reading

A House Divided: Six Belief Systems Struggling for America's Soul, Mark Gerzon, G.P. Putnam's Sons: New York, 1996. Important insights into how society's structure has fed belief systems that each contain strengths and weaknesses that can serve or threaten society.

A Study of History, Arnold Toynbee (abridgment by D.C. Somervell), Dell Publishing: New York, 2 volumes, 1965. Explains the rise and fall of civilizations, particularly as influenced by the role of a creative or dominant minority.

Collapse: How Societies Choose to Fail or Succeed, Jared Diamond, Viking: New York, 2005. How human activity depletes resources and fails to apply existing knowledge to looming problems.

Dedication and Leadership, Douglas Hyde, Notre Dame University Press: South Bend, 1992. Lectures explaining to Catholic missionaries the innovations in group dynamics that enabled the Communist Party to obtain 30 million members in free countries.

Effective Classroom Turnaround: Practice Makes Permanent, John Jensen, Rowman and Littlefield: Lanham MD, 2012. Methods that turn around or accelerate any classroom quickly.

Encounter Groups: First Facts, Morton A. Lieberman, Irvin D Yalom, Matthew D. Miles, Basic Books: New York, 1973. Careful research explains the impact of small group leadership styles on participants' long-term personal change.

Evicted: Poverty and Profit in the American City, Matthew Desmond, Crown Publishing: New York, 2016. A picture of what it is like to be a poor person in America, a vivid account of people struggling.

How to Spend $75 Billion to Make the World a Better Place (2nd edition), Bjørn Lomborg, Copenhagen Consensus Center: Copenhagen, 2014. Scientists evaluate thirty-nine proposals for spending money to improve the world like addressing child malnutrition right away.

Sciencedaily.com. This free website provides current research and thought about the entire range of scientific issues including studies related to society, culture, and politics.

Strangers in Their Own Land: Anger and Mourning in the American Right, Arlie Hochschild, The New Press: New York, 2016. Important book for understanding conservative values in rural communities.

Ted Talks. www.ted.com/talks. Experts from every field offer 2400 leading edge, user-friendly presentations that can impact individual lives and society.

The Brainwashing of My Dad, Jen Senko (90 minute documentary), DVD Blu-Ray and VOD. A resource for understanding how media manipulation for the past thirty years has distorted attitudes about people, society, and government.

The Fix: How Nations Survive and Thrive in a World of Decline, Jonathan Teppernan, Crown Publishing: New York, 2016. Other nations have solved problems like inequality, immigration, corruption, civil war, Islamic extremism, the resource curse, energy, gridlock, political pragmatism, monopolies, education, and tax and banking laws. Unique conditions in other countries may inhibit applying their solutions to the U.S.

The Sixth Extinction: An Unnatural History, Elizabeth Kolbert, Henry Holt: New York, 2014. Documents the ongoing impact of human activity on the disappearance of living things large and small.

Unlimited Power: The New Science of Personal Achievement, Anthony Robbins, Free Press: New York, 1997. Life-changing for individuals, this book explains how to work in harmony with our inherent capacities to reshape our thinking and lives. Inexpensive now in paperback, it is also offered in a free home-study format available on the Internet.

White Working Class: Overcoming Class Cluelessness in America, Joan W. Williams, Harvard Business Review Press: Boston, 2017. An insightful, readable summation of the forces converging on the American middle class that help explain the 2016 election.

APPENDIX I. Promotional Flier

(Promote a lecture with a flier such as the following adapted to local
interests.)

A MOVEMENT FOR CHANGE

Are you tired of excuses from leaders?
Could they show more common sense and cooperation
to get things done for the American people?
Are you concerned about unattended problems, such as

1. reasonable health insurance and care?

2. the growing inequality between rich and poor?

3. an economy working fine for the well-off but not for the rest?

4. an immigration policy governed by fear, bias, and self-interest?

5. a head-in-the-sand climate change policy?

6. a deteriorating infrastructure?

7. politics manipulated by money?

8. an ineffective, inhumane criminal justice system?

The question is how to unite people's effort to bring about change.

At (place and time), (person and their qualifications)
will offer an answer followed by questions and discussion.
There is no charge and all are welcome.

APPENDIX II

Memorize and be able to discuss the Preamble to the Constitution:
**We the people of the United States, in order to form a more perfect
union, ensure domestic tranquility, provide for the common defense,
and insure the blessings of liberty for ourselves and our posterity, do
hereby establish the Constitution of the United States.**

Memorize and be able to discuss the introduction to the Declaration of Independence:

We hold these truths to be self-evident, that all men are created equal, that they are endowed by their Creator with certain unalienable Rights, that among these are Life, Liberty, and the pursuit of Happiness. That to secure these rights, Governments are instituted among Men, deriving their just powers from the consent of the governed.

Explain an idea below, give another time to think about it, inquire if they agree with it, and discuss their answer:

> The basic issue is fair use of society's resources. What does fairness mean?
> Civilizations break down when leaders use their power for their own interests. How are our leaders doing that?
> The system then fails to meet its challenges. How is ours doing that?
> The powerful demonstrate their values by how they treat the powerless.
> The wealthiest 1% in the world own more than the other 99%.
> Unfair sharing of the nation's productivity creates inequality.
> Free enterprise is capitalism with little protection for public needs.
> Many supporters of free enterprise assume that some people have to suffer.
> After World War II, unions helped blue collar people for the first time in history to a secure retirement and college for their children.
> The potential for the disastrous rise of unwarranted power by the military, industrial complex exists and will persist–Eisenhower.
> Good of the whole is society's aim to benefit all people and forms of life.
> Otherism is the basic bias that discounts anyone different from ourselves.
> The public agreement is a belief that society's benefits be shared broadly.
> Evidence tells us if a belief is true or not.
> Our values tell us which evidence matters.
> Mediocre thinking damages all social policies.
> Some use up resources meant for all.
> Government must cope with all the issues left over after people benefit themselves.
> The U.S. government is an oligarchy controlled by the few.
> Trickle down economics is like having three dogs and giving one of them a wiener, expecting him to share it with the other two—Bill Maher.
> Only an active majority can restrain a minority's greed.

——30——

www.ingramcontent.com/pod-product-compliance
Lightning Source LLC
Chambersburg PA
CBHW070809280726
48660CB00015B/21